THE CONFLICT
WITHIN ISLAM

Expressing Religion Through Politics

ISRAR HASAN

iUniverse, Inc.
Bloomington

THE CONFLICT WITHIN ISLAM
Expressing Religion Through Politics

iUniverse books may be ordered through booksellers or by contacting:

iUniverse
1663 Liberty Drive
Bloomington, IN 47403
www.iuniverse.com
1-800-Authors (1-800-288-4677)

ISBN: 978-1-4620-8301-5 (sc)
ISBN: 978-1-4620-8302-2 (ebk)

Printed in the United States of America

iUniverse rev. date: 12/17/2011

Author's Note

There is widely recognized system for the transliteration of Arabic into English, along with specific diacritical markings to indicate long and short vowels; I have endeavored, for the sake of clarity and ease, to present all Arabic words in their simplest and most recognizable English usage. The Arabic letter *hamza,* which is rarely vocalized, will occasionally be marked with an apostrophe ('). The letter *ain*—best pronounced as glottal stop—will be marked with an apostrophe ('), as in the word *bay'ah*, meaning oath. Further, rather than pluralizing Arabic nouns and pronouns in Arabic according to their grammatical rules, I will simply add an *s/es*; thus *Kahins*, instead of *Kuhhan*; *Hadiths* instead of *Ahadeeth*.

Unless otherwise indicated, most translations of the Qur'an are from Abdullah Yusuf Ali and the Holy Bible from the New King James Version. The suffix of 'peace and blessings of God be upon him' after the names of the prophet and messenger are not used in this study, considering that all Muslim believers recite these words spontaneously when they come across such names in writing or hearing.

Israr Hasan
E-mail: hitt2010@gmail.com
20 November 2011

CONTENTS

Preface

Islam for me had never been more than a ritual of Friday prayers and the two *Eid* prayers. My early life partly spent in the undivided India and partly in Bangladesh until I migrated to Pakistan and got a brief opportunity to study Islam under the guidance and patronage of the eminent thinker-scholar, Fazlur Rahman (1919-1988)[1], as a Research Fellow in the Central Institute of Islamic Research, Karachi, Pakistan, in mid-sixties. Practically, I have generously used in this study my old notes taken during his lectures in the class room on various topics. It was only under his stimulating lectures that I developed an interest and awakening to know Islam—to know that Islam is something more than rituals and practices. Only then did I know that this is a religion of the Book, and one cannot be a true Muslim without deep study and understanding of the Qur'an.

I am indebted to my friends and family members here in the United States, especially my granddaughter, Iqra Ahmed, a student of Grade Eleven who took care the formatting of the whole manuscript with Header and Footer. I am especially indebted to a friend-by-chance, Dr.

---

[1] Fazlur Rahman, born on Sept. 21, 1919, and brought up in a Malik family of Hazara district in Pakistan and died on 26th July 1988 in Chicago, Illinois. He was recalled from the McGill University, Canada by the then President of Pakistan, General Ayub Khan and given the charge as Director of the Islamic Research Institute from 1961-68. He also served on the Advisory Council of Islamic Ideology, a supreme policy-making body of Pakistan, which used to propose policies to the Government of Pakistan for implementation. This job proved to be the most tumultuous period in his life because of the bickering between the political parties and religious groups. He became a controversial figure and targeted by the religious parties. After a turbulent period that adversely affected his health and his leadership he resigned in 1968. After a short spell he was appointed as Professor of Islamic Thought at the University of Chicago in 1969. In 1986 he was named Harold H. Swift Distinguished Service Professor at Chicago, a title he held until his death in 1988.

Denny A.Clark, Ph.D., Professor Emeritus of Philosophy & Religion, at The College of Idaho, where he taught for 22 years without whose help and contribution this book could not be as meaningful and poignant as it is now. I am also grateful to my neighbor and native, Lakshmeshwar Dayal, a retiree from Indian Administrative Service and a devotee of Islamic disciplines. His suggestions on critical chapters have been immensely helpful. I have used quotations from his recent book, 'The Truth about Islam'. Lastly, I am grateful to my wife without whose cooperation and patience this book could not see the light of the day. She patiently, though indignantly, tolerated my gross negligence from her home keeping.

The nature of the subject of this book, spread throughout its pages, came to my mind basically after the event of 9/11. All nineteen perpetrators were Muslims. Their victims were largely loving, peaceful, normal famly people of varied faiths and ethnicities, including Muslims. Their attack on the twin towers was basically an attack against the American System and the American injustices with Palestinians, Lebanese and others as much as stationing American forces in almost all Arab and Muslim countries.

Many critics of Islam have pointed to multiple examples of violence in Islam's history, and have used to the label "terrorism" for all of it. That is not an appropriate description, however. A better term would be "militancy" which better expresses its ambiguous combination (in varying proportions) of legitimate moral grievance and illegitimate personal ambition for power and prerogatives, which often cannot be easily distinguished or disentangled.

This is not a book of history; it does not claim to cover every aspect of Islam and does not even deal with the various phases of its historical growth and development. It confines itself to the search for the true mission of Islam and how that mission has been hijacked in the struggle of faith and power. In describing this aspect the historical part naturally cannot be ignored, though I have used history selectively to strengthen my arguments. This is, of course, as it should be. This is not a book of religion either. Since religion and politics overlap each other in the history of Islam, theology and jurisprudence have their interplay in the study.

Introduction

Why a restudy of Islam today when tons of electronic and print media in book, magazine and newspaper formats are available in almost every language in bookshops and libraries throughout the world? It is partly because never before have words of both demonization and praise been heard so loudly and so conflictingly as we hear today; never before has the world been split so sharply into two antagonists as it is now. Islam is all for peace justice, values and happiness, says one, while it is all for war, destruction, blood-letting, intolerance, and injustices, says the other. The gulf is becoming wider and wider with the passage of time. The problem complicates when this divide is not based on faith and prejudices only, but also on sincere and honest scholarship. It is not as if all Muslims praise today's Islam and all non-Muslims demonizing it. It is perplexing to see when a Muslim demonizes Islam and a non-Muslim praises it (e.g., Aiyan Hirsi, Salman Rushdie and likes on one side, and innumerable intellectual numerous non-Muslim scholars of repute on the other.[2] Current scholarship, based on scientific investigation of written and unwritten documents, customs and traditions of centuries-old practices has made the faith-based claims ineffective. Scientific investigation of social phenomena is not meant for finding false or truth, but is a search for the normative of right or wrong in the contemporary history of nations and their state of affairs.

Why Muslim Militancy?

This work provides me with a fitting occasion for restating the perspective which inspired its writing and indicating its relevance to the copious output of opinion and debate that followed in the wake of the tragic events of 11th September, 2001. While going through these debates in the East and the West it is not difficult to discern the polar trends

---

2   A. J. Arberry, John Esposito, Karen Armstrong, Wilfred C. Smith, Andrew Whetcroft, T.W.Arnold, and many others.

of thought between each hemisphere. While one disapproves the events of 9/11, the other justifies them. The overarching theme of these events remains today, at the 10th anniversary of the event, haunting the hearts and minds of both. There are instances of Muslims, Christians and others crossing the line of their faith in the aftermath of 9/11. My intention in writing this book, inter alia, is to draw attention to what remains unimagined and unthought-of, not merely out of neglect, but out of the active resistance of the mythical mind of the current Islamic thought.

Multi-culturalism

It is simply a fact that modern conditions, whether we like it or not, oblige us to strive for some comprehension of each other's presuppositions. Isolationism is gone, and with it gone is the kind of world in which it was feasible for one civilization or culture to ignore the values and convictions of another. Plurality of ethnicity and race, religion and culture, are the phenomenon of today's societies. With the exception of Iran and Saudi Arabia, multiculturalism is the norm of almost all Muslim societies from Morocco to Indonesia. Even the exclusively Muslim states, like Saudi Arabia and Iran, are not completely uninfluenced by other's culture and thought. Almost all the necessities of their life, both personal or public, are imported from industrially advanced countries of Europe and North America, which bear inherent cultural and educational influences. The other Muslim countries having multi-racial and multi-religious society are no better than the first one. They all lag behind in intellectual and industrial developments, in health and education advancement, and in the essentials of modernity, based on democracy and freedom in spite of their being mostly rich in natural resources.

Secularism

Apart from Iran and Saudi Arabia, almost all Muslim societies and states are neither religious nor secular. The Christian world had long ago announced the Christ's oft-quoted words: "Render therefore unto Caesar, the things which are Caesar's, and unto God, the things that are God's" separating religion and politics. Practically, there were no separation of church and state in the medieval Europe. For centuries Christian West was engulfed in fighting between Church and State, resulting in breaking the monopoly of Roman Catholic Church by establishing Anglican Church under suzerainty of the King of England, Henry VIII. Since then, political domination of Roman Catholic on Churches of England and non-Catholic countries disappeared. No one can deny its repercussions on ethical and moral depravations in the affairs of the states in today's democratic societies. This has resulted in a vacuum of values and ethics; it is now felt, from the life of the people who are advancing beyond leaps and bounds in today's technology and its advancement. We, in the supposedly advanced countries of Europe and America feel neither comfortable nor happy. On the other hand, those in Muslim societies feel that in the present state of things, they could neither get salvation in their life hereafter, nor experience prosperity and advancement in their present life.

Muslim experience with politics and religion during the recent past has been varied and contrasting. Whereas Moghal Emperor, Akbar the Great, expelled Islam and introduced his new religion Deen-e-Ilahi, the Emperor Aurangzeb introduced *shari'a* into his legal system. A similar situation occurred in Turkey when *Ata Turk* ended the centuries-old Islamic Caliphate in 1924 and set up a secular state of Turkey. Iran passed from a millennium of an utterly secular state to the current theocratic state. Saudi Arabia remains a fundamentalist state, whereas in our time other Muslim states are passing through various experimental stages of religion and secularism. The battle between religion and politics is an age-old story and Islamic societies and states are not immune of this battle.

Muslim Societies in doldrums

This is a study of a people in the turmoil of today's world. The Muslim community in our day is in serious transition. What confuses today's Muslims is that they face the perplexities and opportunities of modernity as heirs of a unique tradition. Muslim society is characterized by a religious heritage Islam and a great past. What is happening to the community is a confusing situation of how to Islamize the essentials of modern age for development, prosperity, and for a happy life in this world and salvation in the world hereafter. This study is a bird's eye view of the efforts made by the Muslim intellectuals and *ulama* in the medieval and post-medieval periods of Islam to achieve this goal. What is happening to the community and to its religious expression is the subject of this book.

We do not find any difficulty in this study so long as Muslims were masters of the situation and were sovereign over their own state of affairs. The problem arose when Islam began to lose its influence, power and political hegemony with the beginning of nineteenth century, when Europe started its march toward progress and modernity and, at the same time, extended its colonial rule over all the Muslim states except Turkey, Morocco and Saudi Arabia.

The classical and medieval studies by Muslim theologians, jurists and thinkers are insufficient in today's contemporary Muslim states and society. The content, functions and authority of religion are changing profoundly under the impact of the new forces of scientific and technological inventions, electronic and digital revolutions, and options offered by economic and globalization forces. Today, the problem for Muslim societies is to know whether they should or should not resist these forces, as they did with modernity, or whether the new inventions and globalization will be more effective tools in changing the status of the state and political institutions, the collective mentalities concerning traditional beliefs, rituals and values, educational practices, channels of communication and the relationship to scientific knowledge, especially in the domain of human, social, political and legal sciences.

Muslim States: A Brief Survey

Today, throughout the Muslim world the processes of contemporary history is so complex and radical that they are far from easy to understand, whether for the Muslims, or for the outside observers. Yet such understanding is important: for Muslims, in order to participate intelligently in the transformation toward which they are heading to; for outsiders, to observe the Muslim life intelligently and to relate themselves sanely to it; for both, to communicate, understand and live together in peace and happiness. Today's world is a global-body; if one part of the body aches, the other parts are affected. It is the significance of these needs that justifies our present exploratory endeavor to seek such understanding. We do not claim that our treatment of the issues here raised is adequate, but we do insist that those issues are important and worth understanding for all.

History is primarily a human activity, despite its partial conditioning by impersonal forces. For Muslims, faith ramifies through all segments of social, political, economic and cultural developments. One of the distinguishing factors of Muslim world is the Islamic element, persistently significant in the on-going affairs of these nations in a way that the actors in these affairs are persons who are Muslim.

What is special about this century that makes our age so starkly one of critical transition, and what special about Islam, that makes its involvement in this crisis so dramatic? In both cases, a very great deal is special. The Muslim's faith—its development and its dynamism—is until halfway in its ultimate evolution—and we will see to its completion. With respect to the instability of glittering modernity—much is being written and seen. We need not indulge in it except briefly. Much has been said and written on it and much more is forthcoming.

Islam and modernity

Never before in human history or in evolution of human society has change been so swift, so pervasive, and so transparent as today. Not only the development and affluence, since the Industrial Revolution and the recent strides of scientific and electronic inventions and information technology, has been quick and out of all proportion to anything seen before. For Islam, with the dynamics of the past slowly giving way to the swift development of the contemporary scene, consciousness is perforce spreading among Muslims of how fluid is its present, as well as its past. One example: the poet-thinker Sir Muhammad Iqbal speaks of "the enormous rapidity with which the world of Islam is spiritually moving".[3] With these comes an incipient sense of humanity's opportunity for directing change.[4] In addition to these, there are new conditions which Islam in its modern context shares with the rest of the present-day world. We need a clearer understanding of what kind of thing Islam is, as well as what kind of thing modernity is, if we want gain a sensitive insight into the modern condition of the Muslim world.

---

[3] Sir Muhammad Iqbal, *The Reconstruction of Religious Thought in Islam,* 1944, Lahore, p.7; and Muhammad Asad, *Islam at the Crossroads,* Delhi 1934; Lahore 1955.

[4] For instance, the move in Egypt to consider a possible bringing together of the four legal systems of Sunni Islam, and even bringing theology of Shi'a and Sunni together. One expression of this is the monthly journal, *Risalat al-Islam,* Cairo, 1368/1949; and also the statements circulated by the Council of the Academy of Islamic Studies, Hyderabad, Deccan, India, *Toward Reorientation of Islamic Thought: A Call for Introspection, 1954.*

Impact of the West

No doubt, the West and of the last century have implicated Islam and its societies. But there is no denying that Islam has also had a powerful impact on contemporary non-Islamic society. Islam piqued interest among European scholars, setting off the movement of Orientalism. Islamic architecture influenced European architecture in various ways (for example, the Türkischer Temple synagogue in Vienna). The linguistic and cultural influences on Mozarabs in Spain and the influences on the contemporary non-Muslim states and societies are spread in the pages of medieval European history. Islam's thrust in this situation, the stresses and strains generated in its on-going process, and the dynamics of its reaction to the modern world—whether aggressive or cowering, protective or creative—must all be understood in terms both of the crucially new environment, as well as of Islam's own inner quality. Islam is a system with its own inherent shock-absorber.

Manifestly, Islam could never have survived across the past fourteen centuries as one of the five great world religions had it not, like the others, had the quality of having something profound, relevant and personal to say directly to all sorts and conditions of people of every status, background, capacity, temperament, and aspiration. Islam, like the other world religions overflows all definition both because it is open at one end to the immeasurable greatness of the Divine and because it relates at the other end to the immeasurable diversity of human society. An understanding of the present condition of the Muslim society is impossible without an understanding of Islam.

Islamic Civilization

Since the primary characteristic of the Muslim world is that it is Muslim, we begin our study with an attempt to elucidate what it means to be a Muslim and how far this distinguishes the Muslim world from other worlds.

Secondly, because contemporary Muslim society is decidedly the outgrowth of the immediate currents of past events, we need a general survey of the recent background throughout the Muslim world, seeking a common pattern among its numerous diversities, enough at least to justify the concept that Islamic history continues apace. An understanding of current events in the Muslim world involves an understanding of their Islamic quality. We will find that the Islamic factor is persistently significant in the on-going affairs of these nations because the actors of these affairs are persons who are Muslim.

Muslims in Conflict

In contrast to the inherent Islamic character, today Muslim terrorist organizations exist across the world, and have carried out attacks from South Asia across the Middle East, Europe, Southeast Asia, and the United State since at least 1983. These organizations use several tactics, including suicide attacks, hijackings, kidnapping and execution, and recruit new members through the internet and other sources. The best-known organization is Al-Qaeda, which carried out the Sept. 11, 2001 attacks and which envisions a complete break from the foreign influences in the Muslim world while keeping abreast with modern sciences and developments, and the creation of a new Islamic caliphate.

The laws of *Jihad* categorically preclude wanton and indiscriminate slaughter. The warriors in the *Jihad* are urged not to harm non-combatants, women and children, "unless they attack you first." These laws insist on the need for a clear declaration of war before beginning hostilities, and for proper warning before resuming hostilities after a truce. What the classical jurists of Islam never remotely considered is the kind of unprovoked, unannounced mass slaughter of noncombatant civil populations that we have seen recently in both Muslim and non-Muslim countries. For this there is no precedent and no authority in Islam.

The question is: why should Muslims be surprised, incensed or feel the world does not understand Islam, such atrocities or the practices of stoning women to death or beheading Muslims who are open to other beliefs, persist A majority of Europeans and Americans believe that "Islam is negative for them." We are witnessing unprecedented movements across Europe against the infringement of Muslim culture, religion and dress code on European societies. Muslims in their homelands and in other parts of the world do not seem to take notice of other peoples' impatience with their unsolicited way of life.

The question is: what do Muslims want non-Muslims in Europe, America and rest of the world to know about Islam that could change their negative views of Islam? Based on what non-Muslims see on the news media, experience and hear in the streets, in mosques, in Muslim schools in Europe and America—let alone in Iraq, Pakistan, Yemen, Somalia, Afghanistan, Iran, and Saudi Arabia—the overwhelming majority of the European countries do not want to be associated with Islam. Unlike most Muslims, the majority of Westerners relate to each other through social interaction, merits, common values, tangible contributions and tolerance of differences. Most Muslims, however, relate to others through religious orientation, like *Shi'a, Sunni, Ahmadi, Deobandi, Barelvi,* and *Wahabi.* Is it any wonder the West wants to prevent Islam from taking root in their democracies?

There is an escalating conflict within and between Muslims societies over differing interpretations of Islam and religious rituals. Even fifteen centuries could not make *Shi'as* and *Sunnis* reconcile with each other, while outcasting out minority communities, like *Ahmadi, Baha'i,* and others. Muslim-on-Muslim killings, the destruction of minorities' holy shrines and other cultural heritages, as well as the ongoing carnage in Pakistan, Afghanistan, Yemen, Iran, Iraq and Egypt, are but some examples of bloody conflict among Muslims. The rampant oppression of Muslim and non-Muslim minorities in all Arab and Muslim countries bears witness to a religion mired in contradictions and at odds with itself and, by extension, with the rest of the world.

Perhaps no other world religion abhors and warns against violence and injustice of all kinds and strife as unmistakably as Islam does. In fact, if Islam means acceptance or submission to the will of God, it also means peace, literally. More important, it preaches moderation, restraint and reason in everything we do, even in our devotion and prayers. It warns us that killing one innocent human being is akin to killing all humanity and saving one innocent life is like saving mankind. The Qur'an constantly cautions us that Allah does not like those who spread strife and chaos on earth. We are told that killing a fellow human being is waging war against God, and that Allah promises them harshest punishment. We hardly find any logic in recent Muslim feats of terrorism and lack of tolerance against Muslims and minorities in Muslim societies of Asia, Africa and the Middle East.

In their long and eventful history, Muslims have never faced a greater challenge to their identity and existence than now. This sickness within is far more dangerous than what they confront from without.

The Nature of Conflict

On the death of Prophet Muhammad in 632 the question of succession assumed paramount importance; it threatened to be as much religious as political. The trauma of the Prophet's death resolved the problem without any serious dispute. The first two successors of the Prophet, known as caliphs, proved remarkably resourceful; they united the faithful under one banner to spread the faith.

The trouble began after the first two Caliphs, with the reign of Othman. Rival groups took to arms, caliphs were murdered and their murders plunged the Caliphate into a succession of civil wars. Since then the Muslims have never been a united community. As the wars of Caliphate dragged on, temporal and religious factions drifted apart and each faction broke into sub-factions; all of them swore by the shari'a—the canonical law of Islam—but each faction interpreted it differently and went about it in its own way. Those who operated in the temporal domain used Shari'a for their own ends while the theologians busied themselves with the coining of new theories and the charting out of fresh paths for the faithful. The vast majority remained silent spectators to this frenetic activity; they were content with their routine and the simple rituals they practiced. Islam was simple enough for them to follow without much guidance.

For more than two hundred years this state of affairs continued, leading to a plethora of contradictory doctrines, which finally divided the Muslims into two broad groups—one owing allegiance to their temporal rulers, the other opposed to them. The ruling group was not much concerned with the dictates of religion. To them power mattered more than faith. The other group was against the rulers' heathen activities; it aimed at purifying Islam. But the conflict did not much perturb the common people; they kept out of it.

This conflict between religion and politics extends far into the past; it did not begin with Islam or Christianity but existed much earlier. Thus the conflict went on with the passage of History. Temporal power acquired greater authority.

PART—I

ISLAM IN HISTORY

The Making of A History

Islam originated in Arabia in the early seventh century CE. Two broad elements should be distinguished in that immediate religious backdrop: the purely Arab background and the penetration of Judeo-Christian elements. For the most part, however, the Bedouins were a secular people with little idea of an afterlife. At the sanctuaries (*harams*) that had been established in some parts, fetishism seems to have developed into idol worship; the most important of these sites was the *Ka'bah* at *Makkahh*. The Bedouin Arabs believed in a blind fate that inescapably determined birth, sustenance and death. These Arabs also had a code of honor (called *murūwah*, or "manliness"). It was their real religious ethics; its main constituent was tribal honor, the honor of women, bravery, hospitality, honoring one's promises and pacts, and last but not least, vengeance. In southwestern Arabia, a rather highly sophisticated civilization had existed since the *Sabian* period, with a prosperous economy and agriculture.

Jewish and Christian populations existed (Jews in Madina—pre-Islamic *Yathrib*—in the south and in *Khaybar* in the north; Christians in the south, in Iraq, in Syria, and in certain tribes). The *Makkahns* had nevertheless come to know a good deal about Judeo-Christian ideas (6:92); several people in *Makkah* and elsewhere had arrived at the idea of monotheism. The primary background of **Islam** is Arab rather than Judeo-Christian, although the latter tradition has strongly influenced **Islam**. In its genesis, **Islam** grew out of the problems existing in Arab *Makkahn* society.

During a twelve-year struggle in *Makkah* (610-622 CE), the prophet Muhammad had gathered a devoted group of followers. Yet his movement seemed to reach an impasse because of the unflinching opposition of the mercantile aristocracy, which saw in it a threat to both of their vested interests—their Ka'bah-centered religion, from which they benefited as custodians of the sanctuary and recipients of income from the pilgrimage, and their privileged control of trade. After

Muḥammad and his followers emigrated from *Makkah* to Madina in 622 (the beginning of the lunar Islamic calendar, called the *hijrī*, or "emigration calendar"), at the invitation of the majority of the Arab inhabitants there, he became the head of both the nascent community and the existing polity. However, while he gave laws, waged peace and war, and created social institutions, he never claimed to be a ruler, a lawgiver, a judge, or a general; he referred to himself always as a messenger of God. As a result, not only were Islamic "religious" doctrines and rituals in the narrower sense regarded as Islamic but so were the state, the law, and social institutions. **Islam** is thus the name of a total way of life and does not merely regulate the individual's private relationship with God.

In Madina, then, the Prophet was able to institute his social reforms through the exercise of the religious and political power that he had been denied in Makkah. After three battles in which Muslims gained the upper hand over the Makkans and their allies, **Islam,** now in rapid ascendancy, was able to take Makkah peacefully in AH 8th /630th CE along with a large part, if not the whole, of the Arabian Peninsula. In Madina, too, the Muslim community was formally launched in 2nd/624th as the "median community," the only community consciously established by the founder of a religion for a specific purpose, as the Qur'ān speaks of those "who, when we give them power on the earth, shall establish prayers and welfare of the poor and shall command good and forbid evil" (22:41). Finally, Makkah was declared to be the goal of annual pilgrimage for the faithful and also the direction (*qiblah*) for prayer, instead of Jerusalem. Both the constitution and the anchoring of the community were complete.

After a brief lapse into tribal sovereignty following the Prophet's death, Arab resistance to the acknowledgment of Madina's central authority was broken by force. The tribesmen's energies were turned outward in conquests of neighboring lands under the banner of **Islam**, which provided the necessary zeal and incentives for rapid military and political expansion with richness in war booty. Within a century after the Prophet's death, Muslim Arabs were administering an empire stretching from the southern borders of France through North Africa and the Middle East, across Central Asia and into Sind. There was no policy of converting non-Muslims to **Islam**. The purpose of *jihād* was not conversion but the establishment of Islamic rule. Nonetheless,

4

partly because of certain disabilities imposed by Islamic law on non-Muslim subjects (mainly the *jizyah*, or poll tax, was the heavier particularly for the lower strata of the population) and partly because of Islamic egalitarianism, **Islam** spread quickly after an initial period during which conversions were sometimes even discouraged. This was the first phase of the spread of **Islam**; later on, Muslim mystics, or the *Sufis*, were the main vehicles of Islamic expansion in India, Central Asia, and sub-Saharan Africa, although the role of traders in the Indian and Indonesian coastal areas and China must not be minimized. Even in the twentieth century, Turkish soldiers brought **Islam** to South Korea during the Korean War.

Less than half a century after the Prophet's death, political dissensions over succession led to civil war. A number of groups called the *Khārijīs* ("those who went out") declared war on the community at large because it tolerated rule by "unrighteous" men; they claimed that a Muslim ceased to be a Muslim by committing a reprehensible act without sincerely repenting, and that other Muslims who did not regard such a person as non-Muslim also became non-Muslim. In reaction to the *Khārijīs* and the ensuing civil strife, the community (both the Sunnī mainstream and the Shī'a, or party of 'Alī) generally adopted a religious stand that not only was tolerant of religious and political deviations from strict Islamic norms but was even positively accommodating toward them. The net result of this basic development was that excommunication was ruled out so long as a person recognized the community as Muslim and professed that "there is no god but God and Muhammad is his prophet." This formula created or rationalized accommodation for an amazing range of different religious opinions and practices under one God and Muhammad's prophethood.

With the advent of the Abbasids, there were other political, social, and religious changes as well, among them the improvement of the status of the Iranians, who, under Umayyad rule, were denied an identity of their own as "clients" (*mawālī*) of the Arab tribes; and the espousal and implementation of legal measures created by the religious leadership, which had been largely alienated from the *Umayyads*. All of these developments combined to facilitate the rapid spread of **Islam.**

Muslims have always looked for God in history. Their sacred scripture, the Qur'an, gave them a historical mission. Their chief duty was to create a just community in which all members, even the most

5

weak and vulnerable, were treated with absolute respect. The experience of building such a society and living in it would give them intimations of the divine, because they would be living in accordance with God's will. A Muslim had to redeem history, and that meant that addressing the current state of affairs was not a distraction from God's mission but the fulfillment of God's goal. The political well-being of the Muslim community was a matter of supreme importance. As with any religious ideal, it was almost impossibly difficult to implement in the flawed and tragic conditions of history, but after each failure Muslims had to get up and begin anew.

Politics was, therefore, a sacrament: it was the arena in which Muslims experienced God and which enabled the divine to function, through them, effectively in the world. Consequently, the historical trials and tribulations of the Muslim community—political assassinations, civil wars, invasions, and the rise and fall of the ruling dynasties—were not divorced from the inner religious quest, but were related to the essence of the Islamic vision. An account of the external history of the Muslim people cannot, therefore, be of mere secondary interest, since the chief characteristics of Islam has been its sacralization of history.

The past and present militancy of the host of Muslim fundamentalist and militant groups, starting from *Kharijis* in the early period of pious caliphs, *Qarmatians* in the medieval period of *Fatimids* of Egypt, and the *Wahabbis* emerging from Saudi Arabia, and *Ayatollahs* in Iran in the recent past, the emergence of Muslim Brotherhood and its offshoots, PLO, al-Qaeda, Taliban, Islamic *Jihad*, Hammas, Hizbollah, Jama'a Islamia, National Liberation Front, and many others throughout the Muslim world, now spilling into Europe and America, can be seen as the extension of the same phenomenon—the sacralization of history. It is not that all the above mentioned militant groups are fighting today for 'the cause of Allah'. Their methodology to achieve justice through militancy is like fighting a just war with wrong weapon.

The Arab Conquest

After the death of the Prophet, the army that was targeted at Syria was dispatched by *Abu Bakr*, in spite of the protestation made by certain Muslims in view of the then disturbed state of Arabia. This was the first of the series of campaigns in which the Arabs overran Syria, Persia and Northern Africa—overturning the ancient kingdom of Persia and despoiling the Roman Empire of some of its fairest provinces.

Dollinger has put the problem that meets us here, in the following words: "Was it genuine religious enthusiasm, the new strength of a faith now for the first time blossoming forth in all its purity, that gave the victory in every battle to the arms of the Arabs and in so incredibly short a time founded the greatest empire the world have ever seen? But evidence is wanting to prove that this was the case. The number was far too small of those who had given their allegiance to the Prophet, while on the other hand all the greater was the number of those who had been brought into the ranks of Muhammad only through pressure from without or by the hope of worldly gain. Khalid b. Waleed has exhibited in a very striking manner that mixture of force and persuasion whereby he and many of the *Quraysh* had been converted when he said that 'God had seized them by the hearts and by the hair and compelled them to follow the Prophet'. The proud feeling too of a common nationality had much influence. Until more powerful was the attraction offered them only a miserable subsistence, for the fruitful and luxuriant countries of Persia, Syria and Egypt."[5]

These conquests which laid the foundations of the Arab empire were certainly not the only outcome of *Jihad* waged for the propagation of Islam, but they were followed by such a vast defection from Christianity that this result has often been supposed to have been their aim. The spirit which animated the invading hosts of Arabs who poured over the confines of the Byzantine and Persian empires, was no proselytizing zeal

---

[5]   T.W. Arnold, The Preaching of Islam, Kitab Bhavan, New Delhi, India, 1999; p.42.

for the conversion of souls. On the contrary, religious interests appear to have entered but little into the consciousness of the protagonists of the Arab armies. The expansion of Arab political control is more rightly envisaged as the migration of a vigorous and energetic people driven by hunger and want, to leave their inhospitable deserts and overrun the richer lands of their more fortunate neighbors.

Additionally, it is not in the annals of the conquering armies that we must look for the reasons which led to the so rapid spread of Islam, but rather in the conditions prevailing among the conquered peoples. It is not surprising to find that many of the Christian Bedouins were swept into the rushing tide of this great movement and those Arab tribes, who for centuries had professed the Christian religion, now abandoned it to embrace the Muslim faith. The tribe of *Banu Ghassan*, who held sway over the desert east of Palestine and southern Syria, who were "Lords in the days of the ignorance and stars of Islam," after the battle of *Qadisiyyah* in 14 Hijrah, in which the Persian army under Rustam had been utterly discomfited, many Christians belonging to the Bedouin tribes on both sides of the Euphrates came to the Muslim general and said: "The tribes that at the first embraced Islam were wiser than we. Now that *Rustam* hath been slain, we will accept the new belief."[6] Similarly, after the conquest of northern Syria, most of the Bedouin tribes joined themselves to the followers of the Prophet.[7]

That Force was not the determining factor in conversions may be recognized from the amicable relations that existed between the Christian and the Muslim Arabs. The Prophet himself had entered into treaty with several Christian tribes, promising them his protection and guaranteeing them the free exercise of their religion and to their clergy undisturbed enjoyment of their old rights and authority.[8]

In the battle of the Bridge (13 Hijrah) when a disastrous defeat was imminent and the panic-stricken Arabs were hemmed in between the Euphrates and the Persian army, a Christian chief of *Banu Tayy* sprang forward to assist *Muthannah*, the Muslim general, in defending the bridge of boats which could alone afford the means of an orderly retreat.

---

6   Muir, Sir William, *Caliphate: Its Rise, Decline and Fall*, London, 1891 pp.121-22.

7   Caetani, Leon; *Principe di Teano: Annali dell' Islam* (Milano 1905) vol. iii. P.814.

8   Caetani, Ibid. vol. ii, pp. 260, 299, 351.

Winning battles alone could not have made Islam permanent or even strong had there not been a state of affairs awaiting some such message and ready to accept it. Both in the world of Western Asia and in the Greco-Roman world of the Mediterranean, society had fallen, much as our society has today, into a tangle wherein the bulk of people were disappointed and angry and were seeking for a solution to a whole group of social strains. There was indebtedness everywhere; the power of money was glorified with consequent usury. There was slavery everywhere. Society reposed upon it, as ours reposes upon wage slavery today. There was weariness and discontent with theological debate, which, for all its intensity, had grown out of touch with the masses. There lay upon the freemen, already tortured with debt, a heavy burden of imperial taxation; and there was the irritant of existing central government interfering with people's lives; there was the tyranny of the lawyers and their charges. To all this Islam came as a vast relief and a solution of strain. The slave who admitted that Mohammed was the prophet of God, ceased to be a slave. The slave who adopted Islam was henceforward free. The debtor who accepted Islam was rid of his debts. Usury was forbidden. The small farmer was relieved not only of his debts but of his crushing taxation. Above all, justice could be had without buying it from lawyers. Wherever Islam conquered there was a new spirit of freedom and relaxation. It was the combination of all these things, the attractive simplicity of the doctrine, the sweeping away of clerical and imperial discipline, the huge immediate practical advantage of freedom for the slave and riddance of anxiety for the debtor, the crowning advantage of free justice under few and simple new laws easily understood that formed the driving force behind the astonishing social victory of Islam. The courts were everywhere accessible to all without payment and giving verdicts which all could understand. This new movement was essentially a "Reformation," and we can discover numerous affinities between Islam and the Protestant Reformers on Images, on the Mass, on Celibacy, etc.

Although in later years this great empire was split up and the political power of Islam diminished, until its spiritual conquests went on uninterruptedly. When the Mongol hordes sacked Baghdad in 1258 CE and drowned in blood the faded glory of the Abbasid dynasty—when the Muslims were expelled from *Cordova* by Ferdinand of Leon and Castile in 1236 and later from *Granada*, the last stronghold of Islam in Spain, and paid tribute to the Christian king—Islam had just gained a footing in the island of *Sumatra* and through the islands of the *Malay Archipelago*. In the hours of its political degradation, Islam has achieved some of its most brilliant spiritual conquests on two great historical occasion—the *Saljuke Turks* in the eleventh and *Mongols* in the thirteenth century—and in each case the conquerors accepted the religion of the conquered. Unaided also by the temporal power, Muslims have carried Islam into Central Africa, China and the East Indian islands.

At the present Islam extends from Morocco to Zanzibar, from Sierra Leone to Siberia and China, from Bosnia to New Guinea. Outside the limits of strictly Muslim lands, places such as China and Russia contain large Muslim populations. There are a few small communities of the followers of the Prophet, which bear witness to the faith of Islam in the midst of non-Muslims, including the Polish-speaking Muslims of Tatar origin in Lithuania, that inhabit the districts of Kovno, Vilno and Grodno; the Dutch-speaking Muslims of Cape Colony; and the Indian coolies that have carried the faith of Islam with them to the West Indian Islands and British and Dutch Guiana. In recent years, too, Islam has found adherents in Europe, England, in North America, South America, Australia and Japan.

Islam's expansion over so vast a portion of the globe is due to various causes—social, political, and religious: but among these, one of the most powerful factors at work in the production of this stupendous result has been the unremitted labors of Muslim missionaries who, with the Prophet himself as their great ensample, have spent themselves for the conversion of unbelievers.

Though a clear distinction can be drawn between conversion as the result of persecution and a peaceful propaganda by means of methods of persuasion, it is not so easy to ascertain the motives that have induced the convert to change his religious allegiance. Both in Christianity and Islam there have been at all times earnest souls to whom their religion has been the supreme reality of their lives and likewise there have been those without the pale who have responded to their appeal and have embraced the new religion with a like fervor. But, on the other hand, Islam, like Christianity, has reckoned among its adherents many persons to whom religious institutions have been merely instruments of a political policy or forms of social organization, to be accepted either as disagreeable necessities or as convenient solutions of problems that they do not care to think out for themselves. Thus both Christianity and Islam have added to the number of their followers by methods and under conditions—social, political and economic—which have no connection with such a thirst for souls as animate the true missionary.

Islamic Polity
in Post-Prophetic Period

All political theories in Islam start from the assumption that Islamic government exists by virtue of a divine contract based on the *Shari'a*. None, therefore, asks the question of why the state exists. Political science was thus not an independent discipline but a department of theology. There was no distinction between state and society, or between Church and state; and therefore no doctrine of the temporal end which alone belonged to the state and the spiritual end which belonged to the Church. Religion was not separated from politics, or politics from morals. Since the activity of the Muslims relating to the state had a metaphysical and religious basis, it follows that religious dissent amounted to political disaffection and even treason.

The Founder of Islam was his own head of a state. During his lifetime, the Muslims were a political as well as a religious community, with the Prophet as sovereign, governing a place and a people, dispensing justice, collecting taxes, commanding armies, conducting diplomacy, and waging war. In Islam, there was no king, there was only God, and Muhammad was His Messenger, who taught and ruled on God's behalf. When the Messenger died, his spiritual and prophetic function—the promulgation of God's message—was completed. The implementation of God's message was taken by his deputy or successor known as *khalifa* (caliph).

During the period of the first four Caliphs (632-660), the Muslim state and government was indistinguishable from the public body. The senior members of the Companions in Madina advised, controlled and participated in both legislative and executive functions. Law could hardly be separated from politics. Legislation in this period can, therefore, mainly be attributed to the contemporary Caliphs with the joint work of the Community senior members.

With the expansion of the Muslim conquests from the year 657 onwards, peoples and communities of different races and varying cultural and social backgrounds were included within the Islamic empire. Gradually there evolved a body of Islamic political ideas, at the base of which lay pre-Islamic tribal tradition, and Hellenistic and Persian theories of state. All set forth the divine nature of ultimate sovereignty and presupposed the function of the state to (i) guarantee the maintenance of Islam and (ii) the application of the *shari'a*, and (iii) the defense of orthodoxy. The raw materials upon which it built were the scattered verses of the Qur'an dealing with political thought, the traditions of the prophet, the practices of the primitive Islamic community and the interpretation of these sources in the light of later political developments, reinforced by the dogma of the divine guidance of the community and the infallibility of *ijm'a* (public opinion).

The basis of the political structure was the *ummah*, the 'community'—the assembly of individuals bound to one another by ties of religion. Its internal organization was defined by a common acceptance and a common submission to the divine law and to the temporal head of the community. Obedience to rulers was laid down in the Qur'an: "O you who believe! Obey Allah, and obey the Messenger, and those charged with authority among you" (4:59).

The main preoccupation of the constitutional theorists in the first and second centuries of Islam was over the question of election and deposition of the *Imam* and reflects the struggles between the Sunnis, the *Kharijis*, and the *Shi'as*, and the conflicts between the *Mu'tazila* and other schools.

Under the *Umayyads*, with the conquests of Syria, Iraq, Persia and Egypt, Hellenistic and *Sassanian* influences combined with Arab tradition began to shape the governing institutions of Islam, and gradually a semi-official interpretation of the formulations, stated above, emerged. However, no theory of constitutional government was formulated, although some signs of theological problems for the conduct of the state were beginning to emerge.

The rise of the *Abbasids* was followed by a transformation of the administration and society under the influence of *Sassanian* tradition. The Abbasids had come to power with the support of the Khurasan army. While the Abbasid Caliphate was at the height of its power, although the introduction of foreign elements into the practice and

13

theory of government aroused disquiet among the jurists, mainly on theological grounds, problems of constitutional theory do not appear to have attracted their attention.

As the Caliphate declined and the fragmentation of power took place, an imperative need was felt for the formulation of an ideal of Islamic government to which rulers could be appointed and which would enshrine the traditions of the community, which were threatened on all sides.

There was a gap between theory and practice, and in fact there were a number of independent kingdoms and rebellious groups within the state. A rationalization of the conflict between theory and practice was therefore required.

As is the case with all great religions, it was precisely the arguments, the discord, and the sometimes bloody conflicts that resulted from trying to discern God's will in the absence of God's prophet that gave birth to the varied and wonderfully diverse institutions of Islam. Just as the movements that succeeded Jesus' death—from Peter's messianic Judaism to Paul's Hellenistic religion of salvation to the Gnosticism of the Egyptians, and more mystical movements of the East—as "Christianities"—so was it that followed Muhammad's death, splitting Islam into *Kharjites*, *Shi'as*, *Sunnis* and their affiliates.

Throughout Islamic history, as Muslim dynasties—Arabs during *Umayyads*, Persians and Arabs during Abbasids, Turks during Ottomans, Egyptians during Fatimids, Mongols during Moghals of India, and also during *Ghaznavids* and *Saljukes*—tumbled over each other, Muslim kings were crowned and dethroned, Islamic *shuras* (consultative bodies elected and dissolved), only the *Ulama*, in their capacity as the link to the traditions of the past, have managed to retain their self-imposed role as the leaders of Muslim society. As a result, over the past fourteen centuries, Islam as we know it has been almost exclusively defined by an extremely small, rigid, and often profoundly traditionalist group of men who, for better or worse, considered themselves to be the unyielding pillars upon which the religious, social, and political foundations of the religion rest. How they gained this authority and what they have done with it, is perhaps the most important chapter in the story of Islam.

Here we are concerned with the contemporary manifestation of this problem and crisis. First, however, there is value in glancing quickly at the over-all history of Islam in the earlier phase, from the decline of the great medieval period until yesterday. Ever since its inception, Islam has faced and met spiritual and intellectual challenges. From the 2nd/8th to the 4th/10th centuries, a series of intellectual and cultural crises arose in Islam, the most serious and significant was that produced by Hellenist intellectualism, but Islam met all those successfully—assimilating, rejecting and adjusting itself to the new currents. However, very different was the case at the time of the Western impacts on Islam in the 12th/18th and especially the 13th/19th century. The first phase of Western impact was in each case political and military, and in each case the Muslims were vanquished and politically subjugated directly or indirectly. This was followed by religious and intellectual forms of infringements through various channels. The most patent and direct challenges were from the surge of scientific inventions and technological advancements in Europe and the West.

For many centuries the world of Islam had been in the forefront of human civilization and achievement. In the Muslims' own perception, Islam itself was indeed coexistent with civilization, and beyond its borders there were only barbarians and infidels. This perception of self and other was enjoyed by most, if not all, other civilizations—Greece, Rome, India, China, and now we may add the United States and Europe.

For most medieval Muslims, Christendom meant, primarily, the Byzantine Empire, which gradually became smaller and weaker until its final disappearance with the Turkish conquest of Constantinople in 1453. The remoter lands of Europe were seen in much the same light as the remoter lands of Africa from which there was nothing to learn and little even to be imported, except slaves and raw materials. For both the northern and the southern barbarians, their best hope was to be incorporated into the empire of the caliphs, and thus attain the benefits of religion and civilization.

For the first thousand years or so after the advent of Islam, Muslims made repeated attempts to accomplish this goal. In the course of the seventh century, Muslim armies advancing from Arabia conquered Syria, Palestine, Egypt, and North Africa, all until then were part of Christendom, and most of the new recruits to Islam in the west of Iran and Arabia were indeed converts from Christianity. In the eighth century, from their bases in North Africa, Arab forces, now joined by Berber converts, conquered Spain and Portugal and invaded France;

in the ninth century they conquered Sicily and invaded the Italian mainland. A subsequent series of Christian campaigns, started in the eleventh century to recover the Holy Land, from Muslims known as the Crusades, ended in failure and expulsion.

In Europe, Christian arms were more successful. By the end of eleventh century the Muslims had been expelled from Sicily, and in 1492, almost eight centuries after the first Muslim landing in Spain, the long struggle for the Christian reconquest of Spain ended in victory. But meanwhile there were other Muslim threats to European Christendom. In the East, between 1237 and 1240, the Tatars of the Golden Horde conquered Russia; in 1252 the Khan of the Golden Horde and his people were converted to Islam. Russia, with much of Eastern Europe, was subject to Muslim rule, and it was not until the late fifteenth century that the Russians finally freed their country from "the Tatar yoke." The descendants of *Genghis Khan* and *Halagu*, known as Khans, eventually created four large states in the Tigris-Euphrates valley and the mountainous regions of Iran extending up to the river Volga. It was the greatest political upheaval in the Middle East since the Arab invasions. By the beginning of the fourteenth century all four of the Mongol empires had converted to Islam and became the chief Muslim power in the central Islamic heartlands. A third wave of Muslim attack begun when the Ottoman Turks, who conquered Anatolia, captured the ancient Christian city of Constantinople in 1453, invaded and colonized the Balkan Peninsula, and threatened the very heart of Europe, twice reaching as far as Vienna.

At the peak of Islamic power, there was only one civilization that was comparable in the level, quality, and variety of achievement; that was of course China. But Chinese civilization and power remained essentially local, limited to one region, East Asia, and to one racial group. Islam, in contrast, created a world civilization—poly-ethnic, multiracial, international, one might even say intercontinental.

For centuries the world view and the self-view of Muslims seemed well grounded. Islam represented the greatest military power on earth—its armies, at the very same time, were invading Europe and Africa, India and China. It was the foremost economic power in the world, trading in a wide range of commodities through a far-flung network of commerce and communications in Asia, Europe, and Africa; importing slaves and gold from Africa, slaves and wool from Europe, and exchanging a variety of foodstuffs, materials, and manufactures with the civilized countries of Asia. It achieved the highest level to that point in human history in the arts and sciences of civilization. Inheriting the knowledge and skills of the ancient Middle East, of Greece and of Persia, it added to them new and important innovations from outside, such as the use and manufacture of paper from China and decimal positional numbering from India. It is difficult to imagine modern literature and science without one or the other. To this rich inheritance scholars and scientists in the Islamic world added immensely important contributions through their own observations, experiments, and ideas. In most of the arts and sciences of civilization, medieval Europe was a pupil and, in a sense, a dependent of the Islamic world, relying on Arabic versions even for many otherwise unknown Greek works.

Decline of the East
and Rise of the West

With the beginning of the Renaissance and the advent of New Learning, Europeans began to advance by leaps and bounds, leaving the scientific and technological and eventually the cultural heritage of the Islamic world far behind them.

The Muslims for a long time remained unaware of this. The great translation movement that centuries earlier had brought many Greek, Persian, and Syriac works within the purview of Muslim and other Arabic readers had come to an end, and the new scientific literature of Europe borrowed from Arabic literature was almost totally unknown to Muslims. Until the late eighteenth century, only one medical book was translated into Turkish—a sixteenth century treatise on *syphilis*[9], *presented to Sultan Mehmed IV* in 1655.[10] "Apart from that, the Renaissance, the Reformation, the technological revolution passed virtually unnoticed in the lands of Islam, where they were until inclined to dismiss the denizens of the lands beyond the Western frontier as benighted barbarians."[11]

Usually the lessons of history are unequivocally taught on the battlefield, but there may be some delay before the lesson is understood and realized. The final defeat of the Moors in Spain in 1492, the reconquest of Portugal in 1542 and the liberation of Russia from the rule of the Islamized Tatars were seen as decisive victories. Like the Spaniards and the Portuguese, the Russians too pursued their former masters into their homelands, but with far greater and more enduring success. In 1554, the Russians reached the shores of the Caspian Sea and

---

[9] This disease had come to the Islamic world from Europe and is until known in Arabic, Persian, Turkish and other languages as "the Frankish disease."

[10] See Abdulhak Adnan, La Science chez les Turcs Ottomans (Paris: 1939), pp. 87, 98-99.

[11] Bernard Lewis' What Went Wrong? Oxford University Press, 2002, p. 7.

in the following century, they reached the northern shore of the Black Sea, thus beginning the long process of conquest and colonization that incorporated vast Muslim lands into the Russian Empire.

But in the heartlands of Islam, these happenings on the remote frontiers of civilization seemed less important. They were overshadowed in Muslim eyes by such vastly important victories as the ignominious eviction of the Crusaders from the Levant in the thirteenth century, the capture of Constantinople in 1453, and the triumphant march of the Turkish forces through the Balkans toward the surviving Christian imperial city of Vienna.

The Ottoman sultan was not without political rivals and sectarian challengers within his own Muslim world. The sultan was more successful in dealing with these challenges. At the turn of the fifteenth-sixteenth centuries, the Ottomans had two Muslim competing neighbors. The older of the two was the *Mamluk* sultanate of Egypt, with its capital in Cairo, ruling over all Syria and Palestine, and the holy places of Islam in Western Arabia. The other was Persia, united by a new dynasty with a new religious militancy. The founder of the dynasty, *Shah Ismail Safavi* (1501-1524), a Turkish speaking Shi'ite from Azerbaijan, brought all the lands of Iran under a single ruler for the first time since the Arab conquest in the seventh century. He made Shi'ism the official religion of the state, and thus differentiated the Muslim realm of Iran sharply from its Sunni neighbors on both sides—to the East, in Central Asia and India, and to the West, the Ottoman Empire.

The Ottoman Sultan Selim I, who reigned from 1512-1520, launched military campaigns against both neighbors. He achieved a substantial but incomplete success against the Shah, and a total and final victory over the *Mamluk* sultan of Egypt. Egypt and its dependencies were incorporated in the Ottoman realms; Persia remained a separate, rival and hostile state.

The Ottomans and the Persians continued to fight each other until the nineteenth century. The idea of a *possible* anti-Ottoman alliance between Christendom and Persia was occasionally proposed, but to little effect. Shah Ismail of Persia sent a letter to the Emperor Charles V to join hands against Ottomans. The appeal fell on deaf ears and the emperor did not send a reply to Shah Ismail until 1529 by which time the shah had been dead for five years.

The three great empires—the *Safavids* of Iran, the Mongols of Central Asia and Ottomans of Constantinople—were all in decline by the end of the eighteenth century. This was not due to the essential incompetence or fatalism of Islam contrary to the claims by some. Any agrarian polity has a limited lifespan, and these Muslim states, which represented the last flowering of the agrarian ideal, had simply come to a natural and inevitable end. In the pre-modern period, Western and Christian empires had also experienced decline and fall. The Muslim weakness at the end of the eighteenth century coincided with the rise of an entirely different type of civilization in the West, i.e., one based on the rise of innovations in science and technology. This time the Muslim world found it far more difficult to meet the challenge. The rise of the West, coincided with the decline of Muslim power and politics. When the Ottomans tried to reorganize their army along Western lines in the hope of containing the threat from Europe, their efforts were doomed because they were too superficial. To beat Europe at its own game, a conventional agrarian society would have to transform itself from top to bottom, and re-create its entire social, economic, educational, religious, spiritual, political and intellectual structures. And it would have to do this very quickly, an impossible task, since it had taken the West almost three hundred years to achieve this development.

The struggle and occasional wars between the Ottomans and the Safavid Persians continued until the eighteenth century, by which time neither Turkey nor Persia offered any threat to Europe. The Moghal Empire declined in 1707 after the death of Aurangzeb and was officially abolished by the British after the Indian Rebellion of 1857. The *Safavid* Empire ended with the death of its last ruler Ismail III who ruled from 1750 to 1760. The last surviving Muslim empire, the Ottoman Empire, collapsed in 1918 in the aftermath of World War I. On 3 March 1924, the institution of the Caliphate was constitutionally abolished by President Mustafa Kemal Atatürk as part of his reforms. The Turks' entry into World War I (1914-1918) resulted in a deathblow for the Ottoman Empire.

With the defeat of Central Powers, the Allied forces occupied Istanbul (Constantinople) and the Ottoman government collapsed completely. The Empire was divided amongst the victorious powers with the signing of the Treaty of Sevres on 10 Aug. 1920. The fall of the empire led to the creation of the modern Middle East and the Republic of Turkey. The Ottoman Empire lost its Middle Eastern territories, which became mandates of Britain and France; large areas of southern and western Anatolia became an Italian zone of influence; almost all of Thrace was ceded to Greece, which also gained a protectorate over Smyrna; the straits and sea of Marmora were given to the Allied powers as an international zone; Armenia was recognized as an independent state. Britain obtained virtually everything it had sought under the secret Sykes-Picot Agreement it made with France in 1916 for partitioning the Middle East. The Turkish national movement, under the leadership of Mustafa Kemal *(Ataturk)* led the Turkish War of Independence and the foundation of the Republic of Turkey. The Turkish revolutionaries eventually reclaimed the Straits and Istanbul and abolished the caliphate on 3 March 1924. The Sultan and his family were declared persona non grata of Turkey and exiled.

Colonization and Decolonization

As the Europeans occupied more and more Muslim territories after World War I, they inevitably influenced Muslim thinking. Muslims could do little but helplessly witness the disintegration of the Muslim polity and society. Having lost their freedom, they felt downgraded, and now their laws and practices were being ridiculed as archaic and immoral. 'What had gone wrong?' they asked themselves. In the past they had blamed their own rulers who had strayed from the path of the Prophet and the 'rightly guided' caliphs. Now their rulers—inept, cowardly and corrupt—had not only yielded power but were willing to adopt the colonizers' values, laws and institutions. Indeed many of the popular leaders in the post-colonial period, who came to the fore to guide the community began to impress upon their fellow-Muslims the need to befriend Christians and collaborate with the colonizers. They tried to bring about a rapprochement between the two. In the process Islam was pushed aside.

When the new ruling classes, educated and trained in Western ideas, pushed for a reformed Islam, mainly in order to face the challenges of industrialization, they inevitably became admirers of Western-style democracy. Consequently, a conflict arose between the fundamentalists, who wanted to return to the past, and the secularists, who urged assimilation and transformation. What tilted the scales in favor of the secularists was the patronage they received from the colonizers. The social and economic changes generated by the colonizers also brought immediate benefits to the secularists. But this phenomenon did not last very long. The wave of secularism soon transformed into realization of nationalism, the honor and freedom of the motherland. Even so, the occupying powers were more inclined towards the secularists than the fundamentalists, who advocated, as a panacea for all the community's ills a new form of pan-Islamism, which the colonizers felt was far more dangerous than nationalism.

Ironically, the first Muslims to turn secularist and nationalist were the Arabs, among whom Islam first began. They revolted against the Ottoman Turks, and attained an independent Arab identity with the active help of Britain and France during World War I. The rebellious Arabs later discovered to their loss that they had only changed masters from fellow Muslims to colonial alien. They had no alternative but to collaborate with the new rulers. To appease Hussein of *Makkahh* the British installed his two sons, *Faysal* and *Abd Allah*, as rulers of Iraq and Transjordan respectively. But both had to function under the eye of the British, who gave them military protection. The rulers were Arabs, the popular representatives were Arabs, but neither enjoyed any real power. They were dependent on British arms. The king was a showpiece, as were the newly created parliaments, where deputies could debate but not decide; shout but not act.

The situation in the non-Arab world under the European colonizers was somewhat different. The Muslims there did not face the same problems. For instance, in Central Asia, the Czarist regime was overthrown by the Bolsheviks, who were not westernized in the same sense; they were communists, who accepted no religion. Though they had assured Muslims in their area that Islam would be protected, that promise was never really honored.

In India, ruled by Muslim dynasties for more than a thousand years, the Muslims found themselves a minority in the years after the sack of last Moghal emperor in 1857. Their problems were also different from other Muslims. They not only had to cope with British suspicion against them, but also with the rising tide of nationalism, which was essentially a Hindu nationalist phenomenon.

Similarly, in the countries of South-East Asia like Indonesia, which is predominantly Muslim, and Malaysia, which has a Muslim majority, the reactions of Muslims towards the Dutch and the British differed. They were inspired by nationalist fervor and influenced by the West, but their Islam, being of a later origin, had imbibed a lot from the indigenous cultures of Hinduism and Buddhism; this made it more liberal and eclectic, and therefore much more nationalistic. After independence, the fundamentalists did their best to reduce the influence of non-Muslim elements but the nationalists, who were more influenced by secularism than Islam, eventually triumphed and were able to usher in a more composite culture. The struggle that the Muslims—especially the two organizations, *Muhammadiya* and *Sarekat Islam*—in Indonesia waged against secularism was hardly effective in the liberation movement and never reached the dimensions, it had in India before its partition.

The pro-decolonization Labor government elected at the 1945 general election in Great Britain moved quickly to tackle the most pressing issue facing the Empire, that of Indian Independence. When the urgency of the situation and risk of civil war became apparent, the newly appointed, last Viceroy, Lord Mountbatten, hastily announced on 15 August 1947 the partition of India into independent states of India and Pakistan. Burma and Ceylon which had been administered as part of the British Raj, gained their independence the following year in 1948. India, Pakistan and Ceylon became members of the Commonwealth, though Burma chose not to join.[12]

The British Mandate, where an Arab majority lived alongside a Jewish minority, presented the British with a similar problem to that of India. The matter was complicated by large numbers of Jewish refugees seeking to be admitted to Palestine following the Nazi oppression and genocide in the Second World War. Rather than deal with the issue, Britain announced in 1947 that it would withdraw in 1948 and leave the matter to the United Nations to solve,[13] which it did by voting for the partition of Palestine into a Jewish and Arab state. By 1957, Britain felt confident enough to grant independence to the Federation of Malaya within the Commonwealth. In 1963, the eleven states of the Federation together with Singapore, Sarawak and British North Borneo, joined to form Malaysia, but in 1965 Chinese-dominated Singapore was expelled from the union following tensions between the Malay and Chinese populations.[14] Brunei, which had been a British protectorate since 1888, declined to join the union[15] and maintained its status until independence in 1984. However, British Prime Minister Winston Churchill could not ignore Gamal Abdul Nasser's new revolutionary government in Egypt that had taken power in 1952, and the following year it was agreed that British troops would withdraw from the Suez Canal zone and that Sudan would become independent by 1955. Britain's remaining colonies in

---

12 Smith, Simon (1998). *British Imperialism 1750-1970*. Cambridge University Press; p.325.

13 Lloyd, Trevor Owen (1996). *The British Empire 1558-1995*. Oxford University Press; p. 328

14 Ibid. p.396

15 Ibid.

Africa, except for Southern Rhodesia, were all granted independence by 1968.

One major change in the world during the decades that followed World War II in 1945 was the emergence of more than 50 new sovereign states, mostly Muslim. Essentially, this was the result of decolonization. Though Allied forces emerged victorious from the Second World War, the effects of the conflict were profound, both at home and abroad. Much of Europe, a continent that had dominated the world for centuries, was in ruins. Britain was left virtually bankrupt. At the same time, anti-colonial movements were on the rise in the colonies of Europe and Muslim nations. The situation was complicated further by the increasing Cold War rivalry between United States and the Soviet Union. The "wind of change" ultimately meant that the colonial powers adopted a policy of peaceful disengagement from their colonies.

Before World War II the countries of Western Europe and the Soviet Union in the East, had ruled, controlled, or powerfully influenced vast tracts of Muslim territory, including remnants of Ottoman Empire after World War I. Belgium, Britain, France, Italy, Russia, The Netherlands, and Portugal remained imperial powers, holding direct or indirect sway over most of the Muslim states in Southeast Asia, Central Asia, parts of the West Indies, nearly all of Africa, and much of the Middle East. Gradually, what had once been colonies, protectorates, or client states won their independence. Many retained linguistic, cultural, economic or commercial links with Europe; many depended on European investment and aid. But they were politically free of their colonial masters. The Italian colonies in North and East African Muslim states were dismantled fairly quickly. Independence likewise came early to various Middle Eastern countries, although for many years European influence there continued. Egypt, Iraq, Lebanon and Syria gained independence. Iran's independence was guaranteed by Britain and the USSR in 1942. The year 1946 saw Jordan's independence, and 1948, the establishment of Israel. However, historical ties (including the memory of Hitler's Holocaust), strategic pressures, and the need for Middle Eastern oil kept Europe deeply involved in the area long after most of its countries' formal independence. The Suez expedition of 1956 actually brought down a British government in Egypt; oil price rises in the 1970s caused a European recession; and Saddam Hussein's invasion of Kuwait in 1990 for a time seemed to threaten the risk of world war.

France faced similar problems in North Africa. Morocco and Tunisia obtained independence in 1956, but Algeria, legally part of the French republic, took time in getting independence. One feature of the postcolonial period, however, was the reflux into Europe of Muslim emigrants from the former colonies. One of the realities of contemporary world is the fact that Muslim minorities are to be found virtually all over the non-Muslim world. Attention is being given to the presence of Muslims not only in China and in the Russian Federation but also in places such as Japan, Australia, and South Africa. There are substantial Muslim minority communities in the heart of Europe in Germany, Belgium, France, Great Britain, The Netherlands and in both the South and North American continents. The Organization of Islamic Conference (OIC), comprised of fifty-seven states is taking special interest in the circumstances of Muslim minorities throughout the world.

The rise of the West in the sixteenth century was similar to the emergence of the Arabs in the East, as a major world power in the seventh and eighth centuries, but the Muslims had not achieved a world hegemony, as Europe had begun to do in the sixteenth century. Europe's hegemony was basically cultural and social, not territorial.

The new society of Europe and its American colonies had a different economic basis. Instead of relying upon a surplus of agricultural produce as was common in agrarian economy, it was founded on technology and investment of capital that enable the West to multiply its resources. This major change demanded a revolution of the established mores on several fronts at the same time: political, economical, social and intellectual. It had not been planned or thought out in advance, but had been the result of a complex process, which had led to the creation of democratic, secular social structures. By the sixteenth century Europeans had achieved a scientific revolution that gave them greater control over the environment than anybody had achieved before. There were new inventions in medicine, navigation, agriculture and industry. Instead of seeing the world as governed by immutable laws, Europeans had found that they could alter the course of nature. By the time this technologizaton of society had resulted in the industrial revolution of the nineteenth century, Westerners felt such assurance that they no longer looked back to the past for inspiration, as in the agrarian cultures and religions, but looked forward to the future.

The modernization of society also involved social and intellectual change. An increasing number of people were needed to take part in the various scientific and industrial projects at quite humble levels—as printers, clerks, factory workers, civil servants, electrical and civil engineers, etc., and in order to acquire a modicum of the new standards, they had to receive some kind of education. As more workers became literate, they demanded a greater participation in the decisions of government. If a nation wanted to use all its human resources to enhance its productivity, it had to bring groups who had hitherto been segregated and marginalized in agrarian society into mainstream society. Religious differences and spiritual ideals must not be allowed to impede the progress of society, and scientists, monarchs and government officials insisted that they be free of ecclesiastical control. Thus the ideals of democracy, pluralism, toleration, human rights and secularism were not simply beautiful ideals, dreamed up by political scientists, but were necessitated by the needs of the modern social function. In order to be efficient and productive, a modern nation had to be organized on a secular, democratic basis. When societies did organize all their institutions according to the new rational and scientific norms, they became indomitable, and the conventionalwere no match for them.

This had fateful consequences for the Islamic world. The progressive nature of modern society and an industrialized economy meant that it continuously had to expand. New markets were needed, and, once the home countries had been saturated, markets had to be sought abroad. The Western states had already begun to colonize the agrarian countries outside modern Europe in order to draw them into their commercial network, a process that continued after each of the two World Wars. The former politically colonized countries provided raw materials for export to their ex-colonial powers, which fed European industry. In return, they received cheap manufactured Western goods, which meant that their local industries were usually ruined. The ex-colonies, so long they were under colonial powers and influence, they never had the opportunity of technology transfer because of their reliance on manual labor. They also had to be transformed and modernized along European lines, with their financial and commercial life rationalized and brought into the Western system, and at least some of the "natives" had to acquire some familiarity with the modern ideas through education. This neo-colonization was experienced by the agrarian colonies as invasive, disturbing and alien. Modernization was inevitably superficial for two reasons; first, modern ideas needed time, even centuries, to filter down gradually to all classes of society; second, it was beyond the agenda of the masters to modernize their colonies. The vast majority of the populations were left perforce to rot in the old agrarian systems. Society was divided between rulers and ruled. They were ruled by secular, foreign law-codes, which they could not understand. Their cities were transformed, as Western buildings and roads modernized the towns, often leaving the "old city" as a museum piece. Above all, local people of all classes of society resented the fact that they were no longer in control of their own destiny. They felt that they had severed all connection with their roots, and experienced a sinking loss of identity.

It is true that the modern spirit that developed in the West is fundamentally different. In Europe and America it had two main characteristics: innovation and autonomy. It insisted upon independence on the political, intellectual, religious and social fronts. But in the Muslim world, modernity had been accompanied by a loss of independence and national autonomy. Instead of innovations in science, engineering and technologies, the Muslim countries could only modernize by imitating the West. Because the modernizing process has not been the same, democracy, secularism and pluralism were unable to emerge in the way that they did in Europe and America. The modernization process has convulsed Islamic world. Instead of being one of the leaders of world civilization, Muslim states were quickly and permanently reduced to a dependent bloc by the European powers. Now Muslim countries were considered as "backward" just as they had labeled Europe a few centuries earlier. Westerners often took it for granted that they were inherently and racially superior to "Orientals" and expressed their contempt in myriad ways. All this naturally had a corrosive effect. Westerners are often bewildered by the hostility and rage that Muslims feel toward Western culture, which, because of their very different experience, Westerners have found to be liberating and empowering. The Muslim response has not simply been a reaction to the new West, but a paradigmatic reaction.

The European powers had colonized one Islamic country after another. France occupied Algeria in 1830, and Britain took Aden nine years later. Tunisia was occupied in 1881, Egypt in 1882, the Sudan in 1889 and Libya and Morocco in 1912. In 1915, the Sykes-Picot agreement divided the territories of the Ottoman Empire (which had sided with Germany during the First World War) between Britain and France. After the war, Britain and France duly set up protectorates and mandates in Syria, Lebanon, Palestine, Iraq and Transjordan. This was experienced by Muslims as an outrage, since the European powers had promised independence to the Arab provinces of the Ottoman Empire. In the Ottoman heartlands, Mustafa Kemal, was able to keep the Europeans at bay and setup the independent state of Turkey in 1924. Muslims in the Balkans, Russia and Central Asia became subject to the new Soviet Union. Even after some of these countries had been allowed to become independent, the West often continued to control the economy, the oil or resources such as the Suez Canal. European occupation often left a legacy of bitter conflict. When the British withdrew from India in 1947, the Indian subcontinent was partitioned between Hindu India and Muslim Pakistan, which to this day remain in a state of deadly hostility, with nuclear weapons aimed at each other's capitals. In 1948, the Arabs of Palestine lost their homeland to the Zionists, who set up the Jewish state of Israel there, with the support of the United Nations and the international community. The loss of Palestine became a potent symbol of the humiliation of the Muslim world at the hands of the Western powers, who seemed to feel no qualms about the dispossession and permanent exile of hundreds of thousands of Palestinians.

The European colonial empires had allowed communal and legal autonomy to the Muslims living under their rule, especially in matters relating marriage, divorce and inheritance. Today, all the colonial empires that once governed a large part of the Islamic world have ended. After dissolution of Soviet Union, most of its 50 to 60 million Muslims live in six independent republics where, for the time being at least, they are until subject to social and legal systems that are very remote from Muslim holy law. Many remain as minorities in Russia and other non-Islamic republics. Even after breakup of the empires, by no means all Muslim populations are under Muslim rule. Two non-Muslim countries, China and Ethiopia, have ruled over Muslim populations for many centuries. Among the new states established after the fall of British Empire, several non-Muslim countries retain significant Muslim populations, notably India, Sri Lanka, Israel and a number of sub-Saharan African states. Most, if not all, of these have been willing to maintain the system of devolution and legal autonomy, at least in matters of personal status. Their position in these states is significantly different from that of the Muslim remnant in ex-Ottoman southeastern Europe. Today only a few Muslim states with mostly Muslim population like Saudi Arabia, Iran and Sudan are administered by Islamic law while Egypt, Pakistan, Turkey, Syria, Iraq, Malaysia and Indonesia have a blending of a less Islamic and more European system of administration.

The loss of Ottoman territories in Europe was hard but could be borne. The loss of Crimea which was old Turkish Muslim territory dating back to the Middle Ages, was felt as a loss of the homeland. This was the first—but by no means the last—loss of Muslim lands and populations to Christian rule.

Debates in the Ottoman members of the official bureaucracy, about what is going wrong were not new. In a little book[16] written by *Lutfi Pasha*, grand vizier of *Suleyman the Magnificent*, after his dismissal from office in 1541, suggested some acute diagnoses of flaws in the Ottoman structure and remedies that he thought should be adopted. Another was by a civil servant of Balkan origin called, *Kocu Bay*, who in 1630 drew attention to weaknesses in both the civilian and the military services of the state, and proposed reforms to deal with them.[17] The basic fault, according to most of these memoranda, was falling away from the good old ways, Islamic and Ottoman; and the basic remedy was a return to them. This diagnosis and prescription until command wide acceptance in the Middle East.

---

[16] Lutfi Pasha, *Asafname*, edited with a German translation by Rudolf Tschudi, Berlin, 1910.

[17] *Risale-i Kocu Bey* (Istanbul: 1860), translated in German in 1861. On these and other similar works see Virginia H. Aksan, "Ottoman Political Writing, 1768-1808," and Bernard Lewis, "Ottoman Observers of Ottoman decline," in Islamic Studies (Karachi), 1962; reprinted in idem, Islam in History: Ideas, People and Events in the Middle East, Chicago, 1993.

RESISTANCE AND REVIVAL

Napoleon Bonaparte was foremost among the European invaders of Muslim lands. On landing in Alexandria in Egypt in July 1798, he issued a proclamation "in the name of Allah, the Gracious and the Merciful", assuring the Muslims that he would 'restore their religious rights and punish their enemies.' He declared, 'I respect Allah, His Prophet and the Qur'an' more than the *Mamluks* ever did. The proclamation of Bonaparte had the desired effect; the French were warmly received by the theologians and al-Azhar. French rule did not last for more than four years, but it left a permanent impress on the minds of the Egyptians. The British, with the help of a young military officer of the Ottoman army, *Muhammad Ali*, who later became the founder of a modern secular state in Egypt, thwarted the efforts of Bonaparte and cleverly outmaneuvered him.[18]

Expelled from Egypt, the French went into North Africa, took over Algeria in 1830, then Morocco and Tunisia; Czarist Russia followed the French example, and penetrated the Caucasus and Central Asia between 1865 and 1873. The British had already entered India and established themselves as traders in Bengal, gradually spreading in the north and the south. By 1849 they had conquered most parts of the country, which extended up to Burma in the East and Sri Lanka in the south. Later they expanded their territories to the Malay Peninsula, beyond the borders of India. The Dutch, thwarted by the British in Sri *Lanka*, took over Indonesia in 1840. Italians occupied Tripolitania. The grabbing game reached its climax in 1920 at the end of World War I when British troops occupied Damascus and Baghdad, once the two most powerful centers of the Umayyad and Abbasid caliphates. Everywhere Muslims found themselves utterly defeated and thoroughly demoralized. More shameful was their sense of religious subjugation at the hands of Christians, whom

---

18 Rafiq Zakaria. "The Struggle Within Islam: The Conflict between Religion and Politics," Penguin Books, New Delhi, India, 1988.

they had always regarded with contempt. As we have seen, the ruling clique quietly surrendered and corroborated with the foreign rules. It was the religious-minded Muslims, led by the *ulama* and the *sufis* who took up arms against the 'heathen' invaders. They faced heavy odds but they persisted in their rebellion. In Algeria, for instance, *Abd al-Qadir,* venerated as imam by his followers, organized armed resistance against the French colonizers. He succeeded in driving out the French.

In Sudan, the rebellion against the British was led by *Muhammad Ahmad* (1840-45), who claimed to be the '*mahdi*'—divinely guided one. He vowed that he would rid the world of the Christian infidels and restore Islam to its original greatness. He became the master of the Sudan, defeating General Gordon, who was killed in the battle of Khartoum (1885).[19] In Libya, *Muhammad Ali al-Sanusi* (1787-1859), another fundamentalist leader, drove the foreigners from his native land. In Somalia, *Muhammad Abdullah Hasan* (1863-1920) spearheaded the movement against the British. In Central Asia it was *Shamil Waifi* who inspired the Muslims to take up arms against the Czarist forces. This list is not exhaustive but shows that while the deposed rulers and their coteries sat on the fence, it was the men with religious zeal who goaded the faithful to rise in defense of Islam against the 'heathens'. Although all these movements finally crumbled, the heroism with which the fundamentalists fought left an indelible mark in the annals of Islam.

Most of the revolts belonged to the *Naqshbandi* Sufi order, which was directed in the nineteenth century by *Khalid Baghdadi* (1776-1827) who was inspired by the teachings of such spiritual savants as *Shaikh Ahmad Sirhindi*, the arch-rebel against Akbar's liberalism, and other sufis in India. *Baghdadi* imbibed the spirit of rebellion taught by *Sirhindi* and his disciples at Delhi and returned to the heartlands of Islam in West Asia. He gathered together a large number of followers in Syria, Iraq and the Arabian Peninsula. His fame spread to distant regions of East Africa and Southeast Asia. His message was heard all over the Muslim world from Central Asia to the Caucasus and as far East as China. Unlike the old *sufi* orders, which had preached asceticism and non-involvement in worldly affairs, *Baghdadi* exhorted his disciples to take up whatever weapons they could find and sacrifice their lives for

---

[19] Michael C. Hudson, *Arab Politics*, Yale, 1977, p.330. For a fuller picture, see P.M. Holt, *The Mahdist State in the Sudan*, 1881-1898, Oxford, 1958.

the cause of Islam. He turned *sufis* and *ulama* into armed rebels and militant warriors.

The *sufi* rebels fought on two fronts: against the foreign invaders, and against their own people, who had strayed from the right path as set out by the Prophet. Surprisingly, the *Wahhabis* influenced them greatly, despite the fact that their teachings were against Sufism. The *Wahhabi* spirit of rebellion changed the outlook of the rebels, particularly that of the *Naqshbandis*. *Imam Shamil*, a *Naqshbandi* sufi, was both a religious zealot and an able guerrilla commander. He expelled Czarist troops from the Caucasus and ushered in a period of *shari'a* (1885). It lasted only thirty years until the Russians once again overran *Shamil's* kingdom and forced him to surrender. About the same time, *Bahal Din Vaishi* (1804-93), another *Naqshbandi sufi,* organized in *Kazan* a different kind of rebellion against the Russians. He called upon Muslims to stop cooperating with the alien rulers by refusing to pay taxes or enlisting in the army or administrative services. *Vaishi's* movement was essentially non-violent, more or less on lines which Gandhi later adopted and made famous, but when it spread among the Tartars, known for their turbulence, the Russians were alarmed. *Vaishi* was arrested, declared insane and sent to a lunatic asylum.[20]

In India, the role of *Shah Wali Allah* (1702-62) was no less significant. He was an uncompromising fundamentalist, more inclined towards *Sufism* than *Wahhabism*, but influenced by both. He advocated armed rebellion to achieve an Islamic state. His writings were enshrined in his *Tariqa-e-Muhammadiya* or the Way of the Prophet. He wanted an Islamic state to be established in every country where there were Muslims in substantial numbers. One of his followers, *Sayyid Ahmed of Rae Bareli* (1786-1831), organized the *mujahidun* or migration movement. He mobilized his followers in a war against the Sikhs, who had founded a powerful kingdom in the Punjab. They were, however, betrayed by their Afghan allies and defeated by *Ranjit Singh*, the Sikh emperor of North India. The Muslims of Bengal, who were the first to encounter the British, met an equally dismal end. Their leader, *Hajji Shariat Allah* (1781-1840) fought valiantly but was eventually defeated. [21]

---

20 Rafiq Zakaria, *The Struggle Within Islam*, Penguin Book 1989, p.159.

21 Khushwant Singh, *A History of the Sikhs*, Princeton, 1963, pp.273-74.

In China, too, the Muslims led by the *Naqshbandis* declared a *Jihad* against *Manchu* rule in Turkistan. There were five such holy wars in different times from 1820 to 1861. One of the *Naqshbandi* commanders, *Yaqub Beg* (1820-77) liberated the whole of Turkistan and turned it into a puritanical theocracy which he administered for ten years, until its disintegration. Other parts of China witnessed similar Muslim uprising inspired by the *sufis*. A legendary figure was *Ma Ming-hsin* (d. 1781) who rallied his followers round the green flag of the Prophet and called upon them to purify Islam of Confucian accretions.[22]

In *Yunan*[23], *under Tu Wenhsin*, Muslims defeated the emperor's troops and founded an independent Muslim kingdom, which lasted more than fifteen years. *Tu Wenhsin* assumed the name of *Sultan Sulayman* and tried to Islamize the various departments of the State, as well his subjects in general. He drew his inspiration from the teachings of *Ma Teh'sin* and was the first to translate the Qur'an into Chinese; in this he was influenced by his contemporary, *Shah Wali Allah*, who had translated the Qur'an into Persian.[24]

In Africa, the reaction of Muslims to colonial rule was as aggressive and violent as in Asia. But whereas in Asia most of the rebel leaders were *Naqshbandis*, in Africa they belonged either to the *Khalwatiya* or the *Idrisiya* orders. Their order was based in Cairo and was extremely popular among the teachers and pupils of al-Azhar. *Idrisiya* order was founded by the Moroccan sufi, *Ahmad Ibn Idris* (1760-1837) who tried to reconcile *Wahhabism* with *Sufism*. This order rapidly won over the Muslims of Algeria, Morocco, Sudan and West Africa. One of its most colorful leaders was *Hajji Umar Tali* (1794-1864), who repelled a pagan incursion to found a theocratic state in western Sudan. He also conquered and annexed Senegal. In 1893 the French wrested Senegal from *Tali's* successors.[25]

The sufis of the *Sammanya* order were in the forefront of the *Jihad* against the combined might of the Egyptians and the British. This order gained considerable popularity in Sudan, Eritrea and Ethiopia. The *mahdi* of Sudan belonged to it and after his victory over the British, he

---

[22] See M. Rafiq Khan, *Islam in China*, Delhi, 1963, pp.25-26

[23] *Yunan* in <u>Arabic,</u> <u>Turkish,</u> <u>Persian</u> and <u>Urdu</u>—an ancient region of central coastal Anatolia.

[24] Zakaria, Rafiq, *"The Struggle Within Islam"*, Penguin Books, 1989, p.160

[25] Ibid. p.160.

tried to establish a *Mahdist* state, in which he tried to copy the pattern of the city state of Madina. In Libya the rebel sufi, *Muhammad Ali al-Sannusi*, who had successfully repelled the foreigners, inspired by the vision of a rejuvenated Islam, turned his people into devout and militant Muslims. Likewise, in Somalia, Muhammad *Abul al-Hasan* (1864-1920) led the Muslims to fight the British invasion of his country. In Black Africa, the newly converted Muslims were in the vanguard of the fight to save Islam, which gave them for the first time racial equality and a sense of belonging to a universal Islamic brotherhood. One of the most picturesque of the black *sufis* was *Samori Ture* (1830-1900), who founded a purely Islamic state.[26]

There were also many others whose revolts were of no less significance. They were, no doubt, sporadic and petered out after a few years. They were not militarists or freedom fighters, but simply religious zealots to whom nothing in the world mattered except Islam. It is ironic that the *sufis*, who were originally so liberal and tolerant towards followers of other faiths, should have been in the forefront of a militant *Jihad* against them. Yet, this was understandable because they feared that the non-Muslims were bent upon destroying Islam by taking advantage of the ineptitude and weakness of corrupt Muslim rulers. Also, they were dismayed by the latter's cowardice and the readiness with which they surrendered to foreigners. As P. F. Francis Robinson has observed, "As Muslim power crumbled from within, they [the *sufis*] strove to restore it, promoting the Islamic ideal. As old arteries began to harden they built new ones along which they pumped new vitality. As the community lost momentum and direction, they tried to place it once more on the sure base of revelation and the example of the Prophet."[27]

However, no sooner did the *sufis* take to rebellion and power politics, than they lost much of their mystical strength. They became hardened, coarse, and aggressive. However, it must be said to their credit that power did not corrupt them; they did not give up their piety, Spartan living and care for the poor. This was best reflected in the code of conduct that *Abd al-Qadir*, the Algerian *sufi* rebel, imposed upon himself; in a public document he declared that it was his religious duty to despise wealth, despite the power he possessed; be just and fair to all, irrespective of

---

26 Ibid. p. 161

27 Francis Robinson, *Atlas of the Islamic World since 1500*; Oxford, 1982, p.129.

their rank or office; and lay down his life for Islam. Their war was on two fronts—one, against the external enemy who aimed at the subjugation of the Muslims and, two, against the cancer of luxurious living, social immorality and political corruption that was undermining the community. This was the common approach of most of the *sufi* rebels.[28]

In this respect, they stood apart from the other rebels: they did not behave like worldly potentates; they were conscious of the fact that they were men of God and acted strictly in accordance with the Qur'anic teachings and the traditions of the Prophet. The pivot of their rule revolved round the person of the leader who was the mentor, the executor and the exemplar. Hence he could leave no system behind; nor did the possibility exist of sustained popular support without him. In this lay the seeds of their downfall. The rebels were unable to regroup once their top leadership was subdued. This, coupled with their inability to wage modern warfare, proved disastrous. Moreover, the colonial powers had managed, by the use of force and graft, to weaken the rebel resistance. All in all, there was a systematic intellectual indoctrination by the West which the *ulama* failed to counter, and thus it was that the rebellion died. This onslaught inevitably led to the Western powers becoming more firmly entrenched in the lands of Islam.

Although the root of the concept of *Jihad* goes back to the classical period of Islam, the current incarnation as a global force emerged nearly in the twentieth-century with the Islamic revivalist movement known as *Salafism* (the term *salaf* refers to the original Companions of the Prophet Muhammad). *Salafism* began as a progressive movement in colonial Egypt and India whose adherents advocated reform and liberalization of traditional Islamic doctrine. The movement was founded upon the writings of two of the century's most renowned Muslim intellectuals, the Iranian scholar-activist *Jamal ad-Din al-Afghani* (who began his career in India) and the Egyptian reformer *Muhammad Abdu*. *Al-Afghani* and *Abdu* believed that the only way for the Muslim world to throw off the yoke of colonialism and push back against Western cultural hegemony was through a revival of Islam. These "modernists" as they were called, blamed the clerical establishment—the *ulama*—for the sorry state of Muslim society. They sought to challenge the ulama's self-proclaimed role as the sole legitimate interpreters of Islam by advocating an individualized,

---

[28] Rafiq Zakaria, Ibid. p. 162.

unmediated, and highly personal reading of the Qur'an and the *Hadith* (the collected sayings and actions of the Prophet Muhammad).

By far the most successful *Salafist* organization of the time was the Muslim Brotherhood. Founded in the 1920s by the Egyptian school-teacher turned activist, *Hasan al-Banna*, the Muslim Brotherhood began as a grassroots social movement dedicated to the gradual Islamization of society through religious welfare and education programs. *Al-Banna* believed that the only way to create a truly Islamic state was through preaching and good works, not, as some of his fellow Islamists argued, through violence and armed revolt. Although far more conservative in his interpretation of Islam than either *al-Afghani* or *Muhammad Abdu*, *al-Banna* nevertheless agreed that the main obstacle facing an Islamic revival was the *'ulama*, or more specifically, the senior clergy of Egypt's famed al-Azhar University. His reformist outlook and social activism created a stark contrast to the somewhat stilted theology offered by the clergy of al-Azhar.

By the time *Hasan al-Banna* died in 1949, the Muslim Brotherhood was the most dominant social movement in Egypt. Indeed after the collapse of the Ottoman Caliphate in 1924—the symbol of the global Muslim community, or *umma*—the Muslim Brotherhood was the only truly transnational Islamic movement in the world, with offshoots in Syria, Jordan, Palestine, and Lebanon. When, in 1952, a group of Egyptian military officers led by Colonel *Gamal Abd al-Nasser* launched a coup against Egypt's British-backed monarchy, the Muslim Brotherhood helped rally the country under the new administration, resulting in its members' holding a number of senior government posts. But after a failed attempt on his life, allegedly by a member of the Brotherhood, Nasser outlawed the organization altogether and threw its leaders into jail.

In prison, the Brotherhood fractured into competing groups. A new breed of activists, led by the charismatic Egyptian academic, *Sayyid Qutb*, transformed al-Banna's social movement into a revolutionary force dedicated to "setting up the kingdom of God on earth and eliminating the kingdom of man."[29] Qutb declared that Nasser—and in fact every Arab leader—could not be considered a true Muslim unless he was willing to strictly apply and abide by Islamic law. And since

---

[29] Sayyed Qutb, *Milestones* (Birmingham, England: Maktabah, 2006) p/27.

was unwilling to do so, he was an apostate, a *kafir*, and his punishment should be death. Anyone who accepted Nasser's leadership was also a *kafir*. Nasser executed Qutb in 1966 and the Qutb-inspired *Salafists* and radical members of the Muslim Brotherhood fled their home countries in Egypt, Syria, Jordan and Palestine for the only place that would give them refuge, Saudi Arabia. There they encountered an even more conservative strain of Islam commonly called *Wahhabism*.

Born in the vast desert wastelands of eastern Arabia, a region known as the Najd, *Wahhabism* was founded by *Muhammad ibn Abd al-Wahhab* in the middle of the eighteenth century. Claiming that the purity of Islam had been defiled by "un-Islamic" beliefs and practices such as praying to saints and visiting their tombs, *Abd al-Wahhab* sought to strip Islam of what he considered its cultural, ethnic, and religious "innovations" (*bida'*), so as to restore Islam to its original, unadulterated and distinctly Arab origins.

In 1932, just the discovery of oil began to reshape both the physical and social landscape of the Arabian Peninsula; *Wahhabism* became the official religion of the Kingdom of Saudi Arabia. By the 1960s, this kingdom had become one of the richest countries in the world. It soon became the hybridization of *Salafism* and *Wahhabism*, of Islamic political activism and Saudi Puritanism, that gave birth to a new, ultraconservative, ultraviolent social movement of young Muslims called "Global *Jihad*ism."

At first, *Jihad*ism began as just another Islamist movement, focused on establishing an Islamic state. The early *Jihad*ists were "religious nationalist whose fundamental goal was to effect revolutionary change in their own society," said Fawaz Gerges, America's premier scholar of *Jihad*ism.[30] Their primary focus was on what they termed the "Near Enemy"—Arab regimes, hypocrite imams, apostate Muslims—as opposed to the "Far Enemy"—Israel, Europe, and the United States. "The road to Jerusalem goes through Cairo," *Ayman Zawahiri* wrote in 1995, when he was the head of a religious national organization known as Egyptian Islamic *Jihad*.[31]

Throughout the 1980s and 1990s, however, *Zawahiri* and a great many of his fellow *Jihad*ists began gradually to shift their focus from

---

[30] Fawaz Gerges, *The Far Ememy* (Cambridge, England, 2005) p/29.

[31] An article written by Zawahiri in the *Jihad*ist newspaper, *Al-Mujahidun,* April 26, 1995.

the Near Enemy to the Far Enemy—from localism to globalism. This was partly a result of failure of *Jihad*ist movements to bring about the revolution they had promised for so long, partly due to violent suppression of religious nationalism throughout the Arab world and partly due to failures of Islamist movements themselves in Algeria, Egypt and Syria.

The *Salafist* groups that remained uninfluenced by Saudi *Wahhabism* soon began to follow the lead of the Egyptian Muslim Brotherhood, publicly renouncing violence and returning to their roots of preaching and social welfare. Yet, beyond the failure of Islamism, there was a far more significant development in the globalization of the *Jihad*ist movement. The Soviet invasion of Afghanistan in 1979 drew to the region a wave of *Jihadists* from every corner of the world, many of whom, like *Zawahiri* and *Abu Musab al-Suri*, felt increasingly abandoned by the collapse of the Islamist movements in their own countries. The presence on the battlefield of tens of thousands of Muslim fighters from Egypt, Saudi Arabia, Syria, Yemen, Palestine, Algeria, Sudan, Tunisia, Iraq, Pakistan, Jordan, Malaysia, Indonesia—all working together for a common cause—created a sense of global community among the *Jihadists* that they had never before experienced.

Not all *Jihadists* are globalists, of course, nor do all *Islamists* confine themselves solely to nationalist concerns. But for those who continue to count themselves among the growing ranks of the Global *Jihad*ist movement, the strategy of "dragging the Far Enemy onto the battlefield," of expanding the goals and aspirations of *Jihadism* beyond local grievances and nationalist concerns to the Far Enemy both "resolves the mental complex in the *ummah* with regard to defining the enemy," to quote *al-Suri*. [32] It frames the *Jihadist* struggle not as a battle between rival political ideologies but as a cosmic contest between belief and unbelief—or, in *Zawahiri's* words, "between Islam and the infidels." In such a battle, no one can remain neutral. Every Muslim has a duty to respond to the call of *Jihad*, to rally under the banner of Islam, to come to its defense, and to join a cosmic war whose epicenter happens to be in Israel.

---

[32] Quoted in Brynjar Lia, Architect of Global *Jihad*: The Life of al-Qaida Strategist Abu Musab al-Suri (New York; Columbia Univ. Press, 2008), pp.158-159.

The Present and the Future

Independence from foreign rule achieved by Muslim peoples in their homelands is the most fundamental fact about Islam in the present century. What makes this fact significant, however, is that in all these countries, from *Morocco* to *Indonesia*, Islam has played a very important role in the struggle for freedom. The second most important fact of the present, however, is the absence of any workable 'Muslim World', not only politically, but culturally and socially as well. Apart from these facts facing Muslim countries as a whole and whose upshot it is too early to forecast, each individual Muslim society is faced with the internal problem of how to reconstruct itself. With the exception of Turkey, where the secularist basis introduced by Ataturk until persists officially, the majority of Muslim societies have felt that Islam must supply a positive referent in their internal reconstruction programs. Some of them, like Pakistan, have based themselves squarely on an Islamic plea. The real problem of these countries, however, lies in the actual, positive formulation of Islam, i.e., exactly spelling out what Islam has to say to the modern individual and society. The problem is fatefully crucial, indeed, for should these societies fail to provide an adequate answer, the only alternative left to them will be some form of secularism, and there is little doubt that this solution would be tantamount to changing the very nature of Islam.

From the long history of Islam, where it met both challenges and crises of different types—spiritual, intellectual and social—one should naturally expect that Islam, given time for evolving the necessary internal equipment, can resolve the present challenge successfully. But it is absolutely necessary that Muslims be clear as to exactly in what the present challenges lie. To our mind, the challenges are basically two: one stemming from the nature of 'modern' life based on materialism, and the other from the nature of Muslim 'conservatism'. We shall see that the two questions are not entirely separate.

In every growing society, there has been a clash between conservatism and liberalism/modernism. But in all situations of social growth, conservatism must seek not merely to conserve the past, but what is valuable and essential in it. Muslims must decide what exactly is to be conserved, what is essential and relevant for the erection of an Islamic future, what is fundamentally Islamic and what is purely 'historical'. In other words, they must develop an enlightened conservatism. *Wahhabism* failed because it could not separate the fundamentals of Islam from its 'historicals'. Many of the historical events and episodes necessitated by the specific situations were taken into religious history, supported and protected by *Hadiths* comprising from legal details of Sufism, from the *Ijm'a* of the Sunnis to the legitimism of the Shi'a.

Unless, therefore, the problem of the *Hadiths* is critically, historically and constructively treated, there seems little prospect of distinguishing the essential from the historical. But it is precisely this task which the *'Ulama* are resolutely refusing to do. They fear that if *Hadiths* are thus exposed to a scientific investigation, the concept of the 'Sunna of the Prophet', the second pillar of Islam beside the Qur'an, will be destroyed. Some of the recent Muslims and non-Muslims wholesale rejection of *Hadith* and the Prophetic Sunna undoubtedly strengthen these fears. But the point in investigation here is to know the genesis and evolution of a given *Hadith* in order to determine what function it performed and whether present Islamic needs until demand such function or not.

Much more grave than this problem of Muslim conservatism is the challenge to Muslim society of pure secularism and materialism. Most Muslim societies today are neither wholly conservative nor wholly secular (excluding Saudi Arabia, Iran and Turkey). In either case the old spiritual orthodoxy is effective: it is by and large the secularized intellectual who talks of the 'New Society' and, whenever convenient, exploits the name of Islam.

The conservative *Ulama* of today are far more uncompromisingly and even unthinkingly conservative than were their predecessors of the 12th/18th centuries. The only real remedy of the situation lies in a basic reform of the modern educational system and in imparting genuine Islamic values in schools and colleges alongside other subjects. Only in this way can modern secular education be meaningfully integrated into a comprehensive Islamic culture and be creative; otherwise, it is a piece of alien matter arbitrarily grafted on to an organism. It is only in this way that the eternal values and the basic religious experience of Islam may be resurrected from the weight of historical particularity under which they have been submerged.

In carrying out this task of reformulation one more fundamental need will have to be satisfied if Islamic theology and law are to meet the needs of modern humanity and society and to save them from the nihilistic demoralizing effects of crass secularism. In the new reconstruction, the specifically moral and religious emotions must be given due place and incorporated as an integral element. It is because in the previous formulation of Islam, in the old *Shari'a* disciplines, due recognition was not given to this element that Sufism developed as a quasi-separate religion and, in a large measure, in opposition to the official Islam of the *ulama*. That Sufism went at points radically wrong in the course of its development was due to certain broad and deep social factors, but that it originally and fundamentally arose from certain basic religious needs and motives cannot be denied.

After a general view of the contemporary Muslim world, a systematic attempt must be made to elaborate an ethics on the basis of the Qur'an, for without an explicitly formulated ethical system one can never do justice to Islamic law. Muslim legists have not clearly differentiated between the strictly legal and the moral. One advantage of this omission has been the permeation of law with living ethical values (unlike the modern secular systems of law). Law has to be worked out from the ethical systematization of the teaching of the Qur'an and the *uswa* (sunna) of the Prophet, with due regard to the situation currently obtaining. Thus law will adjust to changed social situations, but ethical values or long-range socio-moral objectives will remain constant. This has never been done before; instead, emphasis has been laid on certain dead or purely formal and extrinsic formulae.

It is for this essential task that we most need a recultivation of ideas. Our medieval theological heritage—whether *Mu'tazili,* Sunni or *Shi'i*—is essentially a product of history and bears little direct relationship to the ethics of the Qur'an and the Prophet. Islamic theology/philosophy has to be rebuilt afresh on the basis of the Qur'an, rather than reconstructed from this medieval heritage.

The greatest dilemma of medieval Islamic thought is in the field of ethics. One cannot point to a single work of ethics squarely based upon the Qur'an, although there are numerous works based upon

Greek philosophy, Persian tradition and Sufi piety. Although all these have been, to some extent, integrated with the Qur'an, they cannot be regarded essentially as expressions of the Qur'an. Such a work of ethics will represent the essence of the Qur'an, for the Qur'an is primarily an ethical teaching, not a book of law.

Besides the cultivation of a strong Islamic intellectual base, the creation of some adequate political order both within each country and between Muslim countries is absolutely necessary if Islam is to participate positively in the fashioning of a new world order. At the intra-Muslim level certain developments have occurred resulting in two Islamic summit conferences (Rabat 1969, and Lahore 1974) and the setting up of a permanent Islamic secretariat at Jeddah. But because of the lack of any Islamic vision of an economic-political order, the orientation of many Muslim countries is simply bewildering. The basic requirement of the Qur'an is the establishment of a social order on a moral foundation that would aim at the realization of egalitarian social and economic values. Any system will be Islamic that is based on these values and takes cognizance of the limits of a country's resources. Thus neither socialism nor capitalism is in itself a requirement of Islam.

Sunni political theory, which, like Sunni theological doctrine, emerged as a reaction to certain extremist views of the *Kharijites* and later of the Shi'a, was basically rooted in pragmatism. In opposition to the *Kharijites,* Sunnis asserted that it was not necessary for the ruler to be free from major errors, and against the Shi'a, they denied the infallibility and transcendence of the *Imam*. Why must the ruler be infallible, asks *al-Baqillani*, if he can be advised, admonished and warned by the Community which must wrest its rights from him,[33] and which can depose him? Further, it is also true that the power of the ruler was limited by the *Shari'a* and the constitution of the Muslim Community. But, since *Shari'a* by itself is an impersonal entity, the operative persons in the political field—the military commanders, the high civil servants and sometimes the *Ulama*—may be effective sometimes, but other times may be so weak that a ruler of strong will could both suppress and bypass them. And whose representatives were these personages, created mostly by the rulers themselves? There was in effect no link between the ruler and the community at large, and if

---

[33] Kitab al-Tamhid, Cairo 1947, p.184.

there is a more or less cohesive Muslim community in the world today, it is because of the Ulama and the *Shari'a,* not because of rulers.

Any Islamic reform today must begin with education. Although an Islamic orientation has to be created at the primary level of education, it is at the higher level that Islam and modern intellectualism must be integrated, to generate a modern, genuinely Islamic comprehension. Educational reform is the only approach for a long-term solution of the current problems of the Muslim societies. But educational reform can neither be accomplished nor show results overnight: it is a process which, if undertaken today, will take at least two generations. In the meantime, certain short-term measures can be taken to create an authentic Islamic political orientation and a higher intellectualism as an effective starting point for the islamization of all aspects of life.

As for political life, its foundation is the Muslim community itself. If this community is constituted by its conscious acceptance of the *Shari'a,* or Islamic imperative, as its goal in shaping the Muslim society, most of the problems would be solved. This can be done by an elected president or prime minister who enjoys the community's mandate for a defined and restricted period of time.

The question has troubled many Muslims and non-Muslim scholars as to who is to legislate in Islam, i.e., who is to interpret the Islamic imperative in a legal sense. The source of this trouble does not lie in Islam but in Islamic history, where although the community, at least theoretically, elected an executive head, it did not elect a legislative body. But it was an accident of history that lawmakers in Islam have been private individuals who were able to have their legal opinions accepted by large segments of the community. Indeed, in the early years of Islam after the Prophet, the head of the state did legislate by an informal consultation with the leaders of the community. What can now prevent a legislative assembly chosen by the people from enacting Islamic laws? The claim that the legal interpretation of Islam cannot be left to the assembly members, since it is the function of the *Ulama* to enact Islam into law, is a big and dangerous fallacy. The community based on Islamic imperatives will naturally have the assembly members chosen on their Islamic knowledge and qualifications.

The function of the *Ulama* is not to legislate but to provide religious leadership to the community at large by their teaching, preaching and diffusion of Islamic ideas to the public. It is obvious that the legislation

44

will be genuinely Islamic only to the extent that the public conscience and mind are both Islamic. The ulama's expert advice on difficult matters can be tendered through committees or councils. The Ulama's real creative, direct link will and should remain with the public. If there is more than one opinion on a certain issue, like '*riba*' and 'commercial interest'—and there is bound to be difference of opinion on most issues—let the elected parliament members be persuaded through discussion and debate, for there is no other way in a democratic society. When the parliament/assembly enacts a certain law, that may be right or wrong, but in so far as it reflects the will of the community, it will be both Islamic and democratic, i.e., it will represent the consensus *(Ijm'a)* of the community.

Hopes were aroused in the Islamic world in 1979 with the outbreak of the Iranian Revolution. The violent echoes it produced in some other Muslim countries, it seemed, at least for the first few months following the deposition of the Shah, as though we were about to witness in the third-world a growing tendency to scoff at the idea of the invincibility of the big powers. There was also a growing realization that some means, unthought of before, could enable weaker nations to outwit those who are far ahead of them, both militarily and economically.

But those aspirations were greatly disappointed. The new Iranian regime, by the violent course it chose to take, distorted its own image among Muslims outside Iran. Nevertheless, the Iranian Revolution had the undoubted effect of inducing politicians, experts, scholars and journalists in the West to pay serious attention to these newly aroused aspirations in the Muslim world.

The reasons behind this upsurge are far more simple than some make them out to be. For the past two centuries, the policy of the colonial powers in the Islamic world was based on the plunder of its resources, dissemination of dissension among sects and communities and sowing the seeds of doubt in the validity of Islam itself and in its ability to face the challenges of the modern age. That deliberate colonial policy created artificial barriers between Muslim peoples, making it difficult for them to maintain their ties, thereby undermining the spiritual and moral values of Islam, and forcing on the Muslim *ummah* such institutions, values and ways of life that are foreign to them. This created a schizophrenic attitude towards life and their social problems among Muslims and obliterated their identity.

Several factors made it improbable that this situation could lead to anything but a violent eruption. One was the widening gap between the standard of living of the majority and that of the ruling class, as well as that between the industrialized and underdeveloped countries, partly due to an unjust world economic system. Another was the growing loss of confidence in the political, economic or social solutions imported from capitalist and socialist countries, after long years of vain experiments and painful results. This combined with the growing recognition together with the spreading tendency to believe that the introduction of foreign institutions and ideas, encouraged by the developed countries, had for their aims the continued influence and benefit of those countries, the creation of widening markets for foreign goods, and weakening the hold of Islam on individuals.

Another point to be considered is the waxing tendency among Muslim youth to search for solutions, especially for their spiritual problems, in their own long neglected religion. Somewhat related is the growing awareness among religious Muslims of the sharp contradiction between Islamic tenets which they believe to be adequate for all ages and societies, which cover all aspects of human activity, and the unreligious, worldly tenets adopted by their governments in constitutional, civil, and criminal legislations. This leads them first to wonder how to reconcile the obligatory nature of the religious tenets with the unreligious laws of their so-called Islamic governments, rather than resort to violent means in order to force the government to adhere solely to the tenets of the *shari'a*.

More important, than all the above-mentioned factors, however, is the fact that Islam, in spite of all the setbacks it suffered in past centuries, has always proved itself capable of self-renewal and of responding to a strong stimulus for renaissance or to a powerful leadership, even at times when it seems to have reached the nadir of its career and when all hopes for the future are abandoned. Moreover, there is an ever present belief among Muslims that only Islam can restore to them their lost identity, dignity and self assurance, and provide solutions for their problems—unimported solutions that have their roots in the realities of their own situation.

That Islam could one day represent a real danger to the interests of developed countries akin to that witnessed in the Middle Ages is highly improbable. However, Muslims will constitute the majority of the population of Russia in less than a century, and this will by necessity have its implications for Soviet policies. Nearer in time is the danger of oil sources in Muslim lands falling in the hands of an anti-Western regime or regimes that can cause a great deal of trouble to Western industries as well as the commercial interests of developed countries. As for the danger of this Islamic state or states aligning themselves to the Eastern bloc, one can almost safely assume that an Islamic renaissance along lines exhibited in the revolution of Iran might appear against the traditional enemies of Islam.

What is most regrettable is the tendency among the majority of Muslims to put the blame for the miserable reality of their situation on external considerations that they are unable to cope with, or on foreign powers believed to be responsible for all the ills they suffer. Such attitude is based on a utopian conception of justice that is absolutely unjustifiable, a conception that is insisted upon only by the human victim when it falls in the claws of its enemy as a last resort.

Islam came to see the high power and prosperity of its society brought to an end during the seventeenth and especially the eighteenth centuries by the transformations then going on the West, changes that deprived the Nile-to-Oxus region of its special position in the hemisphere and that throughout islamdom undermined the social and economic structure. While the expansion of European industry had already narrowed down the foreign markets for the products of Muslim workshops, the second and mortal blow was given by Europe's discovery that the Muslim world could be circumvented, both physically and economically, by the opening of the sea route to West Africa and India. The effect was not only to dry up the main artery of economic prosperity, but also to isolate the Muslim World from effective contact with its neighbors and to condemn it to economic stagnation, with all the consequences that economic stagnation has on the intellectual and moral life of a people.

Meanwhile, the economic offensive of the West proceeded apace, and Western countries began gradually to extend their political control over various Muslim territories and to force an entrance for their own products into Muslim lands, in competition with the local industries. By stimulating the production of raw materials for their own manufactures, the Westerners geared the economic life of these lands with their own and fastened upon them an economic weakness and dependence which until now Muslims have not been able to shake off.

By the expulsion of Muslims from Europe, by the Russian expansion eastward and southward at the expense of Iran and Turkey, by opening the sea route to West Africa and India, and by the establishment of colonies there and in territories bordering on Islamdom, Islam was encircled. Then the West began to draw the net by occupying one Muslim country after another, sowing the seeds of political weakness and creating unshakeable cultural and economic ties with them. Later it tried to breed dissension among Muslims, encouraging Arabs to revolt against Turks. Then the state of Israel was created, devouring the energies of Arabs and furthering the dissension between Muslim, and particularly Arab, countries until almost none of them remained on good terms with its neighbors.

The potential for effective protection in the world of today and the possibility to regain a far more powerful position vis-à-vis the West is until very real. The means towards these ends are neither military armaments, nor economic weapon. However much we may boast in our verbal threats of our ability to use the oil weapon to our advantage, as we did in the 1970s, it did not and will not work. The real strength we have that can save our identity from utter annihilation lies in our religion, our heritage, our languages and traditions, our firm determination to hold to them and our taking pride in them.

The West is well aware of this fact of which the majority of our *Ummah* is until ignorant, and is aware that this ignorance on our part is vital to its interests. Clever devices were, and are until, used in order to empty the *Ummah* of its substance without its being conscious of what is going on. We may continue to believe that we are celebrating *Ramadan* if more religious dramas are shown on television. We may think we are Muslims if we abstain from eating pork when our whole style of life has become devoid of all Islamic elements. And we may think our traditions are kept alive if the Sheraton and Hilton hotels in our capitals present daily performance of belly dancing.

The backwardness and decline of the Muslim world is partly due to events and developments for which Muslims themselves bear the full responsibility. The first blow to the commercial prosperity of the Muslim world came from within. First industry and commerce were subjected more and more to the exactions and arbitrary measures of Muslim rulers by monopolies and excessive import and export duties that they were gradually strangled at a time when Europe was hitting hard at them. Impoverished by internal misrule and the armed competition of its rivals, Islam was hard put to maintain equality with its adversary, whose material advantage increased with every year.

Another factor was the closing of the door of *ijtihad*, or use of individual reasoning, which amounted to the demand for *taqlid*, the unquestioning acceptance of the doctrines of established schools and authorities. This caused the *ulama* in the Muslim world to neglect one of their most fundamental duties, that is, to concentrate on developing the doctrinal and intellectual basis of Islam so as to meet the changing needs, problems and circumstances of their contemporaries. For more than a thousand years, the intellectual activity of *ulama* was confined to their fight against innovations, exploiting that inherent mistrust Arabs have for whatever kind of change, or to vain disputes over minor doctrinal questions, absolutely theoretical and without any bearing on the every day life and problems of the *ummah*. The inevitable result was that the *ulama* came to live a kind of life that none but other *ulama* share, separating themselves from the masses, and claiming that no one might be deemed to have the necessary qualifications for independent reasoning in law. This came to be the rule throughout the Muslim world, in spite of efforts to prove the contrary by great Muslim thinkers such as *Ibn Taymiyya, Ibn Qayyim al-Jawziyya, al-Sjhawkani, Jamal al-Din al-Afghani, Muhammad Abduh and Ahmad Amin,* who insisted not only that the door of *ijtihad* was until open, but that it was the duty of all Muslims capable of this task to apply themselves to it.

For almost three centuries following the Ottoman conquest of most of the Arab world, Muslim intellectual life was decadent and the life of the living was more and more confined to narrow grooves. Instead of producing new works in the various branches of knowledge, they were content to write commentaries on older works, and even commentaries on the commentaries. The result of such intellectual stagnation was that, when Islamic countries in about 1800 CE began to respond to the European impact, the religious intellectuals were unable to lead in the adaptation of Islamic life to the new situation. First *Muhammad Ali* in Egypt, then other rulers in the rest of the Islamic world, became convinced of the need to follow the European path, seeing clearly that they could not depend on the *ulama* to help them carry out their mission. What followed was a catastrophic decision, which proved to have sinister and long lasting effects. Muhammad Ali set about providing an education of the European type for the many, utterly unlike traditional Islamic education, leaving the latter entirely in the hand of the *ulama*. Before long there were two competing systems of education in Egypt—and later in almost all other Muslim countries—and the intellectual life of these countries was flowing in two separate channels. The old system began with the Qur'an schools in the villages, and ended with such ancient institutions as *al-Azhar*. The new system had primary schools, secondary schools, and universities, all on the European model.

There was practically no teaching of the Islamic religion in the European type schools, and European model of instructions in the Islamic model of schools. The products of the new educational system had little interest in religion. Thus the Muslim *ummah* came to see an ever-widening gap between the religious and European types of education as well as between their different products.

The thesis accepted in most societies is that laws grow out of and develop along with the life of a community, taking into consideration its changing needs and particular circumstances. Muslim jurisprudence, however, insists that law has nothing to do with historical considerations, that it controls and is not controlled by the needs of the Muslim *Ummah*. Thus the *shari'a* is seen as static and immutable, free from the currents of time, applicable to all societies that accept Islam as religion, whether in Nigeria, Egypt, Turkey or Bangladesh.

Yet no more than approximately eighty verses of the Qur'an deal with legal topics in the strict sense of the term, and these are couched in brief, simple and general terms. If we add the fact that during the twenty-three years of the Prophet's mission verses were abrogated and replaced by others in the light of changes in the circumstances of the Muslim community, and that within a few years following the Prophet's death, the Islamic state came to include peoples of different cultures and legal systems, we can well sympathize with *Abu Hanifa* when he claimed for Muslims the right to use their own judgment in legislation whenever the Qur'an is silent about some point or other.

But then came *al-Shafii*, followed by *Ibn Hanbal*. who both saw that to recognize the right to *Ijtihad* and to take into consideration the different environments and circumstances of different Muslim communities would lead to the dilution of Islam and to the establishment of an Iraqi Islam, an Egyptian Islam, a Syrian Islam, etc. The view they adopted and which was later adopted everywhere in the world of

Islam is that in the absence of a Qur'anic legal decision, a sunna of the Prophet should be searched for and legal rulings on the ground that their intrinsic merits were outweighed by other juristic considerations. But *al-Shafi'i* and *Ibn Hanbal* insisted that these rulings were divinely inspired, were complementary to the Qur'an, and had the same binding force.

Muslims of different backgrounds and of different generations, finding their right to independent judgment reduced to a minimum, and that *al-Shafii's* view would produce a rigid and immutable legal system that ignored new historical circumstances, had recourse to a way out of that dilemma that was both dishonest and quite practical, namely the invention of new Hadiths. They kept attributing sayings and legal decisions to the Prophet that would facilitate adaptation to new social and political developments, and that would lend support to diverse schools of thought and various political doctrines. The Shi'a of the Prophet's cousin, Ali and the descendents of his uncle al-Abbas invented sayings and traditions, giving them the right to the Caliphate. Instead of trying to prove those sayings to be fakes, the *Umayyads* themselves retaliated by inventing *hadiths* that praised *Mu'awiya* and the *Umayyads*, or that urged Muslims to stick to their loyalty to their actual rulers, however unrighteous they might be. Other Pious persons saw no reason why they also should not come up with sayings that praised pious deeds or warned against wicked one, or ascribe to the Prophet wise or merely clever maxims mentioned in the Old or the New Testament. Then appeared traditions that prophesied the course of the events in the Islamic state, and others that supported the views of one or other of the four schools of fiqh. A third group of *hadiths* spoke of the virtues of cities or provinces conquered by the armies of Islam, while a fourth catered for the ever changing requirements of the state or was made at the urgent request of Caliphs and governors. Sufis and other groups or schools of thought then began to attribute to the Prophet sayings depicting their followers as the only true Muslims in the community.

This state of affairs aroused the fear and righteous anger of pious *ulama* who recognized that this enormous number of often conflicting traditions might lead the religion of Islam into the same situation as that suffered by earlier faiths when their adherents turned from their revealed scriptures to follow the writings of their learned leaders. Many of these came to play a major role in shaping the life of Muslims and the mentality and behavior of the youth of our *Ummah*. And so they became a chief source for the younger generation's discontent at so many aspects of modern life and institutions.

The Rise of Sufism

Instead of devoting their energies to the development of the doctrinal basis of Islam in order to meet the new needs and problems of their societies, the *ulama* have busied themselves since the rise of the Abbasids with hunting for positions and lucrative posts, and with gaining promotions and the favor of princes. The result was that the *ulama* became completely isolated and unaware of the problems of the daily life of the masses, losing the respect and awe they once enjoyed. The masses now turned to Sufi shaykhs seeking guidance, the more so as those sufis, especially at the beginning, were less concerned with the things of this world than the *ulama,* more daring in their attitude towards authority, and more occupied with the real issues and substance of religion.

One more serious result of the loss of confidence in the *ulama* and of their failure to help the masses to face new developments was that a growing number of Muslims, especially among the well-educated, turned their backs on Islam altogether and came to believe it to be a thing of the past, fit only for museums, and wholeheartedly accepted the Western way of life as the only way capable of meeting their modern needs.

The only real service rendered by Sufism to Islam was its denouncement of the *ulama's* preoccupation with the exterior elements of religion, with hollow arguments over details that had no spiritual dimension, and over correct behavior in streets and markets that had nothing to do with a live conscience. Thus were their efforts fruitful in evading a danger that threatened Islam. On the other hand, they did not try, as *Ibn Taymiyya* or *Ibn Qayyim al-Jawziyya* did, to clear away the accretions that came to hide the real face of Islam. On the contrary, they added to Islam foreign elements—Christian, Hindu, Persian, or Greek—inventing new *hadiths* that supported their views, reinterpreting the Qur'an, and coming out with a system that the founder of Islam would have found difficult to recognize if he were have come back to life.

By the end of the eighth century the creative phase of Sufism was over, and by the tenth it was on its way to rapid decline. Poverty and contempt for worldly affairs were no longer considered virtues. Sufi shaykhs began to gain the confidence and favor of princes, to own elegant houses and estates, to enter into vain and shallow disputes, to make light of the common standards of morality, and to develop rites and encourage norms of behavior that were quite foreign to Islam.

If a close affiliation between the revival of Sufism and historical periods of political and social decline is recognized, we shall have to agree that Sufism and Sufi orders in the Islamic world ushered a new lease of life as a result of the deterioration of the quality of political life there and in the Arab world. It is a lease of life that reminds us of that given to Sufism by the Mongols' invasion of the Eastern provinces of the Islamic state during the thirteenth century. If we further agree that Sufi ethics made it easier for people to accept—and to facilitate conciliation with—political despotism and forceful subjection, we shall be the more able to discern the real dangers lurking behind the present day revival of Sufi sentiments in our societies.

With the expansion of the Arab state, those new adherents to Islam among the conquered nations who found it too difficult to renounce their previous religious or to accept whole-heartedly the new one, found a convenient solution in a reinterpretation of Islam that made it compatible with their beliefs while appearing, at the same time, to be devout Muslims.

It cannot be questioned that Islam had a deep influence on the life and creeds of the conquered nations. Yet it is also true that these nations succeeded in bringing along into Islam many of their ancient local beliefs. Hindus that forbade the remarriage of widows continued after their conversion to Islam to look down on it, despite the fact that the Prophet himself married nine widows. Some African tribes that used to frown on the killing of cocks until consider them to this day to be sacred birds, but on a new and Islamic basis: that it is the cock that wakens the Muslims at dawn to perform their prayers.

Thus several alien beliefs came to be mingled with Islamic tenets. None of these made it easier for non-Arab nations to retain their creeds than the device of the veneration of saints, a practice clearly in conflict with Islam in which there is no place for intermediaries between God and men. People ignored the obstacle, and so did the *ulama*, as long

53

as this veneration did not come into flagrant contradiction with the concept of the oneness of God.

Once the principle of the veneration of saints was accepted in the Islamic world, non-Arab Muslims began to clothe their old Christian, Jewish, Hindu, Zoroastrian or pagan beliefs with an Islamic garb. Sacred places and graves continued under Islam to be sacred. Persians continued to celebrate the feast of *Nawruz*, but now they gave it an Islamic color, saying that the Prophet chose Ali as his successor on that day! A tree that the populace in Egypt used to worship in olden times was now said to give shade to the grave of a pious Muslim woman called *Saint Khadra* (Saint Green).

There is in the history of Islam not one revolutionary movement inspired by social, political or economic motives, that is not thought of by its adherents as being based solely on religious grounds, aiming at nothing else but the overthrow of an ungodly regime and the reinstatement of the rule of the Qur'an. These sects reinterpreted the Qur'an to suit their own purposes, introduced into Islam ideas quite foreign to it and added until more *hadiths*, until one could hardly tell what was and what was not in accordance with the original tenets of Islam.

Muslim historians of the Middle Ages were not unaware of the methods of historical research. They applied to their materials the same principles laid down and developed by the *Hadith* scholars for the study of traditions. Undoubtedly, Muslim historians achieved great progress in their field during the third and fourth centuries of *Hijra.* Muslim historians could never manage to cast off entirely the influence of the religious disciplines. With the onset of intellectual decline in the Islamic world, historians freely adopted the dogmatic view of the Islamic past formed in religious circles and agreed to serve the aims set down by the ulama for historiography, that is, that it should a means for edification and moral instruction and for preaching the tenets of Muslim sects.

Thus was formed the romantic view of history which many Muslims hold. For them, historical veracity is far less important than the support of faith, edification and the setting up of models and ideals for the believers. As a result, caliphs such as *Umar b. Abdal Aziz*, one of those mainly responsible for the decline and fall of the Umayyad dynasty because of his ill conceived financial policy, came to be considered one of the greatest heroes of Islam and the best of the Umayyad caliphs, merely because he was pious and just to the *Alawids* and *Banu Hashim*. On the other hand, one of the greatest administrators in the history of humankind and the great mainstay of the Arab Umayyad dynasty, al-Hajjaj b. Yusuf, was and until is seen as bloodthirsty enemy of Islam, opposed to all this religion stood for. For similar reasons Yazid b. Muawiya and al-Amin b. al-Rashid were denounced by historians without their having a clear conception of the aims of Yazid's enemies, the followers of al-Husayn, or of al-Amin's enemies, the Persian opponents of Arab rule.

In any case, it seems safe to state that many contemporary Muslims' views of their history and its main characters can never encourage a healthy outlook or a clear understanding of the course of events, and cannot but lead to a superficial glorification of the past and a nostalgia that is hardly justifiable.

The impact of the West's superiority in arms and culture was to lead, during the past two centuries, to a growing doubt in the minds of Muslims as regards their own religion and its institutions. Close contacts with Western civilization had a deep influence on enlightened Muslims and their relation to inherited theories and traditions. They felt an overwhelming need for the adaptation of those theories and traditions to the new situation and to the circumstances they were now facing. Unfortunately, their efforts to achieve that adaptation came at a time when their confidence in their religious heritage was shaken and as they began to look on the Western countries, they found them demi-gods. No wonder that their intellectual efforts were wholly based on Western values and ideas. Even when they tried to defend Islam, their defense concentrated on disproving the accusation that its teachings were an impediment to progress.

Thus almost all Muslim reformers came to preach the same things: to take from both Western and Muslim civilizations what was good for them and leave out what was bad. But what actually happened was that their call opened the way to the wholesale adoption of Western values and institutions, while the reference to their own Muslim heritage was constantly overlooked. As both Muslims and Westerners perceived, unlike the Japanese, the Muslims did not pick up from the West its productivity, scientific spirit and zeal for construction, but only its consumption habits, fashions and its lowest forms of entertainment.

Two considerations made it easy for Muslims to adopt many aspects of Western civilization: one, that the European invader left out the religious element altogether so that their invasion did not take the shape of one faith subjecting another to its rule; second, that the majority of Muslims came to believe the West's claim that its civilization was the climax of all civilization and that it could not possibly suffer such fates as were experienced by preceding ones.

At the time when Muslims and other non-Western nations were well advanced on the road of Westernization, the West itself was in the throes of a painful spiritual crisis, with many seriously doubting its previous claims to perfection and incorruptibility, and its pretense to be able to solve all the world's problems. This spiritual crisis became all the more serious as a result of the now widespread influence of Western civilization. And thus the Muslim nation ended up empty-handed: it had first lost confidence in its Islamic heritage and now had become disillusioned with the Western way of life that now was deemed reprehensible. Hence the bitter feelings towards the West now prevalent among the majority of Muslims.

Such is the picture of the Muslim *Ummah*: a spiritual crisis in the West with resounding echoes in all countries involved in the process of westernization; a verbal, hypocritical loyalty to Islam on the part of rulers who have long since turned their backs on Islamic institutions and modes of government and have opted for Western ones; a loss of confidence and interest in the *ulama* who have little or nothing to say on the more serious issues; young men and women whose faith and respect for their heritage were shaken and without new values to fill the ensuing vacuum; an acquisitive spirit for no useful purpose, and a big demand for consumer goods with no inclination for productivity; women whose sexual ethics are fast approaching those in the West without acquiring the Western women's sense of duty; a fierce struggle on the part of the *ulama* against *ijtihad* while taking a most servile attitude towards their governments; an everyday behavior at home, in office or in the market place, of which nobody can judge whether it has its origin in the Muslim tradition or not; economic problems that have broken the backs of the majority and left them hardly any time or energy to acquire knowledge and seek the advancement of learning.

If that is our predicament, can one until speak of a future, a remedy, and of ways of reform? I certainly believe so, and would like to make a few suggestions as to how to start moving in the right direction. First of all: we must realize that the greater part of the message delivered by the Prophet to his people was unfamiliar to them, contrary to their cherished values and traditions, wholly alien to the ideals and fundamental attitude towards life that they inherited from their forefathers. In so many verses, the Qur'an ridicules people's attachment to inherited beliefs and values that were unreasonable and illogical. Yet there are also sayings attributed to the Prophet that warn against innovation and against departure from the ways of their ancestors. In view of the Qur'anic verses just referred to, one cannot believe that the Prophet could have said such things. He himself had so many times told his companions that they themselves were the best judges with regard to their worldly affairs, and that his commands were binding only when they touched on religious and ethical concerns.

However, we find among Muslims of today those who claim that the conduct and way of *al-salaf al-salih* should be strictly followed, even in such matters as dress, eating, and the putting on shoes, or concerning what should be said to the person who sneezes; and these people accuse those that think for themselves and use their own judgment of not being Muslims at all. They consider as reprehensible innovations anything that was unknown to the Prophet and his companions, and deem as falling under that hateful category of *bid'a,* innovation, such things as coffee, the printing press, newspapers, the electric lamp, the use of forks and knives in eating, and the oil industry. It is clear that this attitude, carried to the extremes, would make impossible life under circumstances different from those witnessed by the Prophet.

Some of us believe that no revival of Islam is possible except by a return to the past. This indeed is correct if it means a search for the true essence of Islam hidden under layers and layers of legends, superstitions, false traditions attributed to the Prophet, false interpretations of the Qur'an, an idealistic view of the history of the *ummah*, and a deliberate distortion of Islamic teachings to suit the purposes of different sects and schools of *fiqh*. These and others have long hid the true essence of Islam. But this is not what these people mean.

The second and final suggestion: "Reformed Islam is Islam no longer," said Cromer. And again this is true if applied to that movement which started in India during the first half of the nineteenth century, and was later taken up by Egypt and other Muslim countries, stressing the

57

conformity of Islamic teachings with the values of Western civilization, and defending Islam and the Prophet on similar grounds. To my mind, though, such a call cannot but lead to a complete surrender of the faith to a wholesale adoption of Western ways of life under the false pretext that Islam itself approved of such ways.

But there is another concept of reform that could not only make Islam relevant to the social and political needs of the present and the future, but could also make it a permanent and ever-effective contribution to world civilization. This necessitates, first, the admission on our part that the purely theoretical thought underlying our faith, as well as other faiths, assumes, whenever it appears in a certain place, at a certain time, and in a society that has its particular characteristics and limitations, certain temporary aspects that are related to these particulars. Therefore it is legitimate for those who live in other ages and places and who are concerned with the religious teachings to start by distinguishing first between what is eternal in them and what is temporary and merely a matter of politics, and second, between what was originally there and what was added later through the centuries. Only then can they decide how to make use of the eternal essence of their religious heritage in their contemporary life and society and how to shape their attitudes in accordance with this essence. Only thus can their faith be as valid and as effective as that of *al-salaf al-salih,* the Prophet's companions, and their successors, *at-ta'biun.*

The word "Islam" means submission to the will of God, recognition of His wisdom and just objectives, acceptance of His decrees, while doing one's utmost in order to make this will prevail. There is no contradiction whatsoever between acceptance of God's decrees and the exertion of effort to make His will prevail by way of resistance, revolution or *Jihad.* For the wise and learned can well discern against the current of history. Such latter trends must be resisted and fought against "in order to make God's will prevail."

There is a Chinese proverb that says, "He who gives me a fish provides me with food for one single day. But he who teaches me fishing provides me with food for the rest of my life." This proverb applies to religious truth more than to anything else. It is by being guided by the spirit of Islam, not by individual tenets, that we can find the right way wherever and in whatever circumstances we live. The one who can, in the light of this spirit, show us the way to face the challenges of our age, is the best Muslim of us all.

If we are asked, "but why Islam at all?" we shall say that it is the religion under the wing of which people in our kind of societies can be both moral and creative. Hence it becomes imperative that we should find "Islamic" solutions to our social and political problems. We have already seen that those who believed the West when it called, "follow us and your problems will be solved," have now come to discover that the West was not sincere in its claim, and that following it has proved, in many ways, to be disastrous.

We have to realize that the problems of our day cannot be solved by ignoring them. What we need now is a kind of vision to be articulated by our intellectuals and scholars that would lead us into new paths. But this vision cannot emerge except in an atmosphere of intellectual freedom and of honest, sober and unromantic discussions that have no place for charges of infidelity and unbelief. In the absence of such atmosphere, we can be sure that our Muslim *Ummah* will stay where it is, and will for a long time to come be in the same precarious state which we all now experience.

PART—II

ISLAM IN FUNDAMENTALS

The Qur'an and the Prophet

It is incontestable that the supreme purpose of the Qur'an and the Prophet was to terminate idolatry and establish the sole worship of God, acknowledged as God alone. Islam was the faith about God to end gods. It was the revelation to finalize revelations. It was the call, in rugged simplicity, to let God be God. This could only be by letting Islam be Islam, and allowing the Prophet be the Prophet. The three demands, unity, community and prophet-hood, were mutual and inseparable.[34]

The Qur'an has no controversy with the earlier faiths which is not implicit in the main contention between Muhammad and his pagan Arab context. The events which are pivotal in the Qur'an are those that relate to the struggle with idolatry. Others, however vital, are only contributor.[35] The Qur'an is primarily seen as a mission to retrieve idolaters for true believers.

All that follows, then, is based on the view that the crux of things Qur'anic lies in the confrontation by Muhammad of the world of the *Quraish*, the custodians of the city of his birth with its shrine and pilgrimage. This was the human constituency of his public mission through its decisive years. It was the scene of the double battle for recognition of prophetic status and divine word. The Qur'an is the document, almost in a sense the sacrament, of both aspects in their unity—God and His messenger. The living context is Arabian paganism, where the prophetic duty must be done, in order that the undivided lordship may prevail and so *Islam* comes to pass.[36]

The concerns of the Qur'an and the exemplary conduct of the Prophet was nothing other than deep God-consciousness which is creatively and organically related to the founding of a socio-political

---

34 Kenneth Cragg; *The Event of the Qur'an;* OneWorld, Oxford, 2006; p.14

35 Ibid. p.15.

36 Ibid. p.16.

order in the world on ethical base. It is this *God consciousness* that sent Muhammad out of the Cave of *Hira* into the world, never to return to that cave or the contemplative life again. What issued from his experience in the cave was not merely the demolishing of a plurality of gods, but a sustained and determined effort to achieve *socio-economic justice*. He aimed at constituting a community of goodness and justice in the world—a socio-political order 'under God's command', that is, according to the principle and moral values that cannot be made and unmade by man at his own whim or convenience and should not be misused or abused for the sake of expediency.

The genesis of the greater Arabic culture during the period of "*Jahiliyya*" or the "time of ignorance" was centered on Muhammad's miracle, the Qur'an. The most important and authentic source of this period is the Qur'an itself, probably the most studied book in today's world. Translation of the Qur'an into any other language from the original Arabic results in loss of effectiveness. A single Arabic word may be a shorthand way of expressing a wealth of connotations and significations. The late Marmaduke Pickthall in the introduction to his translation admits, *"that inimitable symphony, the very sounds of which move men to tears and ecstasy."*

The next most important source of biographical data is the '*hadith*' literature, an act or saying attributed to Muhammad. The most respected collection of *Hadiths* was that assembled by Al-*Bukhari*. Out of 600,000 he selected 7398 traditions. His work is also available in languages other than Arabic. Next comes the collection of *Muslim* (d.261/875), a contemporary of al-*Bukhari*. The genuineness of traditions rests largely on the number and character of the witnesses in agreement in the unbroken chain of transmission.

The principal authority for the life of Muhammad is the *Seera of Ibn Ishaq* (Abu Abdullah Muhammad Ibn Ishaq, (d.768.), a native of Madina, who travelled Egypt, Iraq and Baghdad at the invitation of Caliph al-Mansur. Thus the *Seera* was written under Abbasid patronage.

Unfortunately, none of *Ibn Ishaq's* work is extant in its original form but this has been preserved in a recension by *Ibn Hisham* (d.833), 65 years after *Ibn Ishaq*, entitled *Kitab Seerat Rasulillah*, the Book on the Life of the Prophet.

The basic *elan* of the Qur'an—the stress on socio-economic justice and essential human egalitarianism—is quite clear from its very early passages. Now all that follows by way of Qur'anic legislation in the field of private and public life has social justice and building of an egalitarian community as its end. To insist on a literal implementation of the rules of the Qur'an, shutting one's eyes to the social change that has occurred and that is now occurring before our eyes, is tantamount to deliberately defeating its overall moral-social purposes and objectives. An eminent Islamic thinker-scholar is of the opinion that:

In building any genuine and viable Islamic set of laws and institutions, there has to be a twofold movement: First one must move from the concrete case treatments of the Qur'an—taking the necessary and relevant social conditions of that time into account—deducing the general principles upon which the entire teaching converges. Second, from this deduced general principles there must be a movement back to specific legislation, taking into account the necessary and relevant social conditions now obtaining.[37]

The Qur'an loudly proclaims that it is a highly integrated and cohesive body of teaching (6:114; 12:111; 16:89). Certainty belongs not to the meanings of particular verses of the Qur'an and their content but to the objectives of the Qur'an as a whole, that is, as a set of coherent principles or values. It was for this reason that the men of the first generation of Islam gave judgments in the light of their experience of the Qura'nic teaching *as a whole*. It was, in fact, more to the point on their part to quote a concrete precedent from the Prophet's life, if one was available. Otherwise they relied on the overall understanding of the purpose of the Qur'an. A striking illustration is provided by caliph Umar's refusal after the conquest of Iraq to divide the conquered land among the Muslim soldiers as booty, which was the Prophet's general practice. Under insistent pressure from the opposition, Umar finally appealed to the Qur'an 59:10 to buttress the stand he had taken. In fact, early Muslims acted first upon their experience of the totality of the Qur'anic teaching and introduced the citation of particular verses only at a secondary stage, as described in the Qur'an at 3:17.

---

37 Fazlur Rahman's *ISLAM & MODERNITY: Transformation of an Intellectual Tradition;* Univ. of Chicago Press, Chicago and London, 1984, p.20.

Similarly, if one is tempted to take literal meaning of Sura 9, verses 5, 8, 20, 23, 80, 83 and 93, and given such set of verses into legal code, it will come away with a negative image and meaning of the Qur'an. Such an interpretation would be totally out of place, since it would project backwards the current philosophy of human rights and would ignore the fundamental lesson of the *sura* (chapter) as a whole, which is not outmoded. Muslim theological thought, it seems, has not committed itself to the kind of interpretation that would highlight the pivotal problem until lurking in the contemporary discourse on human rights. Apart from logical and scientific interpretation of the Qur'anic verses and the traditions of the Prophet and his companions the lack of sanctions into civil and criminal law that could be followed by all the Muslim states and countries is also, it seems, one of the factors in divergence in the spirit of Islam.

The place of Islam is unique in the history of religions in a way that its foundation was laid upon a book, and not in the person bearing the book. Man can live and die; scripture can't. It was something unbelievable to the followers of the Prophet of Islam that someday the Prophet will disappear or die. When he died, the crowd of his followings did not believe in the news. One of his companions in the crowd became furious and took his sword in his hand declaring that he would kill the one who says the prophet has died. The commotion among the people was allayed by one senior companion, named *Abu Bakr,* addressing thus:

"O Muslims, if you adored Mohammed, know that Mohammed is dead; if it is God that you adore, know that He liveth, He never dies. Forget not this verse of the Book, 'Mohammed is only a man charged with a mission; before him there have been men who received the heavenly mission and died'—nor forget this, 'Thou too, Mohammed, shalt die as others have died before thee." The enraged gathering was cooled down at this address.[38]

Mohammed was no more with the community of believers, but the Book, as Muslims believe, he received through Arch Angel Gabriel in the form of recitation was with the believers *along with* his sayings and deeds for their guidance. The Qur'an was first memorized by the believers, later compiled in a book, copied and circulated throughout

---

[38] Ameer Ali, *A Short History of the Saracens,* McMillan, London, 1949; p.20.

the centers of the then empire during the third Caliph, *Uthman ibn Affan* (644-656). The verses of the Book were revealed either for moral and spiritual guidance of the community or in answer to practical questions faced by the Prophet during his dealing with the socio-political affairs of the city state of Madina.

When one studies the social aspect of Muhammad's reform, two features appear striking. First, before introducing a major measure of social change, the ground was well prepared first to receive the change. Although Qur'anic warnings against usury were issued in *Makkahh*, it was not legally banned until the Prophet had been in Madina, until he had complete socio-political authority. Similarly the law of the *zakat* tax was not promulgated until well after the Prophet had settled in Madina although the measures of "brotherhood" between the local population and the *Makkahn* immigrants was taken soon after his arrival and a constitutional pact was instituted amongst all the tribes for security of Madina in times of war and peace. Banning of wine and gambling were promulgated in the same gradual manner.

The second feature of the legislation of the Qur'an is that it (like the decisions of the Prophet) always had a background or a historical context, which the Muslim commentators of the Qur'an call "occasions of revelation *(tanzil)*." Most of the time the Prophet decided the day-to-day issues that arose before the new community in the light of the revelations received. Some time in spite of the pressing need of circumstance, he used to hold up his decision until he received the revelation. The real significance of the "occasions of revelation" has never been realized by the interpreters of the Qur'anic verses and there has always been a difference of opinion. The Prophet's immediate followers, the Companions, did not care to record or get them recorded the instances other than revelation, while later generations, successors of the Companions and their successors, although possessing a certain amount of reliable information through a chain of tribal traditions, were left to guess at what these "occasions" might have been. The only reliable or close to reliable was the social and collective behavior of the Arabs, like all tribally organized societies, were custom-bound, and a set pattern of behavior, that was later called *Sunna*, acquired sanctity for them.

There is no doubt that early scholars of Islam and leaders of the community exercised a good deal of freedom and ingenuity in interpreting the Qur'an, including the principles of *ijtihad* (personal reasoning) and *qiyas* (analogical reasoning from a certain text of the Qur'an). There was however, no well-devised system of rules for these procedures, and early legal schools sometimes went too far in using this freedom. For this reason in the late eighth century C.E., *al-Shafi'i* successfully fought for the general acceptance of "traditions from the Prophet" as a basis for interpretation. "The *Umayyads* influenced the Tradition in their own interest."[39] The *Hadiths* multiplied in numbers to accommodate the great diversity of cultures as a result of rapid territorial and racial expansion. Thus many early opinions on the religious law and dogma of Islām as well as sectarian prophecies and other expectations, were cast in the form of *Hadiths*. That the opposing political parties tried to influence public opinion through the medium of *Hadith* and used the names of great authorities of Tradition is a fact no one conversant with the early history of Islam may deny. Yet the real solution lay only in understanding the Qur'anic injunctions strictly in their *context* and background and trying to extricate the principles or values that lay behind the injunctions of the Qur'an and the *Sunna* of the Prophet. But this line of action until awaits the attention of Muslim scholars and jurists.

Instead of giving a progressive interpretation to the Qur'anic texts, the fundamentalists insist on adhering to the outmoded views of classical jurists. One such demand for the banning of interest on investments and deposits; this is being done in Saudi Arabia. The high priest of the *Dawoodi Bohras* has called upon his followers to withdraw their deposits from banks. Allama Abdullah Yusuf Ali, a highly respected commentator of the Qur'an, has opined that the *'usury'* of the old times is not the same as the *'interest'* of today. The one was exploitative, the other is socially productive.

---

[39] I. Goldziher, *Muhammedanische Studien*, 1961, vol.2, p.5

The Authority of Hadith and Sunna

The Qur'an is obviously the foremost foundational source of the Islamic religion. There also exists a second source or foundation (*asl*): the prophetic tradition (*sunna*)known through the *hadiths*, i.e., the prophetic utterances in Muhammad's role as guide of the Community of believers and not as a transmitter of the Word of God. Thus the companions of the Prophet paid heed to his utterances, collected them with great piety, and transmitted them to subsequent generations.[40] After the death of the Prophet these utterances became the object of an intense search so that they could be collected and put into writing, providing a transition from oral tradition to the written, as had occurred with the Qur'an.

The Distinction between Hadiths and the Sunna

Verbal transmission (*riwaya*) concerning the Prophetic model of behavior started early in Islam. Initially, a *hadith* was attributed only to the immediate reporter of a saying or act of the Prophet. The number of Companions of the Prophet who stand at the eyewitness base of any particular *hadith* varies widely. The total number of Companions to whom authoritative Prophetic reports are actually attributed amounts to no more than 1060. At the very top of the list is a companion, *Abu Huraira*, whose chief claim to fame is that he transmitted 5374 *hadiths*. Close by is *Aisha* (the Prophet's wife), credited with 2210. Within a century or so after the Prophet's death, as the growing body of reports began to be systematized and codified, they assumed a standard form that consisted of two parts: a transmissional chain (*isnad*), giving the names of the successive narrators who passed on the initial report, to guarantee its authenticity, followed by the text of what the Prophet

---

[40] "Let him that is present tell it unto him that is absent. Happy he that shall be told may remember better than he who hath heard it." Sermon the Mount; The Spirit of Islam by Syed Ameer Ali, Sang-e-Meel Publications, Lahore,Pakistan, p. 115.

had purportedly said or done. Thus, a typical *hadith* would run like somewhat this: *A* (the narrator) says he heard it from *B* on the authority of *C* who said this on the authority of *D* that the Prophet of God said so and so.

Wherever the Qur'an speaks of the authority of *sunna*, it couples the Prophet with God. The faithful are commanded to obey God and the Prophet of God.

> "Say: Obey Allah and His Messenger"; but if they turn back, Allah does not love those who reject Faith." (3:32)
>
> "And obey Allah and the Messenger; that you may obtain mercy." (3:132)
>
> ". . . So take what the Messenger assigns to you, and deny yourselves that which he withholds from you." (59:7)
>
> "Say: 'If you do love Allah, follow me. Allah will love you and forgive you your sins: . . . . '"(3:31)

The Qur'an also speaks of the 'exemplary conduct of the Prophet of God' so much so that it declares to the believers: "Allah and His Angels send *salat* (blessings) on the Prophet: O you who believe! Send your *salat* (blessings) on him and salute (greet) him with all respect." (33:56)

The Prophet himself distinguished between his own utterance and that of the Qur'an, and it was only at special, critical points that his decisions had to be supported by the Qur'an itself. When a dispute arose amongst the community over a decision of the Prophet with regard to the distribution of booty after a certain expedition, the Qur'an commands, "So take what the Messenger assigns to you, and deny yourselves that which he withholds from you. And fear Allah, for Allah is strict in punishment." (59:7) In another verse the Qur'an says, "But no, by your Lord, they can have no (real) Faith until they make you judge in all disputes between them, and find in their souls no resistance against your decision, but accept them with the fullest conviction." (59:7) This warning refers to a specific case of an internal dispute in the Community. There are many other similar instances in the Qur'an. If the Prophet's authority had been accepted willingly by all faithful normally, without bickering in certain quarters, the Qur'an would not have intervened. In fact, the Prophet had, and normally exercised, an unchallenged authority outside the Qur'an in giving judgments.

During the lifetime of the Prophet people talked about what he said or did as a matter of course. But after his death this talk became a deliberate phenomenon since a new generation was growing up for whom it was natural to enquire about the Prophet's conduct to provide a pattern for their own behavior. The religious orientation of a *hadith*—a verbal transmission—was towards a corresponding *sunna*, a non-verbal transmission, the 'silent' or 'living' tradition, i.e., a religious norm of practice.

We must, therefore, distinguish between the meanings of *'hadith'* and the *'Sunna'*. For later generations, the *Sunna* meant the conduct of the Prophet, from whom it acquired its normativeness. But to the extent that the norm continued to be largely 'silent' and 'non-verbal', the word *'hadith'* was applied to the actual content of the behavior of each succeeding generation, insofar as that behavior claimed to exemplify the Prophetic pattern. The intention of the term *Sunna* was always directed towards the normative status of the Apostolic model.

Hadiths and the Competition for Legal Authority

Muhammad al-Shafi'i (d. 204/820) was the most influential of the early Muslim jurists in underscoring the legal significance of *hadiths*, claiming for prophetic tradition a divine imprint as an extension of the revelation of the Qur'an. It was in line with this conviction that the phrase "the Qur'an and the *Sunna*" became current to describe the fount of authority in Sunni Islam (the major traditionalist sect). The *Hadiths* would necessarily be explanatory or complementary to already revealed verses in the Qur'an. Hence it is this interpretation, the Prophet's own, not some other imagined exegesis of the Book, that should be followed. A *hadith* may simply reaffirm or complement what is already in the Qur'an, or it may render specific what the Qur'an expresses only in general terms—e.g., the exact times of prayer, or the precise terms of the alms-tithe (*zakat*). In legal terms, the *sunna* of the Prophet was full partner with the Qur'an in prescribing Muslim behavior, usually with the *hadiths* being far more detailed and prescriptive than the Qur'an.

In the first two centuries of Islam, during the period of territorial expansion, there arose a need to accommodate a great diversity of cultures in the Muslim community. Thus, once the Prophet's personal example, recorded in *hadiths*, became established as the universal Muslim norm (*Sunna*), many opinions by others on the religious law and dogma of Islam, as well as sectarian prophecies and other expectations, were cast in the form of *hadiths*, attributing these later ideas to the Prophet. In this way, *hadiths* were often fabricated in order to create a normative past that could accommodate the new situations, thereby multiplying in number. Out of the needs and inventiveness of lawyers, the mass of tradition grew apace. When virtually no issues could be argued, until less settled, except by connection with cited acts and opinions of Muhammad, the temptation to require, imagine or allege such traditions became irresistible. The supply of *hadiths* grew to approximate the demand for them, and their mutual growth made the science of supporting attribution both more ingenious and more pretentious.

The selection and editing of the *hadiths* both reflected and contributed to the ongoing controversies among the three great Muslim communities, and cannot be understood apart from those controversies. The great collections of *hadiths* deemed to be authentic by each community were assembled only at the end of the second/ninth century, long after the death of the Prophet. Sunnis finally recognized the compilations of *Muhammad ibn Ismail al-Bukhari* (d. 256/870) and *Muslim ibn al-Hajjaj* (d. 261/875), which they called the 'two authentic ones' (*al-sahihayn*), and within the next century came to view another four as authoritative: the works of Abu Da'ud (d. 275/888), al-Tirmidhi (d. 279/892), al-Nasa'i (d. 303/916) and Ibn Maja (d. 273/886). The Twelver-Shi'a staked their claim on the compilation entitled 'Suitable for the Science of Religion', started by *Kulayni* (d. 939) and supplemented by the collections of *Ibn Babuyi* (d. 991) and *Tusi* (d. 1067). The *Kharijites* used the *Ibn Habib* collection (end of eighth century) called 'The True One of Spring' *(al-sahih al-rabi)*.[41] The differences can be explained by the cultural origins of groups competing for control of the tradition. The ultimate object of the rivalry was leadership of the Muslim political community—caliphate or imamate, as the case might be. Each considered the others to be contrived and false.

---

[41] Muhammad Arkoun, *"Rethinking Islam"* ; Translated and Edited (French to Eng.): Robert D. Lee; p.45.

According to a celebrated *hadith*, the Prophet announced that his community would be divided into seventy-three sects and that the members of all of these would go to hell except one, which was promised salvation. Sunnis use this *hadith* to show that they constitute a unique community called *ahl al-sunna wal-jama'a*, those who follow the prophetic tradition and remain with the community. The *Shi'a* on the other hand, teach that they alone managed to harvest the authentic heritage of the Qur'an and of the prophetic tradition. They call themselves '*ahl al-isma wal-adala*', those who profess infallibility and justice. Finally, the *Khariji* claim to a greater chronological proximity to the founding moment (610-632), a guarantee of superior authenticity. They refused to recognize the Umayyad, whom they viewed as usurpers of the caliphate and went out to fight them. They reject privilege of birth, such as descent from the *Quraysh* tribe or Hashemite family of the Prophet, as a condition for acceding to the caliphate-imamate. They call themselves '*al-shurat*', those who sacrifice their lives to maintain the preeminent authority of God. In all three cases we see the emergence of a religious consciousness bearing competing claims to rightfulness, derived from Islamic teaching and the prophetic model. This consciousness took material form through political institutions and sought fulfillment by them to direct the political community postulated by the Qur'an and the Prophet.

Two undesirable developments ensued from this phenomenon. First, referring every theological, dogmatic or legal doctrine to the authority of the Prophet restricted the free and creative process of interpretation. Second, if the creative process were to go on unrestricted, then a massive and incessant fabrication would be necessary. In fact, both fears interacted. Traditionists attempted to safeguard against both extremes by producing two principles, both embodied in *hadiths* which are probably fictions generated by the principles themselves. According to the first, the Prophet was reported to have said that whatever good sayings exist can be assumed to have been said by him and can be accepted[42] on his authority. According to the second, the Prophet was alleged to have pronounced, "He who tells a deliberate lie about me

---

42 Ibn Maja, vol.4

should be prepared for his seat in Hell".[43] Up to about the middle of the 3rd/9th century, theology and law continued to develop under the aegis of the *hadith*, as did the selective activity of separating the genuine *hadiths* from the weak and the false. This was also the period of the formation and consolidation of the orthodoxy. These were intertwined, and somewhat circular, activities. When the climax of this formulative process was reached, the *hadiths* were finally codified and accepted and, at the same time, the activity of creative interpretation in Islam, in any major sense, almost came to an end.

The earliest record of the warnings against and opposition to the *Hadith* is contained in the works of the jurist, *al-Shafi'i* (d. 204/820). These are highly instructive about the situation obtaining in the 2nd/8th century. The opposition varied from being against particular, individual *hadiths* to being against almost all *hadiths*. Al-Shafi'i was the arch-protagonist of the acceptance of the Prophetic *hadiths* in the field of law, while his opponents in the legal schools claimed that the basis of law should be the Prophetic *Sunna* as it was actually being livedin the practical tradition. By that time the concept of *Ijm'a*, or consensus, had emerged, and they argued that the agreed practice was more entitled to represent the legacy of the Prophet than an obscure *Hadith* which claimed to go back to the authority of the Prophet, but had no basis in the practice. Such *hadiths* if accepted, they contended, would in fact open the door for wholesale fabrication of *hadiths* in the name of the Prophet. Their argument ran as follows: 'The Companions of the Prophet generally and as a whole knew best and were the only and reliable bearers of the Prophetic tradition. The younger generations of the "Successors" saw the Companions in action and also learned from them, even if they could not have access to the Prophet himself, and therefore, were the best immediate source for the Prophetic teaching.[44] This is *Ijm'a* or consensus and against this we cannot accept the testimony of one or two stray narrators of a *Hadith* that may now claim to go back to the Prophet.'

Lawyers in Madina, who claimed a unique position as the depository of the living *Sunna*, did reject the solitary *Hadiths* in certain cases which

---

[43] This Hadith exists in almost all well-known collections of Hadith; see Mishkat al-Masabih, Kitab al-Ilm.

[44] Al-Shafi'i, Kitab al-Umm, Cairo ed. Vii, p.255, also bottom of p.243.

they found in opposition to the 'agreed practice'. *Al-Shafi'i* accused his fellow jurists of lagging far behind these in relating traditions. Once the formalized *Sunna* of Madina was enshrined in the *Hadith*, the position of that city as the home of the Prophetic *Sunna* was established beyond question, although Iraq, with its practice interacting with that of Madina but retaining something of its own entity even in tradition, remained the second major region of the *Sunna*, and independent in law with its *Hanafi* interpretation.[45]

The emergence of the *Hadith* as an all-engulfing discipline led some of the *Mu'tazila*, the rationalistic theologians, to take up a skeptical attitude to the *Hadith* as a whole. *Mu'tazila* were the second group of *Hadith* opponents, separate in kind, from the legists in the preceding paragraph. The *Mu'tazila* were not only theologians, but also lawyers and jurists, as is evident from *al-Shafi'i's* writings.[46] Their basic argument was essentially the same as that of the other legal schools noted above, that the *Hadith*, since its essence is transmission by individuals, cannot be a sure avenue of our knowledge about the Prophetic teaching, unlike the Qur'an, about whose transmission there is a universal unanimity among Muslims. While most of the *Mu'tazila* were originally skeptical of the *Hadith* on their own grounds, they nevertheless accepted the *'Sunna'* and the *'Ijm'a'* (consensus), and indeed they interpreted the Qur'an in the light of both these principles, as was attested by *al-Shafi'i*.[47]

The Development of the Science of Hadith

By the middle of the 3rd/9th century the *Hadiths* had taken definite form, had established almost all its detailed content, and had completely won the field. So far as the content is concerned, it patently reflects the growing and conflicting mass of religious and political views and opinions of the Muslims in their first two centuries. In order to collect, sift and systematize this massive and amazing product, a number of eminent scholars traveled throughout the length and breadth of the then Muslim world. Eager seekers went from place to place to gather *hadiths* and to assess their authenticity.

---

[45] Fazlur Rahman, ISLAM, 2nd Ed. 1979; Uni. Of Chicago Press, Chicago.

[46] Al-Shafi'i; Kitab al-Umm, pp. 250-4

[47] Ibid. p.252.

Imam Malik ibn Anas (93-179 A.H.) was considered, with *Shafi'i* and *Abu Hanifa*, one of "the three most famous imams in Islam because of their contribution to the elaboration of the knowledge that enables the believer to distinguish the permitted from the forbidden." He never ceased to say:

> This religion is a science, so pay attention to those from whom you learn it. I had the good fortune to be born [in Madina] at a time when 70 Companions who could recite *hadith* were until alive. They used to go to the mosque and start speaking: The Prophet said so and so. I did not collect any of the *hadith* that they recounted, not because these people were not trustworthy, but because I saw that they were dealing in matters for which they were not qualified.[48]

Thus, according to *Imam Malik* it was not enough just to have lived at the time of the Prophet in order to become a source of *hadiths*. It was also necessary to have a certain background that qualified you to speak: "Ignorant persons must be disregarded." How could they be considered sources of knowledge when they did not have the necessary intellectual capacity? But ignorance and intellectual capacity were not the only criteria for evaluating the narrators of *hadith.* One of the most important criteria was moral. *Imam Malik* directs suspicion at the transmitters, emphasizes the necessity for Muslims to be on their guard, and even advises them to take the daily behavior of sources into consideration as a criterion for their reliability.[49]

The rising tide of conflicting *hadiths* in the ninth century was threatening to drown the until fresh enterprise of Muslim jurisprudence. To resolve the obvious difficulties, scholars devised a critical method for the study of *hadiths*, that would enable them to sort out the "sound" *hadiths* from the "weak," forged or doubtful ones, based on the considerations identified by *Imam Malik.* The resulting 'Science of the *Hadith*' concentrated almost exclusively on the authenticity

---

48 Ibn Abd al-Barr, Al-Intiqa', p.16.

49 Ibn Abd al-Barr, *Al-Intiqa*, p.16; referenced in *Liberal Islam*: A Source Book; edited by Charles Kurzman, Oxford Univ. Press, 1998; p.119.

and reliability of the witnesses cited in the *isnad* (transmission) of the report in question, since scholars were bound in principle to accept any textually reliable *hadith*. Thus, biographies of the transmitters, the bona fides, their character and their reliability of the memory, along with the continuity in the chain of transmission, were taken into account to determine the genuineness or authenticity of the *Hadith*. On the basis of these investigations, the *Hadiths* were classified into such categories as 'genuine' (*sahih*), 'good', and 'weak'. A *hadith* which has numerous narrators at every stage of transmission is called *mutawatir*, i.e., so certain that doubt concerning its authenticity is almost logically excluded. The work of criticism and the resulting collections were largely for use by lawyers' use, as manifest in the earliest of the collections by al-Bukhari (d. 870), called 'The Sound Collection,' whose 2762 *hadiths* were certified as sound and thus useable in matters of law.

A very large proportion of the gathered *hadiths* were judged by classical Muslim scholars to be spurious and forged and were excluded from the six canonical collections used by Sunnis. The very period in which the *Hadith* discipline reached its full fruition was also the period during which an 'orthodoxy' was emerging from a massive interaction of different, and often opposed, religious doctrines and views,. The traditionalist 'people of the Hadith' (*Ahl al-Hadith*) were actively involved, and indeed the vanguard, in this great drama, entailing a fierce battle between them and the rationalist *Ahl al-Kalam*. By the middle of the 3rd/9th century the ground of the living tradition (*sunna*) had been taken over by the *Hadith* form, but jurists continued to attack individual *hadiths* on the grounds of inconsistency and on the basis of reason.

Apart from the historical criticism of the transmission chains, another principle of selection was at work, i.e., how far a *hadith* was in conformity to the *Sunna* of the period. This principle of selectivity was not primarily historical, but doctrinal. This makes us realize the full import of the claimed *Hadith* according to which the Prophet said, 'Whatever of good speech there be, you can take it to have been said by me'. On no other hypothesis than this can we explain the fact that post-Prophetic developments—the theological positions with regard to human freedom, Divine Attributes, etc.—were all verbally attributed to the Prophet himself—as well as the fact that the *Shi'a,* a major sect of

77

Islam that differs doctrinally from orthodox Sunnis, also has an entirely separate body of *hadiths*.[50]

A further factor entailed was that, between the personality of the Prophet and the Qur'an, on the one hand, and the development of the *Sunna-Hadith*, on the other, there exists a relationship of public historical continuity. The Prophet founded not merely a religion, but also a developing, large-scale Community, and this was done in the broad daylight of history. This public continuity between the Prophet and his Community is the real guarantee of the Prophetic *Sunna*. It was this double connection of spirit and of historical continuity that rendered the *Hadith* impregnable to all attacks in classical Islam.

The Challenge of the Hadiths for Contemporary Islam

As mentioned earlier in this chapter, one of the consequences of focusing on *hadiths* during the competitions within Islam in the 1st-2nd/7th-8th centuries was a loss of creative interpretation. The nearly exclusive focus on *hadiths*, rather than on the wider role of the *Sunna*, led to a nearly slavish dependency on *hadiths*, in which Muslims expected ready-made, explicit answers to later problems in the reported words and actions of the Prophet, without recognizing that some of those reports themselves had been retrojectively projected onto the Prophet. This led them to ignore the dynamics of their own present historical situations, where Islam has immense potency. Many historiographers, who themselves are actors inside the three early ideological streams of Islam, perpetuate the problem by merely restating contemporary issues in the framework of those ideological streams.[51]

Modern Islam yearns for creativity. In the interests of new progress, certain groups[52] have arisen which, if their utterances are taken at their face value, wish to reject *all hadiths* and rely on 'the *Qur'an-only*'. These groups, however, display hardly any awareness of the issues

---

50 Fazlur Rahman, Ibid. p.65

51 Fazlur Rahman; Islam and Modernity: Transfer of an Intellectual Tradition; Univ. of Chicago, 1984; p.47.

52 There is such a group in the Indo-Pakistan subcontinent, who call themselves 'People of the Quran' (Ahl al-Qur'an). They have produced a considerable volume of literature, and also issue an Urdu journal entitled, '*Tulu-i Islam*' from Lahore (formerly from Delhi). This type of thought, however, is not common in the Middle East.

that are at stake. It is not clear whether they deny all historical, doctrinal, and legal validity to the *hadiths*. It seems they have virtually no appreciation of the nature of *Hadith* development. This confused position is considerably similar to that of the *Ahl al-Kalam* in classical times, but with one major difference. The *Ahl al-Kalam* wished to reject the verbal tradition (*Hadith*) in favor of the living tradition (*Sunna*). In our present age, however, the only tradition is the verbal one, since the living *Sunna* now derives its validity from the *Hadith*, through which lies the only avenue of our contact with the Prophet and fundamentally also with the Qur'an. If the *Hadith* as a whole is cast away, the basis for the historicity of the Qur'an is likewise removed with one stroke.

The present unrest, though, is equally genuine and expressive of a vital need. This need for new vitality and fresh interpretation neither can be nor ought to be suppressed. There has never been a general review of all the compilations that would enable scholars to confront the essentially historical problem of exhaustively reconstructing the Islamic tradition. An attempt of this sort would presuppose a systematic comparison of all the *isnads* and all the *matns* (texts of the Prophetic words and actions), carried forward in the three streams of the early Muslim tradition, so that the question of authenticity could be re-examined with modern means of investigation, such as the science of philology.[53] Orthodox guardians of the tradition have vehemently rejected suggestions of this sort already formulated by the Orientalists. The *hadiths*, like the Qur'an, the *shari'a*, and pre-Islamic poetry, are a sensitive point in the Muslim consciousness. These 'guardians' have so far displayed an uncompromisingly conservative attitude and a lack of judgment toward both the new situation and the actual development of the *Hadith*, so that the collections of *Hadith* constitute "official" and "closed" corpora, similar to the Qur'anic Corpus. They do not realize that this attitude, far from maintaining stability (the real reason behind the *Hadith* system), would thoroughly destroy it.

The Modernist also must realize that, although the *Hadith* in part does not represent the pure, verbal Prophetic teaching, it certainly does have an intimate connection with the Prophet. The Modernist may certainly reinterpret the Qur'an and the Prophet's *Sunna*, in so far as it can be disentangled, but they must not disregard the ethos of the

---

53 Ibid. p. 46.

79

Hadith and of the institutions which it guaranteed; no interpretation can take place in a vacuum.

The disentanglement of the historical Prophetic elements is perhaps incapable of complete achievement, for want of early sources. But a candid and responsible investigation into the development of the *Hadith* by Muslims themselves is a logical act of the first order. "Whatever can be achieved in this way will be a sheer gain, for it will reveal the intimate connection between the Community and the Prophet, on the one hand, and between the doctrinal and practical evolution of the Community and the growth of the *Hadith*, on the other. It will illuminate the relationship between these and will clear the way for proper future development."[54]

---

[54] F.Rahman, Ibid. p.67.

The Doctrine of SHARI'A

Introduction

Total and unqualified submission to the will of Allah (God) is the fundamental tenet of Islam. Islamic law is the expression of that will for Muslim society and therefore constitutes a system of duties incumbent on every Muslim. Known as the *Shari'a* (literally, "the path leading to the watering place"), the law constitutes a divinely ordained path of conduct that guides the Muslim toward a practical expression of one's submission to God in this world and the goal of divine favor in the world to come. This path was provided by God to restore justice to the world, i.e., to recognize the 'claims of God' as Creator and Lord and thereby to restore justice to human dealings with one another.[55] It includes all behavior—spiritual, mental and physical. It comprehends both faith and practice; belief in one God is part of the Shari'a, just as are such religious duties as prayer and fasting. Islamic law is the totality of God's commands that regulate the life of every Muslim in all its aspects, including such things as worship and ritual, political and legal rules, details of toilet, formulas of greeting, table-manners and sick-room attendance—all on an equal footing.

Islam typically expresses itself in terms of law, rather than theology; theology has never been able to achieve a comparable importance in Islam. Law remains an important element in the struggle being fought in Islam between traditionalism and modernism under the impact of Western ideas. "One of the most important bequests which Islam has transmitted to the civilized world is its religious law, the Shari'a. It is a phenomenon so different from all other forms of law . . . ."[56]

In classical form the Shari'a differs from Western systems of law in two principal respects. First, the scope of Shari'a is much wider, since

---

55 Q. 16:90.

56 *The Legacy of Islam*, 2nd Edition, Ed.. by Joseph Schacht and C.E.Bosworth, Oxford Univ. Press, 1979; p. 392.

it regulates a person's relationships not only with one's neighbors and with the state (which is the limit of most other legal systems), but also with God and one's own conscience. Ritual practices, such as the daily prayers, almsgiving, fasting, and pilgrimage, are all an integral part of Shari'a law and usually occupy the first chapters in the legal manuals. The Shari'a is also concerned as much with ethical standards as with legal rules, indicating not only what a person is entitled or bound to do in law, but also what one ought, in conscience, to do or refrain from doing. Accordingly, certain acts are classified as praiseworthy (*mandub*), which means that their performance brings divine favor and their omission divine disfavor, and others as blameworthy (*makruh*), which means their omission brings divine favor and commission divine disfavor, but in neither case is there any legal sanction of punishment or reward, nullity or validity. The Shari'a is not merely a system of law, but a comprehensive code of behavior that embraces both private and public activities.

The second major distinction between the Shari'a and Western legal systems is the result of the Islamic concept of law as the expression of the divine will. With the death of the Prophet Muhammad in 632 C.E., communication of the divine will to humanity ceased, so that the terms of the divine revelation were henceforth fixed and immutable. However, application of that divine will and its implications for human society became the key focus of Muslims.

The Formation of Shari'a Law

In the earliest period after the Prophet, two methods were recognized for understanding the Shari'a. On the one hand were the traditional sources of the Qur'an and the Sunna of the Prophet, which must serve as the base. However, since the Qur'an and the Sunna could not suffice for the developing needs of succeeding generations, the second principle—of human intelligence and understanding—was recognized almost from the outset. The first was called 'learning' (*ilm*); the second was called 'understanding' (*fiqh*). Texts from early Islam frequently draw a distinction between *ilm* and *fiqh*, so that one often encounters passages saying, 'so-and-so is good in *ilm*, but not so good in *fiqh*.' Now *fiqh* in this period is nothing other than *ra'y*, or 'personal opinion'. Whereas *ilm* is a process of learning and refers to an objective, organized and disciplined body of data (i.e., the Qur'an and the Sunna), *fiqh* is a process or activity of understanding and deducing, a personal opinion that results from the study of the root sources.[57]

The Qur'an: At the very root of the Muslim conception of law lies the idea that law is inherently and essentially religious. That is why, from the very beginning of Islamic history, law has been regarded as flowing from, or being part of, the concept Shari'a (the divinely ordained pattern of human conduct). It must, therefore, have its basis in the divine revelation. The Qur'an, the final revelation of God to humanity, must accordingly be made the primary source of law.

The Qur'an, however, is not a code of law; it is largely a guide-book of moral, ethical and pious living, and a presentation of humanity's relationship with God. The legal content of the Quran is slender; as out of a total of 6236 verses not more than about 350 are of legal nature, including the verses which were abrogated by subsequent ones, and out of these only about 80 have a specific, legal context. Not all the legally oriented verses are in the form of explicit commands or prohibitions. There are overlaps and even contradictions among them, the latter of which have to be resolved either by exegetical harmonizing, or else by invoking the principle of abrogation, by which a later command cancels or modifies an earlier, apparently contradictory one. This shows that the principal object of the Qur'an is moral in nature; it is concerned to identify the faults in the soul of the believer and to elevate one's conscience and morality in order that it might be its own proper shari'a, in the sense of the way leading to God. The Qur'anic body of statements is both universal and concrete, to inculcate a definite attitude toward life. It enunciates not only eternal spiritual and moral principles, but also guided the Prophet and the early community through their specific struggles against the Makkahn, Jewish and Hypocrite opponents and in the constructive task of the nascent society and state. But still, the legislative portion of the Qur'an is quite small. The scripture, in God's wisdom, has left almost the entire landscape of life free and available as an 'open way' for legislation.

The Sunna: Muhammad, like Jesus, spoke with authority—not his own, but God's authority, and at times with God's very own words. Therefore, the only natural method for freshly applying the Qur'an to

---

[57] Fazlur Rahman, *ISLAM*, 2nd Edition, Univ. of Chicago, Chicago and London, 1979; p. 69.

any given new situation was to see how it had been actually worked in the lifetime of the Prophet, who was its most authoritative exponent and whose conduct was uniquely normative. This was the Sunna of the Prophet, and his religious authority was binding.

While he was alive, this authority was sufficient. But after his death, that living authority was no longer available. Therefore, whatever decisions or pronouncements of the Prophet were authoritative during his lifetime became infallible after his death, and thus were viewed within the framework of a doctrine of infallibility. It is not unreasonable to imagine that his highly respectful contemporaries remembered his words of personal guidance and explanations with the same fervor and fidelity as they remembered his announcement of the words of God. As described earlier, these reports of the Prophet's words and actions constitute the Hadiths.

The Sunna was subsequently expanded to include the precedents of the first four Caliphs and of the earliest Muslim community, known as the 'Sunna of the rightly-guided Caliphs' and the 'Sunna of the Companions', respectively. These precedents were called 'Sunna' in a derivative sense, in which the Companions were regarded as the living embodiments of the Prophetic Sunna. The application of the term was not extended to subsequent generations, except in the sense of their deducing the Sunna from the Hadiths. The agreed practices of the Companions is also known as the '*ijm'a* of the Companions'.

The Qur'an and the Sunna thus served as the indispensable textual sources for accessing the Shari'a by means of *ilm*, and they continue to do so. However, as mentioned above, only a small proportion of the Qur'an pertains to legal issues, and even less of it is formulated as "law." Likewise, most Hadiths are not expressed in legal format. The Qur'an and the Sunna are absolute necessities for the formation of a codified legal system, but they are not sufficient. The expression of Shari'a specifically as "law" also required the exertion of human intelligence and rationality, and this process was *fiqh*, regularly recognized as entailing the activities of *qiyas* (analogical reasoning), *ijm'a* (consensus) and *ijtihad* (independent legal reasoning). The term *fiqh* ultimately came to be used for the science of Muslim jurisprudence itself, underscoring the human interpretive element involved in understanding and applying Shari'a.

Qiyas: The earliest predecessor of *qiyas*, or analogical reasoning, was called 'personal judgment' (*ra'y*), used in the sense of 'I think' or 'I opine'. This type of thinking was relatively very free and produced a wealth of conflicting religious and legal opinion. However, a rudimentary and almost unconscious analogical method was always present. When faced with a new, refined or complicated issue for which the Qur'an and the Sunna provided no clear decision, Muslim jurists engaged in a two-step process of *qiyas,* first identifying the general principle expressed in a specific legal ruling within the Qur'an or the Sunna and second, making a decision regarding the strength of that principle's applicability to the new issue. In this way jurists were able both to remain textually rooted in the Qur'an and the Sunna, as well as to formulate law in ways that effectively addressed new situations.

Ijm'a: After the period of the first four Caliphs, multitudinous differences in legal and dogmatic opinion on details began to appear. The administration of the Umayyad Caliphate left the task of legislation to the recognized religious leaders and jurists of different regions. The jurists, in their turn, employed the method of personal opinion (*ra'y*) on the materials of the Qur'an and the Sunna, which subsequently morphed into *qiyas (*systematic analogical reasoning). But even before the doctrines of *qiyas* ('consensus') and *ijtihad* ('original thinking', discussed below) were formally adopted, a large measure of 'agreed practice', *ijm'a*, had already been achieved. This enabled the jurists and traditionists of the 2nd/8th century to project the doctrine of *qiyas* backwards into the earliest generation of Islam.

The interaction between *qiyas* and *ijm'a* was a natural, dynamic process of assimilation, interpretation and adaptation. Al-Shafi'i, the great unifier of Islamic law, provided the most comprehensive treatment of this relationship, which demonstrated the true nature and all-comprehensive character of *ijm'a,* and he did so within a somewhat well-integrated system of jurisprudence suitable for wide acceptance. By the 8th century C.E., the Muslim *umma* had spread from its epicenter in Arabia, initially a 30,000-member *umma* in Madina, to one that traversed lands as different as Persia, Transoxania, Palestine, North Africa and Spain. As a result, the bewildering variety of local, ethnic traditions now encompassed within the geography of Islam challenged the *umma's* very social solidarity. The *fiqh*, as developed by Al-Shafi'i, allowed a role to two human factors in the interpretation of sacred law:

qiyas, that is (analogical reasoning) and *ijm'a* (consensus), which he viewed primarily as social consensus, rather than as consensus only amongst the *ulama*, as was later frequently claimed. This approach, based on the communal nature of *ijm'a*, is in accordance with the Prophet's famous statement, "Never will God make my community agree upon an error." The articulation of Shari'a by means of *fiqh* thus was based not only on what was written, but also on what had happened and what was happening. Because of this, as *fiqh* developed into a consolidated system, it fulfilled the historic role of maintaining social cohesion for the community of Muslims, whereby early Muslim law was coterminous with the social requirements of the time.

Ijtihad: Ijtihad (independent legal reasoning) is the exertion of effort to interpret the textual sources of *fiqh* and infer legal rules from them, or to formulate a legal ruling on a particular issue. Sometimes *ijtihad* and *qiyas* are used interchangeably, but *ijtihad* is the more comprehensive term, and is the main means by which the divine message has been applied to the changing situations of the Muslim community.

Formation of the Legal Schools

Norms of personal, civil and penal laws which developed with increasing complexity over more than a hundred years after the Prophet's demise arose only partly from the Qur'an and the Sunna and to a great extent from custom and practice, for the society to which the Qur'an was first brought was not without its own version of justice. Mecca was in the process of urbanization, but the prevailing mode of justice there was still largely based on the Bedouin notion of a customary tribal law (*sunna*), administered by an arbitrator (*hakam*) chosen for his sagacity or his charismatic qualities.

The substitution of Qur'anic norms of justice for those of the Bedouins was neither a short nor an easy process. The tribal arbitrator continued to function side by side with fully developed Muslim institutions of justice for many centuries. A good deal of creative legal effort was the crying need of the time. The effort was made, eventually with great success, to convert Arab custom into Islamic law. Judges appointed under Islamic authority were not called *hakams* or arbitrators, but *qadis*, decision-makers, a deliberate echo of *Qada*, used in the Qur'an to describe God's own divine power.

It is an evidence of the characteristic freedom of legal thought in early Islam that during the 1st-2nd/7th-8th centuries a host of accumulations of legal opinion grew up in different centers in Iraq, the Hijaz, Syria and Egypt. The differences in bodies of legal thought were largely due to the various ways in which the Qur'an was interpreted, in the light of local customary law. Hence the local legal formulations differed in detail in the different provinces.

The accumulations of legal opinion in these geographical centers gradually crystallized into schools in the 8th-9th centuries C.E., while at the same time these schools came closer to one another through mutual interaction. In Iraq, the school associated with Abu Hanifa (d. 150/767) called the Hanafi school, developed and systemized by his two disciples Abu Yusuf (d. 181/797) and Muhammad al-Shaybani (d. 189/850). This school, favored by the Abbasids in Baghdad, was most characterized by the exercise of free opinion.

The Syrian school of al-Awza'i (d. 157/774) was later overcome by Maliki school, founded by Malik ibn Anas (d. 179/795) in Madina. Malik himself resembled al-Awza'i in that he placed his reliance on the 'living tradition' of Madina. He collected a body of legal traditions and constructed a system of juridical opinions into a famous work called *al-Mauwatta*—'the leveled path'.

The third major school is called the Shafi'i school, after Muhammad ibn Idris al-Shafi'i (d. 204/819). A pupil of Malik, he formulated the principles of Islamic jurisprudence in the form that these have retained ever since, wherein the verbal tradition was regarded as the sole vehicle of the Prophetic Sunna, and *ijtihad* was thrown outside *ijm'a*. The influence of al-Shafi'i has been incalculable on the development of Islamic Shari'a.

In the 3rd/9th century two new schools arose, but the first and only successful one of these was the Hanbali school, founded by the famous doctor and arch-traditionalist Ahmed ibn Hanbal (d. 241/855). He continued to push the logic of al-Shafi'i's insistence on the Hadith in law. Ibn Hanbal's teaching was systematized after him by his disciples.

The prevalence of four different systems of jurisprudence did not lead to undue controversies or conflict. The four schools of law developed and found acceptance in different parts of the Muslim world, although the territories were not mutually exclusive. By *ijm'a* the four schools (*Madhhabs*) were accepted, and they accepted one another as equally orthodox. There is not only no fundamental difference of jurisprudence between them, but even the differences in detail have largely been turned into a remarkable unity, thanks to the limited *ijtihad* that continued to be allowed and exercised by the schools' scholars. The Hanafi system was officially adopted in the Abbasid Caliphate of Baghdad, and spread to West Asia, Central Asia and to the Indian subcontinent. The Maliki school acquired its main following in North, Central and West Africa. Al-Shafi'i's system got influence in Egypt and Southeast Asia. The Hanbali tradition got centered in Saudi Arabia and later spawned revivalist ideologies, as promoted by Ibn Taymiyya (1263-1382) and practiced by Abd al-Wahhab (1703-1792).

Characteristics of Shari'a Law & its Administration

There is no distinction of legal subject-matters in Islamic law; even a systematic arrangement of the legal subject-matters is lacking. Public/ state powers are reduced to private rights and duties, e.g., the right to give a valid safe-conduct, the duty to pay the *zakat* (alms-tax), the rights and duties of the persons who appoint an individual as Imam or Caliph, and the rights and duties of an Imam or a Caliph. Islamic law did not develop the corresponding legal concept applied to the public/state. For the same reason, the institutions of the Islamic state are construed not as functions of the community of believers as such, but as duties, the fulfillment of which by a sufficient number of individuals excuses the other individuals from fulfilling them. In fact, the whole concept of Islamic state, as an institution, is missing.[58]

Shari'a judicial proceedings differ significantly from other legal traditions, including those in both common law and civil law. Shari'a courts traditionally do not rely on lawyers; plaintiffs and defendants represent themselves. Traditionally, Shari'a law was administered by the court of a single qadi, who was the judge of the facts as well as the law. Trials were conducted solely by the judge, with no jury system. Through his clerk (*katib*), the *qadi* controlled his court procedure. There was no pre-trial discovery process, and no cross-examination of witnesses. Unlike common law, judges' verdicts do not set binding precedents[59]

---

58 Ibid. p. 398

59 Hamzeh, A. Nizar. "Qatar: The Duality of the Legal System," *Middle Eastern Studies*, Vol. 30, No.1, January 1994, pp.79-90

under the principle of stare devises[60] and unlike civil law, Sharia did not utilize formally codified statutes[61] (which were first introduced only in the late 19th century during the decline of the Ottoman Empire). Instead of precedents and codes, Sharia relies on jurists' manuals and collections of non-binding legal opinions or hadiths; these can be made binding for a particular case at the discretion of a judge. There was no hierarchy of courts and no organized system of appeals.

In the field of what, in modern terminology, is called penal law, Islamic law distinguishes between the 'rights of God' and the 'rights of humans'. Only the rights of God have the character of a penal law proper, i.e., a law which imposes penal sanctions on the guilty. This real penal law is derived exclusively from the Quran and the traditions of the Prophet and of his Companions. The second division of penal law belongs to the category of 'redress of torts', a category of civil and penal law which Islamic law has retained from the law of pre-Islamic Arabia.[62] Distinct from the 'rights of God' and the 'rights of humans' is the discretionary punishment of *ta'zir*, a 'claim of the state'. Corresponding to these three, Shari'a law specifies three categories of crimes: *qisas*, *hudud*, and *ta'zir*.

Qisas involves situations of personal injury, and covers several types: intentional murder (first-degree), quasi-intentional murder (second-degree), unintentional murder (manslaughter), intentional battery, and unintentional battery. It is treated as a civil case rather than an actual criminal case, since it is not the state but only the victim or his family who has the right to prosecute and to determine the punishment. They can either demand retribution (*qisas-e-nafs*), which means execution in the case of intentional murder, imprisonment, and in some cases of intentional battery, the amputation of the limb that was lost, or they can request *diyah* (blood money), which is compensation for the loss of life/limb/injury. However, the judge may prosecute for other crimes committed, alongside the murder. If the victim's family pardons the criminal, the guilty party would normally receive a *ta'zir* prison

---

60 Saudi Arabia Basic Industries Corp. v. Mobil Yanbu Petrochemical Co., Supreme Court of Delaware, January 14, 2005 p. 52

61 Fatany, Samar. "Let Us Codify Shari'ah Laws", Arab News, Jan. 31, 2008 *Codification efforts remain incomplete.*

62 Ibid. p. 399.

sentence (such as 10-20 years in prison) for crimes such as "intentional loss of life", "*ta'zir* assault and battery" or "disturbance of the peace".

The second category of crimes is *hudud* (or *hadd*). *Hadd* crimes are crimes whose penalties were laid down by the Quran, and are considered to be "claims against God". *Hadd* crimes are: adultery (*zina*), which includes adultery, fornication, incest/ pedophilia, and rape, pimping; sodomy/lesbianism (or sodomy rape); waging war against God and society (*hiraba*, uniquely known as *moharebeh/ mofsed-e-filarz* in Iran), which includes armed robbery, terrorism, armed violence; theft; use of intoxicants (alcohol/drug use); apostasy/ blasphemy; and defamation (meaning false accusation of any of these things). The consequences of conviction in these cases are not meant as actual punishments, but as deterrents, simply to set an example to the general public and to prosecute the most flagrant violations. The process is extremely exacting; circumstantial evidence is not allowed to be part of the testimony, and a minimum of two witnesses are required to corroborate the evidence, and in the case of sex crimes, four witnesses, thus making it hard, if not impossible in most cases, to receive the violent penalties. When one does receive them, it usually is when the offense was so obvious, obscene or flagrant that it would be impossible not to be convicted.

As a result most countries do not prosecute *hudud* offenses (the exceptions being Saudi Arabia and Afghanistan under the Taliban, which regularly managed to prosecute offenses in the *hudud* manner) Almost all other countries would usually punish the same offense as a *ta'zir* crime.

Ta'zir covers all other offenses not mentioned already. It is a "claim of the state" and conviction results in a discretionary sentence. The punishment may not be more severe than the punishment of a *hudud* crime. It can range, depending on the crime or circumstances, from death to imprisonment to even community service. The *qadi* may punish at his discretion any act which, in his opinion, calls for punishment, whether it can be subsumed under offences against religion (e.g., morals or good manners) or under torts committed against others. The *ta'zir* belongs therefore to penal law proper, but even here Islamic law has never envisaged the imposition of fines. *Ta'zir* belongs neither to ancient Arabian customary law (which was ratified by Islam} nor to Islamic legislation (which appeared in the Quran and in the traditions).

It was the first Muslim *qadis* in the Umayyad period who found themselves called upon to punish, at their discretion, all kinds of acts which threatened the peaceful and orderly existence of the new Islamic society which was coming into being. But the needs of the Islamic society did not stop there, and further extension of penal law, and the creation of agencies which were to apply them, such as the office of the *muhtasib* (an officer responsible for Islamic morals and good behavior) and the *nazar fil-mazalim* (investigation of complaints—a jurisdiction parallel to that of the *qadi*), became inevitable. By the time the functions of these organizations were fully defined, the outlines of the Shari'a had already been firmly laid down.[63]

Circumstantial evidence is allowed for *ta'zir* crimes. Most countries prosecute their crimes as *ta'zir* crimes, due to the flexibility of the evidence-gathering and sentencing. The punishment is meant to fit the crime. For example, a rapist may not be able to be prosecuted for *zina*, but would still be convicted of *ta'zir* rape, or in theft, they would be found guilty of *ta'zir* theft and given prison time rather than amputation. A convicted murderer would still spend time in prison, even if he had received the forgiveness of the family. The heavy *hudud* penalties of amputation and stoning are generally not applied, although some countries do use corporal punishment. Most modern countries, such as Iran, have a fixed penal code that regulate what sentences should be given, depending on the crime and circumstances of the case.

Shari'a courts' rules of evidence also maintain a distinctive custom of prioritizing oral testimony.[64] A confession, an oath, or the oral testimony of a witness is the main evidence admissible in a *hudud* case; written evidence is only admissible when deemed reliable by the judge.[65] Testimony must be from at least two witnesses, preferably free Muslim male witnesses, who are not related parties and who are of sound mind and reliable character; testimony to establish the crime of adultery (*zina*) must be from four direct witnesses.[66] Forensic evidence (e.g.,

---

[63] Ibid. p.400

[64] Benjamin C. Fortna, Education and Autobiography at the End of the Ottoman Empire, Die Welt des Islams, New Series, Vol. 41, Issue 1 (Mar., 2001), pp. 1-31

[65] Ibid. Introduction to Islamic Law

[66] Alhaji A.D. Ajijola, *Introduction to Islamic law*. Karachi, Pakistan : International Islamic Publishers, 1989. p. 133

fingerprints, ballistics, blood samples, DNA) and other circumstantial evidence is likewise rejected in *hudud* cases in favor of eyewitnesses, a practice which today can cause severe difficulties for women plaintiffs in rape cases.[67] Testimony from women is given only half the weight of men, and testimony from non-Muslims may be excluded altogether (if against a Muslim).

In some countries, Shari'a courts—with their tradition of *pro se* representation, simple rules of evidence, and absence of appeals courts, prosecutors, cross examination, complex documentary evidence and discovery proceedings, juries proceedings, circumstantial evidence, forensics, case law, standardized codes, exclusionary rules, and most of the other infrastructure of civil and common law court systems—have, as a result, comparatively informal and streamlined proceedings. Shari'a court can provide significant increases in speed and efficiency, and can be an advantage in jurisdictions where the general court system is slow or corrupt, and where few litigants can afford lawyers. In Nigeria, where imposition of Shari'a was highly controversial, even Nigeria's Justice Minister was compelled to admit that in Shari'a courts, "if a man owes you money, you can get paid in the evening. Whereas in the regular courts, you can sit in court for ten years and get no justice."[68] Other countries, such as Iran, Iraq, and Pakistan, use a civil Shari'a code similar to western countries, and do have defense attorneys, prosecutors, and appeals courts. They also have a Supreme Court, and a definite civil law style penal code, but are still heavily based on the informality and simplicity of a "pure" Shari'a court, and trials often still take a matter of hours or sometimes days.

Shari'a classically recognizes only natural persons, and never developed the concept of a 'legal person' or 'corporation', i.e., a legal entity that limits the liabilities of its managers, shareholders and employees, that exists beyond the lifetimes of its founders, and that can own assets, sign contracts, and appear in court through representatives.[69]

---

67 Muhammad Hashim Kamali. *"Punishment in Islamic Law: A Critique of the Hudud Bill of Kelantan, Malaysia." Arab Law Quarterly,* Vol. 13, No. 3 (1998), pp. 203-234

68 *"The attractions of Sharia: Nigeria's sharia courts are harsh, but quicker and cleaner than secular ones"*

69 *Kuran, Timur.* The Absence of the Corporation in Islamic Law-Origins and Persistence (www.en.wikipedia.org)

Thus, Shari'a has no native tradition of corporate law. This, combined with egalitarian rules of inheritance for male descendants, hindered the concentration of wealth and the development of larger and more sophisticated enterprises, according to Timur Kuran of Duke University. Prohibitions of *riba* (interest) also disadvantaged Muslims *vis-à-vis* non-Muslim minorities in accessing banks and insurance when these services were first introduced by Westerners. Interest prohibitions also imposed secondary costs, by discouraging record keeping and delaying the introduction of modern accounting.[70] Such factors, according to Kuran, have played a significant role in retarding economic development in the Middle East.[71] Some have argued, though, that the West's economic crises at the outset of the 21st century occurred when many of the aforementioned economic policies backfired on a global scale and threatened to bankrupt entire countries.

The Ulama and the Governing Authorities

Islamic law represents an extreme case of a 'jurists' law,' created and developed by private, pious specialists (the Ulama) who usually had no direct political authority. Islamic jurisprudence (*usul al-fiqh*) did not grow out of an existing law, but itself created the law. The formation of Islamic law took place neither under the impetus of the needs of practice nor under that of juridical technique, but under that of religious and ethical ideas. At the time Islamic law came into existence, its perpetual problem—the contrast between theory and practice—was already posed. Because Islamic law is a jurists' law, its legal science is amply documented.

Islamic law provides the unique phenomenon in legal science of scholarly handbooks having the force of law, rather than the state playing the part of a legislator. This depended on two conditions: that legal science guaranteed its own stability and continuity, and that the place of the state was taken by another authority, high enough to impose itself on both government and governed. The first was met by the doctrine of consensus (*ijm'a*), the highest authority among the

---

[70] Kuran, Timur. "The Logic of Financial Westernization in the Middle East," *Journal of Economic Behavior and Organization,* Vol. 56 (2005), p. 600

[71] "Kuran, Timur Why the Middle East Is Economically Underdeveloped-Historical Mechanisms of Institutional Stagnation"

'roots' or principles of Islamic jurisprudence, and the second was met by the fact that Islamic law claimed to be based on divine authority (the Qur'an and the Sunna).

The lifetime of the Prophet was unique in that he was both the recipient of the revelations from God (i.e., the Qur'an) and the leader of the Muslim community. This was followed by the turbulent period of the Caliphs of Madina 632-61C.E., in which the recognized head, the Caliph, was the chief judge (*qadi*) of the community, just as Muhammad had been, but he did not possess any special religious authority, unlike the Prophet. The Caliph delegated this judicial power to others in what were emerging as the provinces of the new Islamic empire. How the *qadis* rendered their judgments was likely on the basis of local custom, their pre-Islamic predecessors' methods and norms, Caliphal instruction, and their own understanding of how independent jurists had interpreted legal issues and cases on the basis of the Qur'an and Sunna of the Prophet. As a result, the practice of these early Islamic judges was of a very mixed quality. Their powers did not end with rendering judgment on cases brought before him. He possessed as well a kind of extraordinary jurisdiction that extended into such religious matters as superintending public prayer and mosques, the charge of orphans, widows, and the divorced, and even such secular matters as finances and administration.

The rule of the Umayyads (661-750 C.E.) represented, in many respects, the consummation of tendencies inherent in the nature of the community of Muslims under the Prophet and the pious Caliphs. During their rule the framework of a new Arab Muslim society was created, and a new administration of justice, an Islamic jurisprudence, and through it, Islamic law, came into being. With the Umayyads, however, the government became vested in the ruling autocracy, which became increasingly distinguished from the public, as well as from the Ulama. The Umayyad rulers carried out their administration from Damascus, largely guided by the Qur'an and the Sunna, but these were interpreted by their advisers and officers on the principle of expediency and in light of local practices in different provinces. In face of this lay authority, the *ulama* of the religious community centered in Medina began to construct the body of Islamic law. Soon, religious legislative activity also arose in Basra and Kufa (now in Iraq). The Umayyad state was influenced by this legislative activity, but the first Umayyad Caliph to apply Shari'a law seriously and systematically was 'Umar ibn 'Abd al-Aziz, around close of the 1st/early 8th century. Tradition credits him with sending out emissaries to all the outlying provinces to teach people the Shari'a law and to record traditions from the Prophet.

The administration of the law was carried out in the Courts by the *qadis*, who were appointed by the state, but drawn from the ranks of the Ulama. Because they were appointed by the state, the *qadis* could be used as instruments of the ruler's will, and in every age, beginning with the early Umayyad times, there were recurring condemnations of the *qadis* by pious Ulama and jurists, many of whom refused to accept government offices, holding that their integrity was thereby in danger of being compromised. In the early years after the Abbasids overthrew the Umayyads, there were striking examples of Ulama who defied the governing authorities. Malik ibn Anas, during a rebellion in 762 against Caliph al-Mansur (754-775) came up with a ruling against the Caliph. For this Malik was persecuted and sentenced to flogging.[72] Likewise, Imam Hanbal was harassed for about fifteen years during the period of Caliphs al-Mamun, al-Mutasim and al-Wathiq for not assenting to the state-approved doctrine that the Qur'an was 'created'.

The early Abbasids attempted to implement Islamic law, which was then still in its formative stage. They were successful insofar as the *qadis*, the administrators of justice, were henceforth bound to the sacred law, but they did not succeed in achieving a permanent fusion of theory and practice, of political power and sacred law. The result was that Islamic law became more and more removed from practice. But several new developments did take place in the Abbasid period. New titular and powerful sultans emerged and began to enact special laws of their own from time to time to cope with exigencies, while owing only nominal allegiance to the Caliph. Thus, a new body of law emerged, devised by the lay authorities to supplement the Shari'a law, which had been articulated by the Ulama. Later Muslim lawyers (*fuqaha*) attempted gradually to integrate this new body of laws into Shari'a law, but the fact that it had originally arisen outside the Shari'a was a significant development.

---

[72] W. Montgomery Watt, *The Majesty That was Islam*, London, Sidgwick and Jackson, 1974, p. 123.

The gradual dismemberment of the Islam Empire was well on its way by about the year 900. With the gradual supremacy of titular heads and powerful sultans over Abbasid caliphs, Shari'a laws were replaced by the new lay-constructed laws. Large-scale lay legislation by the state was effected by the Ottomans, who assumed the title of Caliph in the 10th/16th century. This lay body of law was called the *qanun* (canon). The function of *ijtihad,* which later constitutional theorists attributed to the Caliphal office, was never used. The Ottomans, insofar as they functioned in the field of positive law, did so only as Sultans.

Islamic law profited from its remoteness from political power; by that distinction, it preserved its stability and provided the main unifying element in the divided world of Islam. The changes which did take place were concerned more with niceties of legal theory than with positive law. However, the lively, creative legal interpretive activity of the 1st-3rd/7th-9th centuries became increasingly rigid thereafter. One may readily grant that this rigidity helped Islam maintain its stability over the centuries in which saw the decay of its political institutions. However, taken as a whole, Islamic law reflects the social and economic conditions of the early Abbasid period, and has grown more and more out of touch with later developments of state and society.[73]

The literalist and imitative approach to established legal and theological dogma emerged under the influence of Ibn Hanbal in the 9th century. There was anxiety to discourage personal intellectual initiatives so as to save social unity in the midst of the on-going cultural diversification. The inclination of Abu Hanifa, Ibn Anas and Al-Shafi'i was to keep the social responses stable through resilience and inclusiveness. The Shafi'i school of law created a balance in which the Qur'an, the Sunna and human reason all move in tandem, whereas the Hanbalists intended to keep free inquiry outside religious law by focusing far more on Hadiths. In an extension of the labors of Bukhari and Muslim, Ibn Hanbal devoted great deal of effort at the authentication of Hadith sayings, and he himself produced a collection of 29,000 of them. Legend has it that about eight hundred thousand men and sixty thousand women attended the funeral of Ibn Hanbal in Baghdad in 855. Hanbalism had triumphed, leaving a legacy of legal and theological

---

[73] J. Schacht and C.E. Bosworth, *The Legacy of Islam,* 2nd Ed., Oxford Univ. Press, Oxford, 1974; p. 395.

dogmatism, which stalled the modernization of Sunni Islam and became an inspiration for extremist Islamism in later centuries.

By the 10ᵗʰ century it was claimed within many Sunni circles that the 'doors of *ijtihad*' had closed, and Shari'a law became viewed as a rigid and static system in which one could only repeat that which has been previously stated in the medieval legal manuals. The dynamism and creativity of how Shari'a law actually arose in relation both to the divine revelation and to society became ignored, and Shari'a law came to be viewed as something merely imposed from above. In Islamic jurisprudence a false dichotomy arose, claiming that it is not society that moulds and fashions the law, but the law that precedes and shapes society. Such a philosophy of law clearly poses fundamental problems of principle for social advancement in contemporary Islam. How can the traditional Shari'a law be adapted to meet the changing circumstances of modern Muslim society? This is now the central issue in Islamic law.

Despite the continuous effort of orthodox ulama to stem the development of the principle of *ijtihad*, it has survived. The Shi'as, who followed their Imams for their legal systems, were not constrained that attempt. Eminent Iranian scholar, Seyyed Hossein Nasr, has pointed out that within Shi'a tradition, *ijtihad* has never ceased; its doctrine of the Imamate provided an umbrella of guidance whereby the *mujtahid* (i.e., one who does *ijtihad*) was in inner contact with the Imam (even though the latter was in a state of invisible existence).[74] Within Sunni Islam, as well, *ijtihad* has never fully ceased to be practiced, although it has frequently been marginalized.

Law in Contemporary Islam

The modern period, in the Western use of this term, saw the rise of two great Islamic states on the ruins of Abbasid Empire, the Ottoman Empire (1281-1924) in the Near East and the Moghal Empire (1526-1858) in India. In both empires in their heydays Islamic law enjoyed the highest degree of actual efficiency it had ever possessed since the early Abbasid period in a high material civilization. The synthesis of Islamic law and of Western law in British India and in

---

[74] Seyyed Hossein Nasr, *Ideals and Realities of Islam*, New York, Frederick A. Praegar, 1967, p. 173.

Algeria (in the 18ᵗʰ and 19ᵗʰ centuries C.E., respectively) gave birth to two autonomous legal systems, *Anglo-Muhammadan law* and *Droit Musulman Algerien.*

During the 19th century the impact of Western civilization upon Muslim society brought about radical changes in the fields of civil and commercial transactions and criminal law. In these matters the Shari'a courts were felt to be wholly out of touch with the needs of the time, not only because of their system of procedure and evidence but also because of the substance of the Shari'a doctrine which they were bound to apply.

As a result, the criminal and general civil law of the Shari'a was abandoned in most Muslim countries and replaced by new secular codes based upon European models, with a new system of secular tribunals to apply them. Thus, since the beginning of the 20th century, the application of Shari'a law has mostly been narrowly confined to personal and family law, including marriage, divorce and inheritance, and the particular institution of *waqf* endowments—with the notable exception of the Arabian Peninsula, where the Shari'a law is still formally applied in its entirety. Such Western influences have impacted not only the law of the orthodox Sunni majority, but also to the laws of the Shi'as and of the Kharijis as well. The positive law of Shi'a and Khariji developed in close contact with that of the Sunnis, just as their respective communities lived and remained in close social and cultural contact with each other. Only the law of inheritance of the Shi'a represents an independent systematization of the common principles found in the Quran.[75]

In most countries, too, the court system has been, or is being, reorganized to include, for instance, the provision of appellate jurisdictions. In Egypt and Tunisia the Shari'a courts, as a separate entity, have been abolished, and Shari'a law is now administered through a unified system of national courts. In India and Pakistan it has always been the case that Shari'a law has been applied by the same courts that apply the general civil and criminal law.

Contemporary Legal Systems

---

[75] Ibid. p. 395

The legal systems in 21st-century Muslim-majority states can be classified as follows:

Shari'a in the secular Muslim states: Muslim countries such as Mali, Kazakhstan, Bosnia and Herzegovina and Turkey have declared themselves to be secular. Here, religious interference in state affairs, law and politics is prohibited.[76] In these Muslim countries, as well as the secular West, the role of Shari'a is limited to personal and family matters, e.g., marriage, divorce, family inheritance.

Muslim states with blended sources of law: Muslim countries including Pakistan, Indonesia, Afghanistan, Egypt, Nigeria, Sudan, Morocco, Malaysia and Bangladesh have legal systems strongly influenced by Shari'a, but also cede ultimate authority to their current constitutions and the rule of law. These countries conduct democratic elections, although some are under the influence of authoritarian leaders. In these countries, politicians and jurists make law, rather than religious scholars. Most of these countries have modernized their laws and now have legal systems with significant differences when compared to classical Shari'a.[77]

Muslim states using classical Shari'a: Saudi Arabia and some of the Gulf states do not have constitutions or legislatures. Their rulers have limited authority to change laws, since they are based on Shari'a as it is interpreted by their religious scholars. Iran shares some of these characteristics, but also has a parliament that legislates in a manner consistent with Shari'a.[78]

The Fundamentalist movement: Fundamentalists, wishing to return to basic religious values and law, have in some instances imposed harsh Shari'a punishments for crimes, curtailed civil rights, and violated human rights. These movements are most active in areas of the world where there had been contact with Western colonial powers.[79]

---

[76] Otto, Jan Michiel. Sharia and National Law in Muslim Countries: Tensions and Opportunities for Dutch and EU Foreign Policy. Amsterdam University Press, 2008, p. 9

[77] Otto, Jan Michiel. Sharia and National Law in Muslim Countries: Tensions and Opportunities for Dutch and EU Foreign Policy. Amsterdam University Press, 2008, p. 8

[78] Otto, Jan Michiel. Shari'a and National Law in Muslim Countries: Tensions and Opportunities for Dutch and EU Foreign Policy. Amsterdam University Press, 2008, pp. 8-9

[79] Chris Horrie and Peter Chippindale. *What is Islam? A Comprehensive Introduction*, pg. 4. Virgin Books, 1991.

Extremism: Extremists have used the Qur'an and their own particular version of *Shari'a*[80] to justify acts of war and terror against Western individuals and governments, and also against other Muslims believed to have Western sympathies. Friction between the West and Islam, particularly with regard to the Palestinian question, continues to fuel this conflict.[81]

Contemporary Abuses of Shari'a Law

The reception of Western political ideas in the Near East has provoked, in the present century, an unprecedented movement of modernist legislation.[82] To the chagrin of modern fundamentalists, secular considerations continue to dominate the affairs of state now, whether in the national or international sphere. In reaction, Muslim states that have tried to reassert the place of Shari'a law have given rise to numerous abuses, which ironically have made a mockery of the wider moral framework of Shari'a. For example, In Pakistan, Zia al-Haq introduced the *Hudud* Ordinance, under which theft was made punishable with the amputation of hands and adultery and slander with flogging and death. Soon after its promulgation the Pakistani courts were inundated with cases alleging all kinds of atrocities against women. According to the influential Pakistani daily, *Muslim* of Islamabad, dozens of Muslim women kept in jail without trial, and it pointed out that unscrupulous men were taking full advantage of the *Hudud* ordinance to indulge in the sexual exploitation of women.

A second 'achievement' of Zia al-Haq was introduction of Blasphemy Law in 1980. The Criminal Code of Pakistan's Penal Code provides penalties for blasphemy ranging from a fine to death, making Pakistan the nation with the strictest anti-blasphemy laws among Muslim-majority countries. The Federal *Shari'a* Court was created and given jurisdiction to examine any existing law to ensure it was not repugnant to Islam. A person can be charged with blasphemy on testimony alone. Under this law, the only evidence needed is one 'reliable' man's word. Ahmadis regard themselves as Muslims and observe Islamic practices, a 1974 Constitutional amendment during

---

80 Chris Horrie and Peter Chippindale. Ibid. p.100

81 Chris Horrie and Peter Chippindale. Ibid. pp. 96-100.

82 Ibid. p.395

the time of Zulfiqar Ali Bhutto declared Ahmadis to be a non-Muslim minority because, according to the Government, they do not accept Muhammad as the last prophet of Islam. In 1984 the Government passed an amendment prohibiting Ahmadis from calling themselves Muslim and banning them from using Islamic words, phrases, and greetings. The punishment for violation of this section is imprisonment for up to 3 years and a fine.[83] Salman Taseer, the Governor of Punjab, advocated that the clause in the Constitution declaring the Ahmadi community to be non-Muslims should be revoked, and commented in a TV interview about the country's blasphemy law. He was assassinated on Jan. 4, 2011 in Islamabad by Mumtaz Qadri, who reportedly said he killed Taseer due to the latter's vocal opposition of the blasphemy law in Pakistan.[84] The *Jama'at Ahle Sunnat* threatened mourners with the same fate as that of Taseer, and warned that 'No Muslim should attend the funeral or even try to pray for Salman Taseer or even express any kind of regret or sympathy over the incident.' It said anyone who expressed sympathy over the death of a blasphemer was also committing blasphemy."[85] Supporters of the assassin, Qadri, blocked police attempting to bring him to the Anti-Terrorism Court in Rawalpindi, and some supporters even showered him with rose petals.[86]

In November 2010 the Lahore High Court in Pakistan barred President Asif Ali Zardari from pardoning a Christian women, Asia Bibi, a 45-year old mother of four, sentenced to death on charges of insulting Islam; Salman Taseer had declared to file an appeal for Asia Bibi. This was not an isolated incident; allegations of blasphemy against the Prophet and desecration of the Qur'an have often been used against Christians and other minority groups in local and personal disputes.

Numerous other examples, from multiple countries, could easily be cited. Prof. Ziauddin Sardar of King Abdul Aziz University of Jeddah, Saudi Arabia, has well described the predicament in which Muslims find themselves today as the result of attempts by some to implement

---

[83] Ibid.

[84] "Governor assassinated in Islamabad, Pakistan". IndiaVoice. 2011-1-4.

[85] *BBC News South Asia*, 5 January 2011. Retrieved 2011-01-07.

[86] "Demonstrators Prevent Court Appearance of Alleged Pakistani Assassin". Voice of American, 6th January 2011.

Shari'a law in ways that actually undermine the wider ethical and moral values of Shari'a:

> By emphasizing the precision in the mechanics of prayer and ablution, length of beard and mode of dress, they have lost sight of individual freedom, the dynamic nature of many Islamic injunctions . . . . They have founded intolerant, compulsive and tyrannical orders and have provided political legitimacy to despotic and nepotistic systems of government. They have closed and constructed many enquiring minds by their insistence on in-objective parallels, unending quibbles over semantics. They have divorced themselves from human needs and conditions. No wonder then that the majority of Muslims today pays little attention to them and even foster open hostility towards them.[87]

The potential for misunderstanding and negative reaction by non-Muslims, of course, is likewise high.

Theologians have complicated the definition of a Muslim with various rules on how he should bathe, shave, keep his beard, trim his moustache, clean his nostrils, wash his private parts, dress, talk, walk and sleep; to them *Ghazali* has replied in his *Faysal al-Tafriqa* thus:

"Among the most extreme and extravagant of men are a group of scholastic theologians who dismiss the Muslim common people as unbelievers and claim that whoever does not know scholastic theology in the form they recognize and does not know the prescriptions of the Holy Law according to the proofs which they have adduced is an unbeliever.

"These people have constricted the vast mercy of God to His servants and made paradise the preserve of a small clique of theologians. They have disregarded what is handed down by the *sunna*, for it is clear that in the time of the Prophet, may God bless and save him, and in the time of the Companions of the Prophet, may God be pleased with them, the Islam of whole groups of rude Arabs was recognized, though they were busy worshipping idols. They did not concern themselves with

---

[87] Ziauddin Sardar, *The Future of Muslim Civilization,* London, 1979, p.58.

the science of analogical proof and would have understood nothing of it if they had.

"Whoever claims that theology, abstract proof, and systematic classifications are the foundation of belief is an innovator. Rather belief is a light which God bestows on the hearts of His creatures as the gift and bounty from Him, sometimes through an explainable conviction from within, sometimes because of a dream in sleep, sometimes by seeing the state of bliss of a pious man and the transmission of his light through association and conversation with him, sometimes through one's own state of bliss."[88]

[88] Rafiq Zakaria; *The Struggle Within Islam: The Conflict Between Religion and Politics;* Penguin Books (India) Ltd. ; 1989; p.303

Jihad: In Theory and Practice

In the later part of Muslim history, when Christian Europe turned their attention from Muslim menace to their Reform Movements and there appeared a break in the incessant hostility and conflict, the classical doctrine of *Jihad* was vigorously challenged by a new generation of Muslim scholars. One of the most important of these was *Ibn Taymiyya* (1263-1328), whose influence in shaping Muslim ideology is matched only by *St. Augustine's* influence in shaping Christianity. *Ibn Taymiyya* argued that the idea of killing nonbelievers who refused to convert to Islam—the foundation of the classical doctrine of *Jihad*—not only defied the example of the Prophet, but also violated one of the most important principles in the Qur'an: *"there can be no compulsion in religion"* (2:256). Indeed, on this point the Qur'an is adamant. *"The truth is from your Lord,"* it says; *"believe it, if you like or do not"* (18:29). The Qur'an also asks the believers rhetorically, *"Can you compel people to believe against their will?"* (10:100). Say to those who do not believe, *"To you, your religion, to me mine"* (109:6).

Ibn Taymiyya's rejection of the classical doctrine of *Jihad* fueled the works of a number of Muslim political and religious thinkers, like *Sayyid Ahmed Khan* (1817-98) and *Chiragh Ali* (1844-95) in India, and *Mahmud Shaltut* (1897-1963) in Egypt. They contextualized the Qur'an to show that Islam outlaws not only wars that are not made in direct response to aggression, but also those that are not officially sanctioned by a qualified Muslim jurist, or *mujtahid*.

However, after the colonial experience in the nineteenth century gave birth to a new kind of Islamic radicalism in the Middle East and North Africa, the classical doctrine of *Jihad* went through a massive resurgence in the pulpits and the classrooms of prominent Muslim intellectuals. In Iran, the *Ayatollah Khomeini* (1902-89) relied on a militant interpretation of *Jihad*, first to energize the anti-imperialist revolution of 1979 and then to fuel his destructive eight-year war with Iraq. It is Khomeini's vision of *Jihad* as a weapon of war that helped found the Islamic militant group *Hizbollah*, whose invention of the suicide bomber launched an appalling new era of international terrorism. In Saudi Arabia, *Abdullah Yusuf Azzam* (1941-89) promoted an uncompromisingly belligerent interpretation of *Jihad* that, he argued, was incumbent on all Muslims. "*Jihad* and the rifle alone," Dr. *Azzam* proclaimed to his students. "No negotiations, no conferences, and no dialogues." *Azzam's* views laid the foundations for the Palestinian militant group *Hammas*, which has since adopted *Hizbollah's* tactics in their resistance against the Israeli occupation. His teachings had an exceptional impact on *Osama bin Laden*, who eventually put into practice his mentor's ideology by calling for a worldwide campaign of *Jihad* against the West and their allied autocrats in the Muslim lands by issuing his *fatawa*. Thus they launched a series of horrifying wave of terrorism since the bloody event of 9/11 throughout Europe, America and Muslim countries.

The notion of *Jihad* in the early formative period of pious caliphs, "grew up without any pre-vision;" wrote Thomas Arnold.[89] It developed with the development of the historical events spread throughout the life of the Prophet. Linking up the various messages of this period in the Qur'an, a somewhat complete code of war and peace would seem to emerge, the different elements arising not from theoretical or *a priori* considerations, but from real events which were taking place. This code, which achieves a synthesis between duty and ethics, may be regarded as one of the many everlasting gifts of Islam for mankind. *"And fight in the cause of Allah those who fight you, but transgress not the limits. Truly, Allah likes not the transgressors."*[90] 'These principles seem to address all the three dimensions of war and peace justification of war, degree of force which can be permitted, and restraint, forgiveness, and settlement.'[91] The doctrine of *Jihad*, as it slowly developed in the Qur'an with the events on the ground, was specifically meant to differentiate between pre-Islamic and Islamic notions of warfare. It was "ideological-cum-ethical dimension" that, until that point, did not exist in the concept of warfare throughout the then world.

The concept of *Jihad* evolved at different levels at different time. At the individual level, the transformation, in terms of values and ethics of a

---

[89] Thomas W. Arnold, The Preaching of Islam; Kitab Bhavan, New Delhi, 1999.

[90] Q. 2:190

[91] L. Dayal, Ibid. p.111

Bedouin into a believer required an up-hill spiritual endeavor. He had to leave off his age-old traditions of multifarious local gods, bloody vendetta, suppression of women and total submission to the tribal leader. He had to move over to a singular divinity, equality amongst all, use of reason and intellect, and the virtues of forgiveness and peace. This was a steep climb indeed. This required believer not only to strive, but strive hard.

The spiritual message of *Jihad* entered into a practical phase when the Prophet and the new community of Muslims were pitted against hostile forces. The Qur'an declares permission to wage war in self-defense, *"Fight in the cause of Allah those who fight you"*(2:190). The ever-changing situations of hostility with pagan Arabs, Jews and Christian tribes made the revelations changing accordingly. Several verses in *sura* 9 guide the believers as per situation. They *"violate their oaths after their covenant..."* (9:12); and they *"plotted to expel the Messenger...."*(9:13). There should, therefore, be no hesitation to proclaim a *"grievous penalty"* against them (9:1-3). They should suffer severe retribution, *"then fight and slay the pagans, whenever ye find them..."*(9:5).

The ethical justification for going to war is abundantly emphasized in the scripture. The Qur'an would appear to be one of the earliest documents which addressed the question of essentiality of war.

The vehemence of conflict has to be related to the needs of war, and should be marked by restraint—*"In the law of equality, there is saving of life to you, O ye men of understanding, That ye may restrain yourselve."*(1:179). Retaliation has to be in proportion to the assault; *".... attack him as he attacks you .... And Allah is with those who restrain themselves"*(2:194). The Qur'an, even while justifying war in self-Defense, forbids undue violence, *"Fight in the cause of Allah those who fight you, but do not transgress limits; for Allah does not love transgressors."*(2:190)

Restraint and forgiveness are laid down as a constant requirement for a Muslim, in all circumstances of life, including war. While proportionate retaliation is permitted, forgiveness is the ideal to aspire for as in verse (42:40). Usually patience does not place the aggressor at an advantage. On the other hand, it benefits those who show such patience. *"That is indeed the best course for those who are patient"*(16:126). *".....if anyone remits the retaliation by way of charity, it is an act of atonement for himself."*(5:45) Islam brings out forgiveness as divine attribute and therefore, it requires man to reach spiritually up to such level.

The truth is that the battles fought during Prophet's time were all defensive in character. The practice of using the expression *Jihad* for struggles other than *'the Cause of God'* must be taken to be outside scriptural sanction, and therefore, un-Islamic. For example, at the commencement of the First World War in 1914, the ruler of Turkey, Abdul Hamid II, decided to join with Germany and declared *Jihad* against Britain and France. This was countered by the Sharif of *Makkahh, Hussayn ibn Ali,* who called for *Jihad* against Germany and Ottoman Turks, since he was under British protection.

Today Muslims are engaged in violent conflicts against their Muslim dictators of Morocco, Tunisia, Egypt, Libya, Bahrain, Syria and Yemen making free use of religious vocabulary. The legality of attacks carried out by al-Qaeda, Hizbollah, Islamic *Jihad* and others on combatants and non-combatants as well, are debatable. They did neither carry approval of a head of Islamic State nor *ijm'a* of Muslim *ummah,* a pre-condition of *shari'a* for such attacks.

Whenever Muslim groups are in conflict with organized states, and with powerful nations, their mode of operation has been uncontrollably violent; terrorist actions have not distinguished between combatants and civilians, the guilty and the innocent, men, women, old and children. The Qur'an forbids this in a voice which is loud and clear. Suicide-bombing which is increasingly carried out in such conflicts is wholly un-Islamic; being violative of the principle contained in verse 4:29, *"O you who believe! . . . . do not kill (or destroy) yourselves: for verily Allah has been to you Most Merciful."* There is not a single incident under any circumstances, no matter how extenuating, in which Prophet permitted suicide.[92]

Whenever Muslims are in conflict with organized states, and with powerful nations, their mode of operation has been uncontrollably violent. They go for bitter choice of practices than precepts. They go for a cosmic war. For them a 'cosmic war' is a total war.[93] It is a conflict in which God is believed to be directly engaged on one side over the other. A cosmic war partitions the world into black and white, good and evil, us and them. In such a war, there is no middle ground; everyone

---

[92] Imam Feisal Abdul Rauf, *What's Right with Islam*; New York, Harper, 2004; p. 139.

[93] The term "cosmic war" belongs to Mark Juergensmeyer, *Terror in the Mind of God* (Berkeley: Univ. of California Press, 2003).

must choose a side. Soldier and civilian, combatant and noncombatant, aggressor and bystander—all the traditional divisions, that serve as markers in a real war, break down in cosmic wars. The ultimate goal of a cosmic war was not to defeat an earthly force but to vanquish evil itself, which ensures that a cosmic war remains an absolute, eternal, unending, and ultimately unwinnable conflict."[94]

After the tower had collapsed and the rubble and ash had settled, a curious document was discovered in the baggage of one of the hijackers, detailing the final instructions for carrying out the gruesome *sacrifice*. I say sacrifice because the anonymous document reads like the script of a ceremonial rite, every mindful act, every rehearsed moment meant to underscore the *ritual drama* taking place in the minds of the hijackers.

"Purify your soul from all unclean things", the hijackers were told. *"Tame your soul. Convince it. Make it understand. Completely forget something called "this world."*

"Pray the supplication as you leave your hotel. Pray the supplication when riding in the taxi, when entering the airport. Before you step aboard the plane, pray the supplication. At the moment of death, pray.

"Bless your body with verses of scripture. Rub the verses on your luggage, your clothes, your passport. Polish your knife with the verses, and be sure the blade is sharp; you must not discomfort your sacrifice.

Remember they may be stronger than you, but their equipment, their security, their technology—nothing will keep you away from your task. How many small groups have defeated big groups by the will of God?

Remember, this is a battle for the sake of God. The enemy are the allies of Satan, the brothers of the Devil. Do not fear them, for the believer fears only God.

And when the hour approaches, welcome death for the sake of God. With your last breath remember God. Make your final words, "There is no god but God!"[95]

---

94 "How to Win a COSMIC WAR: God, Globalization, and the End of the War on Terror." by Reza Aslan. P. 5.

95 The complete text in English can be found on the *Guardian* website, www.guardian. co.uk/world/2001/sep/30/terrorism.september113.

Those responsible for 9/11 can be said to have had a single overriding ambition, "to accomplish their mission and to unite the Muslim world" and to maintain, at any cost, the perpetuation of their cosmic war, for there is no more definite means through which their identity can be sustained and have no other weapon more winnable than the human sacrificial missile.

PART—III

ISLAM IN CONFLICT

Islam in Conflict

Nature of the Conflict

On the death of Prophet Muhammad in 632 the question of succession assumed paramount importance; it threatened to be as much religious as political. The successor had to be both a temporal and a spiritual leader. But who, among his companions, could come up to this ideal? A consensus among the faithful was difficult to arrive at; but eventually, because of the trauma of the Prophet's death, the problem was resolved without any serious dispute. The first two successors of the Prophet, known as caliphs, proved remarkably resourceful; they united the faithful under one banner to spread the faith. But after them there was trouble: rival groups took to arms, caliphs were murdered and their murders plunged the Caliphate into a succession of civil wars. Since then the Muslims have never been a united community. As the wars of Caliphate dragged on, temporal and religious factions drifted apart and each faction broke into sub-factions; all of them swore by the shari'a—the canonical law of Islam—but each faction interpreted it differently and went about it in its own way. Those who operated in the temporal domain used Islam for their own ends while the theologians busied themselves with the coining of new theories and the charting out of fresh paths for the faithful. The vast majority remained silent spectators to this frenetic activity; they were content with their routine and the simple rituals they practiced. Islam was simple enough for them to follow without much guidance.

For more than two hundred years this state of affairs continued, leading to a plethora of contradictory doctrines, which finally divided the Muslims into two broad groups—one owing allegiance to their temporal rulers, the other opposed to them. The ruling group was not much concerned with the dictates of religion. To them power mattered more than faith. The other group was against the rulers' heathen activities; it aimed at purifying Islam. But the conflict did not much perturb the common people; they kept out of it.

From the beginning of the Umayyad rule the Companions of the Prophet disapproved of the former's activities, particularly the way in which they had turned the Caliphate into a *muluk* or kingdom. Mu'awiya was aware of the adverse effect of such an attitude. Why then did he decide to opt for the kingship? His explanation was that he feared that tribal jealousies, rampant among the Arabs of the time, would plunge the Caliphate into fratricidal wars and weaken the structure of administration in an empire which now extended from West Asia and North Africa to Central Asia and parts of India. These could not be left to the whims and caprices of tribal leaders or the theological disputations of the jurists and theologians. He was convinced that only a monarchical pattern of administration could assure continuity of rule. Shi'ites, Kharjis, Sunnis and their affiliates were in conflict with each other in the domain of temporal power as well as in theological metaphysics. Broadly speaking, the conflicts were confined to two opposing forces: temporal versus religious. The former was more pragmatic; the later more rigid.

The world of Islam today faces the same challenge it had in the past. Only it is more intense. It has affected every Muslim in every land. The future depends on how its followers respond to this challenge. The fundamentalist have one solution, the secularists another. The question is: are their differences irreconcilables? In the past the fight of the fundamentalists was with the rulers who readily made compromises with doctrinal obligations to achieve their own ends; today their dispute is with the modern secularists over norms of social behavior and systems of government. The conflict within Islam for the soul of Islam continues. Will the struggle be resolved in the present and the foreseeable future, as it was resolved in the past? Or will it make life more difficult for the faithful? This book attempts to find the answer.

Contemporary Developments

Introduction

The history of Islam in modern times is essentially the history of the Western impact on Muslim society, especially since the 19th century CE. There is a genuine reason why things should appear in this light. Ever since its inception, Islam has faced and met spiritual and intellectual challenges. From the 2nd/8th to the 4th/10th centuries, a series of intellectual and cultural crises arose in Islam, the most serious and significant was that produced by Hellenist intellectualism, but Islam met all those successfully; assimilating, rejecting and adjusting itself to the new currents. But the Muslims were, at that time, psychologically invincible, politically masters of the situation and the content of religion was not encumbered by a dead weight of tradition. It was largely the new elements and currents of thought that supplied and built up the content of the Muslim tradition itself. Very different was the case at the time of the Western impacts on Islam in the 12th/18th and especially the 13th/19th century. The first phase of this impact was in each case political and military and in each case the Muslims were vanquished and politically subjugated directly or indirectly. This was followed by religious and intellectual forms of impingement through various channels. The most patent and direct challenges were from the Christian missionaries, the modern thought of Europe and the study and criticism by Westerners of Islam and Islamic society itself.

The unsettlement that ensued from the political defeats and subjugation rendered the Muslim psychologically less capable of constructive rethinking his heritage, and meeting the intellectual challenge of modern thought. If politically Islam had not been shaken yesterday, the story would have been very different today.

Challenges of Modernization

It is true that the positive line of a reconstitution of society universally proclaimed by pre-Modernist reform attempts was in terms of a return to the pristine Islam, to 'the Qur'an and the Sunna', including varying degrees of the Sufi legacy, and thereby brought about a general resurgence of fundamentalism. Now, this fundamentalism itself has constituted and until constitutes in one sense a problem for Modern Islam and is, in fact, the problem for the modernist. We must not overlook the fact that this fundamentalism is not merely an impediment in the way of modernization of society and outlook, but constitutes a basic point of reference in the process of this modernization.

Yet the fundamental character of the modern challenge and the pervasiveness of the Western influence is also a stark fact. The channels through which this influence has come in are legion—the political structure, the administrative and judicial machinery, the army, the press, the education, the information technology and the electronic media, modern thought, and above all, the present indispensible contacts with Western society. At a general level, the problem has been posed both by Western observers and by most modernist Muslims in terms of a conflict between Reason and Faith. There is undoubtedly a great deal of justification for and truth in thus formulating the problem. But it is equally true that this problem has been exaggerated and over-emphasized both by Muslim Modernists and apologists and by Western critics.

The real challenge the Muslim society has had to face and is facing is at the level of social institutions and social ethic as such. The real nature of this crisis is not the fact that the Muslim social institutions in the past have been wrong or irrational but the fact that there has been a social system which now needs to be modified and adjusted. This social system has, in fact, been perfectly rational in the past. The disadvantage of the Muslim society at the present juncture is that whereas in the early centuries of development of social institutions in Islam, Islam started from a clean slate, as it were, and had to carve out a social fabric, an activity of which the product was the medieval social system, now, when Muslims have to face a situation of fundamental rethinking and reconstruction, their acute problem is precisely to determine how far to render the slate clean again and on what principles and by what methods, in order to create a new set of institutions.

The modern challenge had direct bearing on the social institutions of Islam, its laws of marriage and divorce, the position of women and certain economic laws such as t banking, commerce, taxation, insurance, etc. This challenge assumed purely intellectual proportions since a change in social mores involves a re-thinking of the social ethic, which touches the foundational ideas of social justice. The whole problem was raised to a most general level as to whether 'faith' and 'reason' can accommodate one another. Western critics contended that the social and economic backwardness of the late medieval Muslim society was due to the inherently inferior character of the Islamic civilization, seen as a 'Bedouin' phenomenon alien to reason and tolerance. The medieval Muslim conflicts between philosophers and orthodox theologians were unreservedly identified as war between 'reason' and 'religion' and the net conclusion drawn was that Islam inherently opposes reason.

A general summons to the Muslim Community to raise their intellectual and moral standards in order to meet the dangers of the Western expansionism was issued by *Jamal al-Din al-Afghani* (1839-97), the first genuine Muslim Modernist. He made a powerful appeal for the cultivation of philosophical and scientific disciplines by expanding the curricula of the educational institutions and for general educational reforms. He affirmed in his fiery speeches and articles that there was nothing in the basic principles of Islam that is incompatible with reason or science. He reasserted his faith in the transcendental truth of Islam.

If to state that Islam is not against reason and science was the task of *al-Afghani*, it fell to the Egyptian *Muhammad 'Abduh* and the Indian *Sayyid Ahmad Khan* to prove this statement. Both these men agree that Islam, as it was actually believed in and practiced by most of its adherents, would certainly be threatened by the modern advances in thought and science. "If people do not shun blind adherence, if they do not seek that Light which can be found in the Qur'an and the indisputable *Hadith*, and do not adjust religion and the sciences of today, Islam will become extinct in India", *Sayyid Ahmad Khan* said.[96] Both were equally convinced that the dead weight of time had encumbered the true and original Islam with later developments that were no essential part of it and both wished to reveal the true Islam primarily to Muslims but also to non-Muslims.

Need for Political Reform

From the very beginning of the Western expansionist impacts on Muslim land, the Muslims, after the failures of their early military and political resistance to the West, have been preoccupied with the problem

---

[96] Khutabat-I Sir Sayyid, Bada'un, 1931; p.55.

of effective political organization. The problems led to an awareness of the necessity of political reform, and political reform was found impossible without social reform and economic modernization. And since socio-economic modernization could not be carried out without new legislation (besides education) which depended again on political authority. The issues of social and legal reform are inextricably bound up with political problems. The purely political and social developments in the Muslim world are intimately related to the questions of nationalism and secularism, they have direct bearing on the religious history of Islam. Further, the authority to legislate, which in the history of Islam has never been islamically vested in the elected members of legislature, is of intrinsic importance for Islam as a social phenomenon.

The first modernist idea of political reform was voiced by Jamal al-Din al-Afghani. There were two salient elements in his political thought: the unity of the Muslim world and populism. The doctrine of the political unification of the Muslim world, known as *pan-Islamism*, is urged by al-Afghani as the only effective bulwark against foreign encroachments and domination of Muslim lands. The populist impulse can arise only by popular constitutional governments, that can be strong, stable and a real guarantee against foreign force and intrigue. Al-Afghani's influence contributed directly to the Arabi Pasha rebellion in Egypt, the constitutional movement in Persia, Turkey and India.

But despite pan-Islamism sentiment, nationalism has made powerful inroads into the Muslim world and has been officially incarnated in the state-ideologies of certain Muslim countries, like the ideology of Pakistan. It is this political concept of nationalism with a sense and respect of pan-Islamism that has developed in the conflict with the colonial powers in the Muslim countries. European type of nationalism influenced by secularism won an official victory in Turkey through a conglomeration of causes, the most immediate of which was the rebellion of the Arabs against the Turks in the midst of World War I and, above all, the personality of Ataturk himself.

Although there is little explicit secularism in the Muslim world, no Muslim country, excepting Saudi Arabia and Iran, has exclusive political system based on *shari'a*. This problem is basically as to how the religion must be secularized if the secular is to be made religious. But Islamic theology and dogmatism, like those of other religions, have not yet undergone this transformation to be acceptable to the modern mind.

The Rule of Law and Civil Society

The rule of law and civil society are a modern historical construct; they are until in the process of construction on the basis of the new needs and demands of various societies and the political culture available in each tradition of thought. Apart from the advanced European and North American democratic regimes, large-scale on-going experiments are taking place in many contemporary societies, such as China, India, Brazil, and Mexico. Yet, there is no one recognized model of Civil Society with its related rule of law. On the other hand, there are societies in which political thought is paralyzed, dangerously diverted by a perverted religious tradition. This is the case in several of the so-called Islamic regimes or rather regimes which claim Islam to be the official religion of the state. The ideological competition between the two blocs constructed under the names of 'Islam' and the 'West' is increasingly distorting, disrupting and breaking down any positive experience that may be emerging in certain countries ruled by precarious political regimes.

Such simple and current words as democracy, rule of law, human rights, citizenship, justice, liberal philosophy, and free market, such ideals and representations cannot be transferred from one culture to another unless and as long as the process of assimilation has not become deep rooted, initiated by the historical experience that shapes the living collective memory of each social group, community or nation. This is not the case with the majority of Muslim societies. It has obviously failed to develop in contemporary Muslim contexts.

Which memory of Islam was alive in Muslim societies before and immediately after the independence of each country? And which *desires* inspired and motivated the political decision-makers, compared to the desires and expectations of various social groups that were until subject to the tribal solidarity, patrimonial and patriarchal archaic systems? Very few of these questions have been adequately considered so far in the current literature about political Islam.

These are the prevailing conditions in which the debates about a civil society are engaged in Muslim contexts. The geopolitical strategies of the West have clearly accelerated the dialectic answers of radical political Islam; the geopolitical sphere called 'the Middle East' is particularly affected by several ongoing conflicts over vital stakes: oil, the strategic positions of western forces, the place of Israel in the whole area, the conflicting religious memories since the emergence of Islam as a new rival. It is an explosive mixture of material interests, the desire of authoritarian rule and a dispute over jointly held symbolic capital all of which are disputed and dismantled by the modern ideologies that are designed to support self-promoted national interests.

In Muslim cases, the role of tradition changed radically during the struggle for liberation (1945-67) followed by the so-called socialist and Islamic fundamentalist revolutions (from 1970 onward). The changes and their consequences have not yet been studied; it would be enlightening, for example, to compare the progressive, critical attitude of the reformist Muhammad 'Abdu to the regressive, dogmatic positions of his so-called disciple Rashid Ridha, or the later conservative sage Muhammad 'Amara. Even more significant would be the comparison between the liberal writer and thinker Taha Hussein and the fundamentalists who rejected his contributions as too favorable to Western culture and anti-socialist ideology. If we agree on the principle that a civil society and the rule of law should both be founded on the defense of and strong support for a humanist, liberal culture, then the culture, like knowledge, is a subject of continuous inevitable conflict. The best result achievable in this domain is to restrict the conflict to peaceful, constructive debate and enlightened rivalry.

The ethics of responsibility means that any political, scientific, religious, ecological or economic decision engaging the future of all living generations should evaluate all the consequences of each decision for the immediate present and foreseeable future. The immediate pressures of *Realpolitik* have made obsolete any reference to the ethics of responsibility not only in matters of decision-making at the highest level of government, but also in the domain of scholarship, scientific research and the teaching or scholarly transmission of the knowledge produced by the most reliable scholarship. In other words, the rule of law is more the product of a political philosophy than ethics of responsibility.

The majority of the Third World regimes had to replace their so-called Socialist liberation plans by a reversion to a traditional faith-driven 'national identity'. This ideological leap prevailed in Muslim contexts in which the demographic explosion provided a large sociological basis for the so-called 'Islamic revolution'.

The failures of post-colonial states to foster a democratic civil society should be clearly identified with their actual internal genesis and external contexts. Describing the opposition of fundamentalist defenders of a so-called 'Islamic model of state' to the existing regimes accused of introducing Western secularized norms and institutions, is insufficient. In fact, all states in all countries have more or less used and imposed Islamic references and a will to protect the *Shari'a.* This debate on old theological, exegetic and legal issues has overwhelmingly occupied the political space and eliminated the intellectual and scientific endeavors to trace a clear-cut line between the ideological so-called Islam.

There is a reluctance to trust 'Western' scholars on Islamic matters of 'faith'. Faith is not considered a matter of critical knowledge, but only of orthodox reproduction of what the Tradition has preserved from any criticism and has transmitted since the age of the 'pious ancestors' *(al-salaf al-salih).* The result of this policy and mental attitude is that the modern conceptualization of the rule of law and civil society is continuously avoided. Another contradiction: many intellectuals, writers, artists who stand on the side of democratic values prefer to stress the responsibility of the West in supporting conservative regimes than to insist on the role of national 'elites' who have monopolized political power since the independence of each country.

Some Muslim states, like Morocco and Turkey, are candidates to the European Union. As long as Islamic institutions, laws, customs and culture officially prevail in these regimes, it will be impossible to harmonize the legislative process to the admission of new members. This is a very significant and concrete case study. A contemporary society claiming an Islamic identity is to radically rethink this identity in the framework of a criticized, enlarged, eventually revised intellectual, scientific and secular modernity.

Modern revolutions have substituted their own 'regimes of Truth' to the religious ones, which are until claiming full validity in many Muslim societies. For this purpose the French Revolution is a rich case study: it was violent and radical in its will to overthrow the 'old Regime' and a king invested with the divine Right as sacralized by the Church. When Louis XVI had been judged and executed by the courts in the name of the sovereignty of the people, the sacralizing power of the divine Right was finally abolished. When Khomeini came to power in Feb. 1979 he did just the opposite of what the French revolutionaries imposed: he decided to arrest the Shah, and enforced God's law on earth. That way the Shah could be arrested, judged and executed in the name of God as represented by the Imam.

These short historical remarks show clearly that religion and secularism are mostly handled as polemical concepts referring to contingent ideological regimes of Truth.

Liberalism and Islam

"Liberalism contradicts Dogmatism," which is true and trivial. Trivial since it is always true and since it says nothing about the future. A pure idea, potent as it might have been in the past, influential as it may be at present, cannot by itself prevent a people from adopting liberalism and democracy. Only a material force can stop other forces working in a giving society.

Liberal Islam means more than tolerant or moderate Islam; People focus their attention on particulars like marriage, human rights, secularism etc. and seem to think that these are the content of what a liberal Islam should be. In my opinion there is confusion between religious reform and political revolution. Even when dogma and law are closely linked, there are ways to introduce under the veil of 'temporary necessity' (*Darura*) or expediency (*Maslaha, Istihsan*) topical reforms without tampering with the dogma (*Aqida*).

Liberalism is a situation in which society is set free to operate according to its own rules. I think that in circumstances of rapid change we need only to open our eyes to be convinced that society doesn't obey our orders, even when we believe that these come ultimately from God. Miracles just do not occur. To acknowledge the fact amounts to a mental revolution, which opens all doors? Everything becomes possible. I don't understand otherwise what occurred lately in Russia and before that in Germany and Spain. What economists and statisticians call transition in these countries seems to me the mere translation of the following statement: Ideology is, in the long term, less powerful than sociology. As soon as this fact is recognized the reforms just mentioned become inevitable because they serve the interests of all, including those who oppose them for ideological motives. From this standpoint I don't see in Islamic countries so much the pre-eminence of a *"Da'wa"* (religious message) or the ascendancy of clerical elite, as the direct consequence of poverty and economic backwardness.

However, the West doesn't pursue the same policy as regards the economic development of non-Western nations. It is seen as a necessary step towards liberalization and therefore is actively sought in China, Eastern Europe, etc., whereas it is felt as a threat when Islamic countries are concerned, even before the ambitions are translated into reality.

The collapse of the Berlin wall was not due to the policy of containment, blockade, propaganda as much as to a wise policy of easy term loans, free trade and enhanced cultural exchanges. The same strategy should secure the same results elsewhere. Sooner or later a developing society frees itself from ideas and ideals that do no longer correspond to its new aspirations. What is going on from Morocco to Yemen in the shape of political uprising and social unrest from the very beginning of Jan. 2011, can be seen in the same context.

For reasons I need not detail here such an evolution/revolution will probably occur more easily in the "Ajam" countries of Asia than in the Arab Middle East and North Africa, not because the former are less religious but simply because the latter are on the whole less fortunate to social development and modernization. Seeing that happening sometime in the future, somewhere in the vast Islamic world, seeing that the law of society has at last prevailed over the orders of tradition or the commands of ideology, many will, I am sure, cry out, as they do now, facing the staggering performances of some Asian nations: Well, the seeds were always there; we failed to see them before, but now we take notice and we cheer.

Islam and Mondernity
Are They Compatible?

Political Modernism:

From the very beginning of the Western expansionist impacts on Muslim land, the Muslims, after the failures of their early military and political resistance to the West, have been preoccupied with the problem of effective political organization. The problems led to an awareness of the necessity of political reform, and political reform was found impossible without social reform and economic modernization. And since socio-economic modernization could not be carried out without new legislation (besides education) which depended again on political authority. The issues of social and legal reform are inextricably bound up with political problems. The purely political and social developments in the Muslim world are intimately related to the questions of nationalism and secularism, they have direct bearing on the religious history of Islam. Further, the authority to legislate, which in the history of Islam has never been islamically vested in the elected members of legislature, is of intrinsic importance for Islam as a social phenomenon.

The first modernist idea of political reform was voiced by *Jamal al-Din al-Afghani.* There were two salient elements in his political thought: the unity of the Muslim world and populism. The doctrine of the political unification of the Muslim world, known as *pan-Islamism,* is urged by al-Afghani as the only effective bulwark against foreign encroachments and domination of Muslim lands. The populist impulse can arise only by popular constitutional governments, that can be strong, stable and a real guarantee against foreign force and intrigue. Al-Afghani's influence contributed directly to the *Arabi Pasha* rebellion in Egypt, the constitutional movement in Persia, Turkey and India.

But despite pan-Islamism sentiment, nationalism has made powerful inroads into the Muslim world and has been officially incarnated in the state-ideologies of certain Muslim countries, like the ideology of

Pakistan. It is this political concept of nationalism with a sense and respect of pan-Islamism that has developed in the conflict with the colonial powers in the Muslim countries.

Although there is little explicit secularism in the Muslim world, no Muslim country, excepting Saudi Arabia and Iran, has exclusive political system based on *shari'a*. This problem is basically as to how the religion must be secularized if the secular is to be made religious. But Islamic theology and dogmatism, like those of other religions, have not yet undergone this transformation to be acceptable to the modern mind.

The way of dissidence was prevalent within Islam from the beginning. But as intellectual opposition was repressed and silenced, only political rebellion and terrorism had any success, as we see so well today. Only the violence of the subversive could interact with the violence of the caliph/ruler. This pattern, which is found throughout Muslim history, explains the modern reality, in which only religious challenge preaching violence as its political language is capable of playing a credible role.

Once colonization had ended after World War II, the newly independent Muslim states did not renounce their vendetta against reason. They fought against the advances of Enlightenment philosophy and banned Western humanism as foreign and "imported" calling the intellectuals who studied and tried to promote it, like *Syed Ahmed* in India and *Taha Hussein* in Egypt, as enemy agents and traitors to the nationalist cause. At the same time, they committed themselves to the massive importation of weapons from the West. The Arab states allocate a higher percentage of their gross domestic product to military expenditure than do the Western countries. This makes them doubly dependent, since Western nations use the income from arms sales to finance research and development and boost their aeronautic and space industries.

The majority of the colonized Muslim countries never experienced that phase of history so indispensable to the development of the scientific spirit, during which the state and its institutions became the means of transmitting the ideas of tolerance and respect for the individual. Above all else, colonial governments were brutal and culturally limited. The nationalist governments that supplanted them were just as brutal and just as hostile to the flowering of the scientific spirit and individual initiative. This produced a virtual cutoff of the Third World from the advances of humanism in the last centuries in both its aspects: the scientific aspect (promoting the use of government resources to invest in scientific research and encourage freedom to explore and invent), and the political aspect (establishing representative democracy, with citizens' exercise of the right to vote and to participate in political decision making). The result was the rampant malaise that now besets the once colonized nations.

The nationalist movements at the end of the nineteenth and beginning of the twentieth century in Egypt, Morocco, Algeria, Syria, Iran and India tried to modernize Muslim culture without breaking with the past, which was burdened with despotism and manipulation of the sacred. These movements introduced institutions and concepts of West representing democracy, like "constitution", "parliament", and "universal suffrage", while yet failing to educate the masses about the essential point: the sovereignty of the individual and freedom of opinion that are philosophical basis of these institutions and concepts. The nationalists failed to think the problems through. We must not forget that the Arab world, like the rest of the Third World, saw the accession to power of the military *janta* in the 1950s and 1960s after decolonization by the West. The debate for modernization never became a social philosophy and social philosophers were never invited to play the role of reformist. That role went to the *fuqaha*, the religious authorities.[97]

Taha Hussein, (d.1972) one of our great defenders of the rationalist tradition, was harassed during his lifetime and judged and condemned after his death "as a manipulator of heathen, Hellenic idea . . . a collaborator devoted to French thought and American thought"[98]

Muslims have been discussing democracy for a century and a half. It came to them, paradoxically, in the baggage of the French, Italian and English colonial armies, the armies that brought other strange things, like the telephone, electricity, railway and automobile. Although the Muslim states are found of these along with electronic surveillance and sophisticated telecommunications systems, some of them nevertheless feel the need to base their political legitimacy on the

---

[97] Ali Umlil; *Islam et etat national* (Casablanca: 1991) p. 47

[98] Anwar al-Jundi, *Muhakamat fikr Taha Husayn* (Cairo: Dar al-Islam, 1984);p. 15.

past. Why does Saudi Arabia, which moved heaven and earth during two US administrations (President Carter and President Reagan) to buy the AWACS missile system, feel a stronger need to adhere to Islam than does Tunisia? What hides behind this outcry for religion and culture that reverberates in the Arab and Muslim world? One thing is certain. The call for Islam in the 1990s expresses diverse needs that are not always archaic and are certainly not always of a spiritual nature.

There are some Muslim regimes that find their interests better protected if they base their legitimacy on cultural and symbolic grounds other than on democratic principles. The sacred, the past, ancestor worship seem to be the chosen grounds in most cases. This category groups together regimes as different as the Kingdom of Saudi Arabia, the Iranian regime of Imam Khomeini and his successors, the military regime of Zia al-Haq in Pakistan, and the Sudanese regime that terrorizes its people in the name of the *sharia.*

Considering how often Islam has been used to rationalize the brutal policies of oppressive totalitarian regimes like the *Taliban* in Afghanistan, the *Wahhabis* in Saudi Arabia, or the *Faqih* in Iran, it is hardly surprising that the term "Islamic democracy" provokes such skepticism in the West. Some of the most celebrated academics in the United States and Europe reject the notion that the principles of democracy cannot be reconciled with fundamental Islamic values. When politicians speak of bring democracy to the Middle East they mean specifically an American secular democracy, not an indigenous Islamic one. The dictatorial regime in the Middle East and North Africa never seem to tire of preaching to the world that their anti-democratic policies are justified because "fundamentalists" allow them but two possible options: despotism or theocracy. The problem with democracy is that if people are allowed a choice, they usually choose regime change. So free democratic elections were suspended in Algeria when it seemed imminent that they would be won by an Islamist party; while in Egypt a permanent application of the country's emergency laws (until recently in 2011) had made free elections inconceivable. The current surge of revolutions which are going on through Morocco, Algeria, Tunisia, Libya, Egypt, Syria, Yemen, Oman and Jordan are all, but the expression of the age-old clashes between the hereditary rulers and their democratically awakened people.

When fourteen centuries ago Prophet Muhammad launched a revolution in Makkahh to replace the archaic, rigid, and inequitable strictures of tribal society with a radically new vision of divine morality and social egalitarianism, he tore apart the fabric of traditional Arab society. It took many years of violence and devastation to cleanse the *Hijaz* of its "false idols." It will take many more to cleanse Islam of its new false idols—bigotry and fanaticism—worshipped by those who have replaced the Prophet's original vision of tolerance and unity with their own ideals of hatred and discord. But the cleansing is inevitable, and the tide of reform cannot be stopped. The Islamic Reformation is already here. We are all living in it.

Rationalism

Muslim Brotherhood ideologue *Sayyid Qutb* (d. 1966) describes modernity as responsible for stripping humanity of its spirituality and its values and reducing human beings to the level of animals—perhaps rational, but animals nonetheless. In his words:

"There is no doubt that man has attained great conquests by virtue of science. He has made immense progress in the field of medicine and treatment of physical diseases. In the same way, man has also made tremendous progress in the field of industrial products. But despite all these, the question arises what man has actually got out of these struggles and progress? Have they caused any spiritual growth? Has he gained the wealth of peace comfort and satisfaction? The answer to all these questions is nothing but an emphatic 'No.' As a result of his material progress, instead of getting peace and ease, man is confronted [by] troubles, restlessness and fear."[99]

In *Qutb's* analysis, the root of this modern malaise is the replacement of the guidance of revelation with the dictates of human reason. This negative appraisal of modernity is predicated on the assumption that Western rationalism relies solely on reason and rejects faith. As such, it is seen as excessive intellectualism, the "de-spiritualization" of humanity. In Islamist discourse, the antidote to this essentially inhuman rationalism is Islam's deep spirituality, which does not preclude reason but subordinates it to faith. In this perspective, Islamic values keep

---

[99] Sayyid Qutb, Islam: The True Religion, trans. Ravi Ahmad Fidai (Karachi, Pakistan: International Islamic Publishers, 1981), 25-26.

reason in its proper place: in the service of faith. Although *Sayyid Qutb's* analysis is typical of modern Islamist discourse, other Islamic analyses reflect a more nuanced view of rationalism.

The complementarity of faith and reason is the traditional Islamic position. Nevertheless, the value of reason in human life was a dominant value in Islam from the earliest times. Fourteenth-century legal scholar Ibn Khaldun, taking inspiration from al-Ghazali, claimed that faith and reason are both necessary for a balanced human life. The ultimate goal of the Islamic community is justice, he said. Scriptures tell us that God established the Muslim community and commissioned Muslims—as his stewards—to spread justice throughout the world.[100]

To do that, Ibn Khaldun says, people were given reason. Reason is necessary to achieve the goals established through revelation. He says in The *Muqaddimah* that people's ability to think is what distinguishes them from animals. It allows human beings "to obtain their livelihood, to cooperate to this end with their fellow men, and to study the Master whom they worship, and the revelations that the Messengers transmitted from Him."

Reason and Religion

Closer examination of condemnations for modernity indicates that it is not reason as such—or even modernity, as it is understood in the West—that is being condemned, but the actions of Western countries that colonized the Muslim world. Islamist condemnations must be recognized as protests against imperialism and the continued problems of post-colonial life, which are also blamed—rightly or wrongly—on the West. Virtually, all of the Muslim world was colonized, and this is the dominant reality in its modern history; developments in twentieth-century Islamic thought can be viewed as a series of efforts to deal with its results.

Prior to World War I, Islamic reform efforts were characterized by appeals to Islam's inherent rationality and commitment to science and learning. A prominent proponent of this perspective was Jamal al-Din

---

[100] The reference here is to two fundamental tenets in Islam, amanah and khilafah. The former is based on the Qur'an's description of creation wherein God entrusts the world to human beings (33:72). The second refers to the Qur'an's designation of human beings as God's representative or stewards on earth (2:30; 6:165).

al-Afghani (d. 1897). Afghani noted that it was Islam's commitment to learning that had produced the highest scientific culture in the Middle Ages. According to Afghani, science "is continually changing capitals. Sometimes it has moved from East to West, and other times from West to East." Science does not belong to any single culture; it is a world heritage to which various communities have contributed at various times. Noting Muslims' major contributions to science, Afghani concludes that Europeans are mistaken when they claim that Islam is inherently unscientific or backward. In fact, he says, of all the major religions Islam is the most supportive of science.

Egyptian religious scholar Muhammad Abduh (d. 1905) also encouraged Muslims to revive their spirit of intellectual independence, and cautioned against traditionalism. He said that "traditionalism can have evil consequences as well as good and may occasion loss as well as conduce gain. It is a deceptive thing, and though it may be pardoned in an animal, is scarcely seemly in man."[101]

According to Abduh, it was intellectual creativity that within a few centuries had allowed the Islamic community to become one of the world's major political and cultural forces. But when Muslims began to simply imitate their ancestors, elevating tradition to the status of virtue, they lost their intellectual vigor and fell into obscurity and became easy prey for more energetic forces. Abduh noted that the universe is inherently rational. He described rationality as a reflection of divine unity. Based on the Qur'anic command to "read the signs" and "seek knowledge," Abduh considered the exercise of reason to be essential to the practice of Islam. Failure to exercise one's reason was a religious failing.

There are two identifiable strains of Islamist discourse. One phase stands in stark contrast to the confident optimism of its reformist predecessors. It is defensive, bordering on xenophobic, characterized by deep distrust of a stereotypical "West" that seem bent on undermining and even destroying the Muslim world. It blames virtually all of the Muslim world's problems and shortcomings on the West. Another strain of Islamist discourse is more self-critical, rational, and practical. It recognizes the positive role of reason in Islam and stresses the need

---

[101] Muhammad Abduh, The Theology of Unity, trans. Ishaq Musa'ad and Kenneth Cragg (London: George Allen & Unwin, 1966), 39-40.)

to exercise it. For example, Iran's president Muhammad Khatami espouses reform and development in the context of what he calls a total transformation of society.[102]

He notes that Iran, like all Islamic societies, is until struggling with economic, social, and political underdevelopment. While admitting the legacy of colonialism as one of the sources of these problems, *Khatami* maintains that the persistence of underdevelopment is the responsibility of Islamic societies themselves. In contrast to those Islamists who totally reject Western society, he says that Western societies have positive strengths and achievements, and identifies modernity specifically as something Muslims should try to emulate. Thus, *Khatami's* approach differs from the earlier Islamist ideology. Modernity, he points out, is not a rejection of religion in favor of godless reason but rather is merely a rejection of the "autocratic and whimsical rulers." Two essential elements of modernity, he says, are freedom and reason. Freedom is necessary for people to be able to use reason as God intended it to be used: to examine societies and find out what is necessary to remedy their problems. "Transformation and progress require thought," he says.[103]

Algerian reformer Mohamed Arkoun also bemoans the negative effect that defensive, militantly anti-Western activists have had on Islam's present intellectual climate. He speaks of their "intellectual poverty" and considers their views a deviation from Islam's intellectual traditions. He says, "There is a need to encourage and initiate audacious, free, productive thinking on Islam today." The task now, as it has always been, is to "integrate . . . new disciplines, new knowledge, and new historical insights into Islam."[104]

Similarly, Moroccan philosopher Mohammed 'Abed al-Jabri calls upon Muslims to examine their intellectual and scientific heritage. They must distinguish between the content of that knowledge, by now quite outdated, and the process of developing that knowledge. Those wishing to assert an authentic Islamic identity vis-à-vis the West, he

---

[102] Muhammad Khatami, *Islam, Liberty, and Development* (Binghamton, NY: Institute of Global Cultural Studies, Binghamton University, 1998), 3).

[103] Ibid., 11.

[104] Mohamed Arkoun, *"Rethinking Islam Today,"* in Charles Kurzman, ed., Liberal Islam: A Sourcebook (New York: Oxford University Press, 1998), 205-7.)

says, would do well to reactivate that intellectual enterprise.[105] Iranian intellectual and reformer Abdolkarim Soroush agrees. He traces the roots of modernity, including secularism, to the use of reason. Human beings were created with reason, and reason demands freedom: "We are impassioned about freedom and consider it the sine qua non of humanity because reason and freedom are inextricably intertwined."[106] "Our mission as rational human beings is to search actively for the truth."[107]

In sum, while anti-rational viewpoints appear in some Islamic discourse on modernity, they do not represent an essentially Islamic position on the subject. Understanding of basic Islamic teachings on the human responsibility to exercise reason, along with both classic discussions of the role of reason in society and the broad range of contemporary discourse on the subject, reveals that Islam cannot be construed as an impediment to rationality. Just as in Western heritage, faith and reason are seen as complementary in Islam.

Secularism

In Europe's modernity, the reliance on reason was accompanied by the development of secularism. Reason was considered the secular replacement for the eternal authority of church authorities, and demanded the separation of religion and state. Must secularism therefore be considered an essential component of modernity and its concomitant democratization? Some modern Islamic thinkers condemn secularism. Fazlur Rahman equates secularism with atheism and attributes the atrocities of colonialism to the West's secularism. For him it is "the bane of modernity."[108] Abdolkarim Soroush, a proponent of democracy, likewise rejects secularism. He says: It is amazing that some consider the democratization of the religious government contingent upon the

---

[105] Mohammed 'Abed al-Jabri, Arab-Islamic Philosophy: A Contemporary Critique, trans. Aziz Abbassi (Austin: University of Texas Center for Middle Eastern Studies, 1999).

[106] Mahmoud Sadri and Ahmad Sadri, trans, and eds., Reason, Freedom, and Democracy in Islam: Essential Writings of 'Abdolkarim Soroush (Oxford: Oxford University Press, 2000), 88.)

[107] Ibid., 90.

[108] Fazlur Rahman, Islam and Modernity: Transformation of an Intellectual Tradition Chicago: University of Chicago Press, 1982), 15.)

secularization of religion and religious law. Liberal democracy draws inspiration and strength from the authentic axiom that states: human beings are naturally free and unique . . . . Is the religious society not, by nature, plural and pluralistic? . . . Belief is a hundred times more diverse and colorful than disbelief. If the pluralism of secularism makes it suitable for democracy, the faithful community is a thousand times more suitable for it . . . . We no longer claim that a genuinely religious government can be democratic but that it cannot be otherwise.[109]

Religious Pluralism

Religious pluralism is rooted in the Qur'an's explicit acceptance of religious diversity: "For each of you [religious communities: Jews, Christians, Muslims] we have appointed a law and a ritual. If God had willed it, he could have made you all one religious community. But [he has not] so that he may test you in what he has given you. So compete with one another in good works" (5:48 cf. 11:118). Therefore, the Qur'an says, "Do not argue with the People of the Book unless it is with something that is better, except with such of them who do wrong. And say: We believe in what has been revealed to us and revealed to you. Our God and your God are one, and to him we surrender" (29:46). Rejecting exclusivism, the Qur'an exhorts all monotheists to work together for the common good: "O People of the Book [Jews, Christians, Muslims], let us come together upon a formula that is common among us, so that we may serve only God" (3:64).

The normative model established by Prophet Muhammad—the Sunna—confirms this acceptance of pluralism. When the newly formed Muslim community moved from Makkah to Madina to escape religious persecution there, Prophet Muhammad dictated a constitution to guide inter-communal relations. In the constitution, Muhammad said, "The Jews . . . are a community along with the believers. To the Jews their religion and to the Muslims theirs."[110] The constitution then confirmed that the various tribes would cooperate in mutual support and loyalty,

---

109 Sadri and Sadri, Reason, Freedom, and Democracy, 144-45.)

110 For the entire text of the Constitution of Madina, reportedly dictated by Muhammad, see W.Montgomery Watt, Islamic Political Thought: The Basic Concepts (Edinburgh: Edinburgh University Press, 1968), pp. 130-34.

but that each group was free to practice its religion. Only those who were disloyal to the community would lose their rights.

Based on the Qur'an and the example of the Prophet, Islamic legal scholars institutionalized religious freedom. That included the freedom of non-Muslims to live according to their own laws of religious practice and personal status, although in civil and criminal matters they were bound by Islamic law. Islam maintained its essential pluralism, and because Islamic sources accepted the validity of other revealed religions, Islamic political theory protected the rights of non-Muslims to practice their respective religions.

Despite that essential pluralism, hostility toward the West stemming from the colonial experience and postcolonial condition has raised questions about pluralism in modern Islamic thought. This hostility often takes on an ideological caste in contemporary Islamist discourse, where an elision is made between the degenerate nature of Western society and secularism itself. In many cases, secularism is construed in such a way as to make it utterly and hopelessly immoral.

This attitude was reflected in the views of early Islamists such as Abu'l-A'la Mawdudi (d. 1978). Some legal scholars in colonial India had determined that as long as Muslims were free to practice their religion under British rule, the territory remained liveable by Muslim.[111] Mawdudi rejected this view. Assuming the classical identity of Muslims as those living subject to an Islamic state, he viewed Muslims as a special community that must keep itself separate from non-Muslims, characterized generally as non-believers. Mawdudi believed that this was necessary to preserving Muslims' religious and cultural identity. However, there are many Islamic voices that challenge this exclusivism on Islamic grounds.

Sheikh Rachid Ghannouchi, the exiled leader of Tunisia's *al-Nahda Party*, is one of these voices. He argues in favor of Muslims' participating in non-Muslim governments. He says that Islam has given Muslims the responsibility to protect certain essential human rights through the ages and in whatever circumstances. He cites fourteenth-century

---

[111] Majid Khadduri, War and Peace in the Law of Islam (Baltimore: Johns Hopkins University, 1955; New York: AMS Press, 1979), 157, where he references Abdur Rahim, Principles of Muhammadan Jurisprudence (Madras, 1911), 396-97; William W.Hunter, The Indian Musalmans (London: Trübner, 1871), 120-25.)

Andalusian legal scholar al-Shatibi's list of the essential human rights to be protected by any non-Islamic government: religion, life, family, wealth, and the mind (or reason). Ghannouchi insists that in all historical circumstances, the critical issue for Muslims is "the fulfillment of the needs of humans and serving their best interests."[112] It would be ideal, he says, to live in a truly Islamic government. But since that is not possible today, Muslims must work with what is available, and that is what he calls "power-sharing." Ghannouchi bases his claim on another essential Islamic principle, *shura,* which he defines as the authority of the community. Muslims must work with whoever is willing to help achieve essential goals, such as "independence, development, social solidarity, civil liberties, human rights, political pluralism, independence of the judiciary, freedom of the press, or liberty for mosques and Islamic activities."[113]

Ghannouchi concludes that "the community of believers may participate in any alliance aimed at preventing injustice and oppression, at serving the interests of mankind, at protecting human rights, at recognizing the authority of the people and at rotating power-holding through a system of elections. The faithful can pursue all these noble objectives even with those who do not share the same faith or ideology."[114] Dismissing the conclusions of *Mawdudi,* he says, "A just government, even if not Islamic, is considered very close to the Islamic one, because justice is the most important feature of an Islamic government, and it has been said that justice is the law of God."[115] Therefore, "The best option for such minorities is to enter into alliances with secular democratic groups. They can then work towards the establishment of a secular democratic government which will respect human rights, ensuring security and freedom of expression and belief—essential requirements of humanity that Islam has come to fulfill."[116]

European Muslim scholar Tariq Ramadan takes this argument farther. Rather than justifying Muslim participation in just non-Muslim

---

[112] Rachid Ghannouchi, "Participation in Non-Islamic Government," in Kurzman, Liberal Islam, p. 91.

[113] Ibid.

[114] Ibid., p. 93

[115] Ibid.

[116] Ibid., p. 94.

governments merely as a temporary phenomenon resulting from the lack of a truly Islamic government in the present era, Ramadan views it as a historic development consistent with Islamic principles. The roots of Islamic jurisprudence, *usul al-fiqh*, provide the means to do that. They "make clear that Islam allows us to consider its intrinsic possibilities for adaptation to space and time."[117] Islam's principles constitute a way of life that not only can but must be lived in all contexts. *Fiqh* has prescribed the methodology, ijtihad, for devising ways of accommodating changing circumstances while maintaining fidelity to Islamic principles.

Tariq Ramadan offers pertinent examples of Muslims living under non-Muslim rule during the time of Prophet Muhammad. He does not dispute that in the Prophet's time these were temporary arrangements. Ramadan believes that there is no reason to make the same requirement today, as it would be "a methodological mistake," not accounting for today's realities.[118] For example, it would allow no space for European converts to Islam. Rather than requiring Muslims who live under secular European law to consider themselves in exile or diaspora, Ramadan insists that "there is absolutely no contradiction . . . between their citizenship and their being Muslims; the law allows them to act in this sense, their faith commands it."[119]

Why then do some Muslims claim Islam is opposed to secular democracy? Ramadan says it is because they are failing to take into consideration differences in the historical circumstances in which Islam and Western democracies developed. In the latter case, it was necessary to develop political institutions independent of religious authorities because of the oppressive coercive authorities the institutionalized church had supported. But this is not the case in Islamic history. Because religious authorities were not affiliated with coercive power for the most part, Muslims were never required to separate themselves from it.

Ramadan concludes that Islam is completely opposed to theocracy and adds that although there is no unique model of Islamic government, basic principles have been provided, which he calls "a framework to

---

[117] Tariq Ramadan, *To Be a European Muslim* (Leicester: Islamic Foundation, 1998), p. 65.

[118] Ibid., p. 126.

[119] Ibid., p. 175.

run pluralism."[120] For example, Islamic government must be conducted through consultation and, as Ghannouchi claims, also requires freedom of conscience. This is based on Ramadan's reading of the Qur'an's prohibition of compulsion in matters of religion (2:256). Thus, he says, people must have the right to choose their leaders, express their opinions, and live—male and female, Muslim and non-Muslim—under equal protection of the law. The exact forms taken by government must adapt to the circumstances.

What constitutes a just and merciful government in today's world? For Abou El Fadl, as for Ghannouchi, it is one that protects the basic human rights identified by Islam's classical jurists. Traditional interpretations of these rights, however, are no longer tenable. For example, early scholars interpreted the protection of religion as the prohibition of apostasy on punishment of death, and the protection of mind or reason as the prohibition of alcohol. Nowadays, those interpretations would not achieve a just and merciful society. Those rights must be "re-analyzed in light of the current diversity of human existence." In particular, he calls for equal rights for all citizens. Any government that does these things reflects the divine mandate. By recognizing the human responsibility for articulating, executing, and adjudicating that government, divine sovereignty remains intact. In other words, "Democracy . . . offers the greatest potential for promoting justice and protecting human dignity, without making God responsible for human injustice or the degradation of human beings by one another."[121]

These scholars agree not only that Islam is compatible with secular democratic principles, but that Islamic principles demand secular democracy in today's world, although they disagree on the details of the working of democracy. Ramadan says that the role of the scholars may now be taken up by elected assemblies, while Abou El Fadl believes that the scholars should remain an identifiable body and should have only advisory function to Muslim voters. However the details are worked out, these views are typical of such modern Muslim thinkers who call for political participation with non-Muslims to achieve Islamic goals

---

120 Tariq Ramadan, *"The Notion of Shura: Shura or Democracy?"*

121 'Khaled Abou El Fadl, *"Islam and the Challenge of Democracy,"* BostonReview(April-May2003; http://www.bostonreview.net/BR28.2/abou.html (accessed October 2, 2003).

of justice and mercy and who believe that in order for a government to conform to Islamic principles, it must fully and equally protect the rights of Muslims and non-Muslims. That is, as Soroush says, they believe a government does not have to be secular to protect religious pluralism, but it has to be pluralist to be Islamic.

This discussion has argued that there are no essential impediments in Islam to the development of either rationalism or secularism, key components of modernity. However, Western and Islamic experiences of pluralism have diverged in critical ways. Unlike pre-modern Western law, classical Islamic law protected pluralism. As a result, the West's modernity stresses the separation of religion and politics, while voices of modern Islam find that separation unnecessary. While pluralism is considered essential to modern Islamic democracies, secularism as such is not.

Modernity and Democracy in Islam

Since the nineteenth century the question of Islam and modernity has been at the heart of intellectual debates in both the "Muslim" world and the "West." Throughout this time-span three distinct but somewhat analogous strands of debates have emerged. One believes that the religion of Islam is incompatible with modern thinking and scientific rationality. The second posits the opposite view (i.e., a compatibility thesis). A third view posits that there are some elements that can be incorporated, adapted, and adopted by the Islamic world but simultaneously rejects other elements of modernity or deem them as alien. These three views have advocates both within and outside of the "Muslim" world. Their rationale to adopt a particular view may differ; Muslim advocates of the incompatibility thesis would advance their view in the name of cultural "authenticity," while Western counterparts would advance their view in the name of ethnocentricity or secularism.

The efforts in mid-2003 to construct a new political order in Iraq provide an important case in which some of the fundamental issues are highlighted. There was fear that the active participation of the *Shi'a* majority in democratic elections might result in the establishment of a theocracy. It also makes the same assumption made by the Islamic fundamentalists that if something does not fit within the pattern of the medieval canonical synthesis of Islamic thought as reflected in the medieval definitions of the *Shari'a*, it is not "authentically" Islamic.

Iran is a less successful example of efforts to synthesize Islam and democracy. Nevertheless, compared to secular authoritarian regimes of the Middle East, Iran has a good deal of public participation in politics. The ideas of the Iraqi leader Ayatollah Muhammad Baqir al Sadr represent another effort at synthesis. Muslims, in other words, are convinced that there is an Islamic democratic alternative that is neither a copy of Western-style secular-liberal democracy nor the theocracy of Islamist extremists.

Sayyed Abdol Majeed al-Khoei, the *Shi'a* cleric who was murdered in *Najaf* in April 2003, also stated that "if we want to evaluate suitability, or unsuitability, of secularist plans vis-à-vis Muslim countries, a careful revision and scrutiny is necessary for Muslim problems in a way that is altogether different from dealing with those known in Europe. If secularism means a precondition that excludes religion, this is unacceptable . . . . But if secularism is without a precondition, it will then mean pluralism . . . . There is no objection to that."[122] Thus, the challenge is to define a democratic system that does not have the precondition of excluding religion.

"Islam," "democracy," and "modernity" are all contested terms. In many discussions, it is assumed that there is a fixed and single definition of each of these terms. In the old standard format of the debates about the relations between Islam and democracy, the answers were simple and depended on the definitions rather than analysis. However, the more recent conceptualization of the issues can recognize that while Islam, as defined by radical reactionaries, may not be compatible with democracy, Islam and democracy are compatible in the faith and aspirations of most Muslims in the contemporary world.

In the concrete contexts of contemporary Muslim societies, there are many obstacles to creating participatory democratic societies. Some of them are the result of deeply rooted institutions and attitudes. Yet some of the most authoritarian regimes in the Muslim world are neither traditional Muslim regimes nor Islamist in program.

Democracy is an infected wound that the East has been carrying for centuries. Opposition forces have constantly rebelled and tried to kill the leader, and he has always tried to obliterate them. This dance of devil between authority and individuality is for the Muslim repressed.

---

[122] Sayyed Abdol Majid Al Khoei, "Islam and Secularism," islam21 3 (December 1997):14-15.

The West is frightening because it obliges the Muslims to exhume the bodies of all the opponents, both religious and profane, intellectuals and obscure artisans, who were massacred by the caliphs, all those who were condemned, like the Sufis and the philosophers, because, the palace said, they talked about foreign ideas from Greece, India, and ancient Persia.

Since the beginning Muslims have given their lives to pose and solve the question that has remained an enigma up until the present: to obey or to reason, to believe or to think? The West with its insistence on democracy seems to us eminently *gharib*, foreign, because it is a mirror of what frightens us, the world that fifteen centuries have not succeeded in binding: the fact that personal opinion always brings violence. Under the terror of the sword, political despotism has obliged Muslims to defer discussion about responsibility, freedom to think, and the impossibility of blind obedience. That was called the closing of the gates of *ijtihad*, "private initiative".

Throughout its history Islam has been marked by two trends: an intellectual trend that speculated on the philosophical foundations of the world and humanity, and another trend that turned political challenge violent by resort to force. The first tradition was that of the *falasifa*, the Hellenized philosophers, and of the Sufis, who drew from Persian and Indian culture; the second was the *Kharijite* tradition of political subversion.

The two traditions, the *Sufis* and the *Kharijites*, raised the same issues that we are today told are imports from the West, issues that Islam has never resolved: that of *ta'at* (obedience to the *Imam*), and that of individual freedom. Political Islam resolved these issues neither in theory nor in practice, for the idea of representation was never implemented, although the idea that the imam is chosen by the community is deeply rooted in Sunni Islam

Two ways lay open to the Muslims: the way of rebellion taken by the *Kharijites*, which leads to violence and murder; and the way of *'aql*, glorifying reason, which began with the *Mutazila*, the philosophers who intellectualized the political scene. Instead of preaching violence against an unjust *imam* like the *Kharijites*, the *Mu'tazila* held that the thinking individual could serve as a barrier against arbitrary rule. Muslims would use both these approaches at different times, both were extremely important, recurring throughout the centuries. In the modern

140

Islamic world only the violent, rebellious way is being taken by those who loudly proclaim their wish to rule. The rationalist tradition is apparently not part of their Muslim heritage. That is why outlining it and thinking about it is so critical.

In theory, obedience is required only if the *imam* follows the *sharia*, which leads to justice, happiness, harmony, and prosperity. The obedience owed to the *imam* must in no way be considered equal to that owed to God. The *imam* is never infallible in Sunni (orthodox) Islam. This is a fundamental difference between Sunni and Shi'a.

A senior American diplomat enters one of the grand presidential palaces . . . from which president Hosni Mubarak ruled over Egypt . . . Then the American gently raises the issue of human rights and suggests that Egypt's government might ease up on political dissent, allow more press freedoms and stop jailing intellectuals. Mubarak tenses up and snaps, 'If I were to do what you ask, the fundamentalists will take over Egypt. Is that what you want?' The diplomat demurs and the conversation moves back to the last twist in the peace process.

When President Bill Clinton urged Yasir Arafat to sign on the Camp David peace plan[123] in July 2001, Arafat is reported to have responded with words to the effect, 'If I do what you want, *Hamas* will be in power tomorrow.' The Saudi monarchy's most articulate spokesman, Prince Bandar bin Sultan, often reminds American officials that if they press his government too hard, the likely alternative to the regime is not Jeffersonian **democracy** but Islamic theocracy.

In Tunisia, too, (before the current Arab Unrest) Bin Ali has exploited the "Islamist threat" to justify his authoritarian rule. In Jordan, on August 15, 2002, the king postponed the elections until spring 2003 citing "regional circumstances" as an obstacle.[124] Ironically, on August 20 (5

---

[123] Palestinian officials deny that there was a genuine peace deal on offer at Camp David; the Palestinian Minister, Nabil Shaath said in an interview with the Time Magazine: "the Israelis did not offer Palestine on a silver platter. There was no sovereignty over the air, over the sea, over the borders. Nothing for the Palestinian refuges. It was a bum deal" Time Magazine, April 15, 2002, p. 63).

[124] Many observers of Jordanian politics interpret the decision to postpone the election and leave the country without an elected parliament for the period between June 2001 and spring 2003 is attributed to the regime's fear of the opposition (Islamic, Pan-Arab, and Left parties) wining a majority because of the Palestinian and Iraqi crises.

days later) the PM of Jordan said. "difficult regional circumstances must not hamper Kingdom's reforms."[125] The PM'S words are understood as including political reform. Since the dissolution of Jordanian parliament in June 2001, the government introduced more than 100 provisional legislations restricting public freedoms, increasing prices, doubling compulsory insurance on cars among host of other issues. No elected body approved these legislations.[126] The apparent pattern of behavior of the regimes in many Arab Middle Eastern countries is that they use a democratic discourse to justify undemocratic practices. They do everything possible in order to stay in power. The practices of these regimes are the main reason why democratic aspirations in the peoples of the Middle East are not transformed to democratic institutions. One may ask why the peoples of the Middle East do not take action to force the regimes to democratize? There are many important reasons. One important reason is the well-spread fear of security and authorities. To be sure, 79 percent of the Jordanian population reported that they could not criticize the government verbally without fearing economic security and governmental punishment. Moreover, three-quarters could not take part in peaceful political activities (i.e., authorized demonstrations) for the same reasons[127] This evidence suggests that there is more to the story than just culture and religion.

The current surge of revolutions which are going on through Morocco, Algeria, Tunisia, Libya, Egypt, Syria, Yemen, Oman and Jordan are all, but the expression of the age-old clashes between the hereditary rulers and their democratically awakened people.

---

[125] Given the fact that he was brought up and live most of his life in the U.K. and United States, the king was perceived to be a democratic ruler, but his endorsement of his government recommendation to postpone the elections twice evaporated the hopes of most of those who had hoped that he will enhance democracy in Jordan.

[126] Muslims and Democracy in International Journal of Comparative Sociology; Dec. 2002; p.269;

[127] Center for Strategic Studies 2002.

THE ISLAMIC RESURGENCE

The fundamental spiritual crisis of Islam in the twentieth and twenty-first century stems from an awareness that something is wrong between the religion of Islam and the historical development of the world. The problem of modern Muslim is how to rehabilitate that history: to set it going again in full vigor, so that Islamic society may once again flourish as a divinely guided society.

Will they perhaps leave it as an ambiguous tradition, its adherents torn between a loyalty within and a world without—a loyalty that they cherish but do not know quite how to apply, and a world by which they find themselves surrounded but with which they do not know quite how to cope? Or will they perhaps emotionalize it into a closed system, by which they retreat from modernity into a fanaticism of crippling isolationist violence? Or will they construe it into an open, rich, onward vision, an effective inspiration for truly modern living: bringing themselves spiritual integrity and fulfillment, and their society's progress, justice, and honor in the world? Such questions, we believe, will turn not only the religious but also the worldly welfare of the Muslim people. Worldly problems cannot be solved by men whose ideological and moral outlook is seriously inappropriate to their solution. The economic, political, military, demographic, and other kinds of question that unrelentingly press on each of the various Muslim nations cannot be under-estimated by anyone familiar with the area or concerned with the welfare of its people. It would be absurd to belittle these issues. Yet for Muslims, none of them is more consequential than the religious question. Indeed, all go hand in hand. While Islam in each locality moves in conjunction with the life of its community, the world around persists in marching too.

The Wahhabiyah Movement.

The first Islamic movements to rehabilitate history in the modern period were protests against the internal deterioration. They called a halt to decadence, summoning Muslim society back to its first purity and order. One of the earliest of these, and the most major was the *Wahhabiyah*[128] *movement in eighteenth century Arabia. It was puritanical, vigorous, and simple. Its message was straightforward: a return to classical Islam. It rejected the corruption and laxity of his contemporary Arab society. It rejected the accommodations and cultural richness of the mediaeval empire. It rejected the warmth and piety of the mystic way. It rejected also the alien intellectualism not only of philosophy but of theology. It rejected all dissensions, even the then well-established Shi'a domination. It insisted solely on the Law. The classical Law, said the Wahhabis,* is the sum and substance of the faith—and in its most rigid *Hanbali* version, stripped of all innovations developed through the intervening centuries. Obey the pristine Law, fully, strictly, singly; and establish a society where that Law obtains. This is Islam, they preached. All else is superfluous and wrong. Apart from preaching, they set out to establish that society—to bend early life once more to the classical purposes of God. The founder, Muhammad Ibn Abd al-Wahhab,[129] (1703-1787) effected an alliance with a local

---

[128] For an analytical and critical bibliography of the Wahhabi movement, see the master's thesis in the library of the Institute of Islamic Studies, McGill University, Montreal: Hisham A. Nashshabah, "Islam and Naitonalism in the Arab World: a selected and annotated bibliography". 1955, pp.7-26 and the original work of Muhammad ibn Abd al-Wahhab, published by the Maktabat al-Nahdah al-Ilmiyah at-Sa'udiyah, *Makkah*.

[129] Muhammad Ibn Abdal Wahhab, born in the city of *Unaynah* in 1703, got his early education from his father, later from Muslim scholars in Basra, Makkahh and Madina. Like most scholars in Najd, Saudi Arabia, at the time, Ibn Abd-al-Wahhab was a follower of Ibn Hanbal's school of jurisprudence but condemned *taqlid*. He returned his hometown in 1740 and began to attract his followers including the ruler of *Unaynah*. He persuaded the ruler of his town, to level the grave of a companion of the Prophet, Zayd Ibn al-Khattab, who was highly revered by the locals. Secondly, he ordered an adulteress be stoned to death, a practice that had become uncommon in the area by that time. These actions gained the attention of the surrounding rulers. The chief of Al-Hasa and Qateef who held substantial influence in Najd, threatened Ibn Mu'ammar that he would not allow him to collect a land tax for some properties that he owned in al-Hasa if he did not kill ibn 'Abd al-Wahhab. Ibn Mu'ammar declined to do this, but ibn 'Abd al-Wahhab was forced to leave. Foremost among his detractors were his own father and brother. Upon his expulsion from 'Unaynah, Ibn Abd al-Wahhab was invited to settle

ruling prince, Muhammad Ibn Sa'ud (d.1765) so that theory and practice should go hand in hand.

They were able to hew for themselves in the desert a community that should carry forward the divine program. Their isolation allowed them to execute their experiment relatively undistracted. Not until the 1930's, with the discovery of oil and consequent rise of modern technology and modernity on their borders, was the career of their reversionary social order seriously interrupted.

Shah Waliyullah of Delhi (1703-1762)[130] was promoter of one of the purification movements who rejected the degeneration of post-classical Islam but not rejecting its achievements. He grew up watching the Moghal empire crumble. Unlike Ibn Abd al-Wahhab, he thought and worked from within one of the passing mediaeval empires, rather than outside. He would refashion and revive rather than reject. His Islam is therefore more comprehensive and richer than the Wahhabis; also more flexible. He would, for instance, embrace and enliven all the schools of law in his new amalgam. He accepted more Islamic development. He was more mediaeval than classical. His political ambition was to restore Muslim power in India more or less on the Moghul pattern. It was the next century before some of his reform ideas were organized

---

in neighboring town Dir'iyya by its ruler Muhammad ibn Saud in 1740. Upon arriving in Diriyya, a pact was made between Ibn Saud and Ibn Abd al-Wahhab, by which Ibn Saud pledged to implement Ibn Abd al-Wahhab's teachings and enforce them on his and his neighboring towns. Beginning in the last years of the 18th century Ibn Saud and his heirs (The House of Saud) would spend the next 140 years mounting various academic and military campaigns to seize control of Arabia and its outlying regions, finally taking control of the whole of modern day Kingdom of Saudi Arabia in 1922. This provided the movement with a state. Vast wealth from oil discovered in the following decades, coupled with Saudi control of the holy cities of Makkahh and Madina, have since provided a base and funding for Salafi missionary activity. The current Saudi minister of justice and the current grand mufti of Saudi Arabia are also descendents of Ibn Abd al-Wahhab.

[130] For a bibliography, see the master's thesis in the library of the Institute of Islamic Studies, McGill University: Mo'inuddin Ahmad Khan, "A Bibliographical Introduction to Modern Islamic Developments in India and Pakistan", 1955; and Maulana Abdur Rahman's introduction to his Urdu translation of Shah Waliyullah's greatest work, Hujjatullah al-Balighah, Lahore, 2 vols. 1953.

into socio-political movements, to some extent, under the leadership of his son, Abdul Aziz (1746-1824) and his grandson, Ismail (1781-1831). By this time the decline of Indo-Muslim society had gone until further, where the weakness was of course attracting aggressive outside powers, such as Sikh regime in the North-west, British East India Company in Bengal and revival of Hindu power in western India. Accordingly, one finds this movement for Islamic regeneration expressing itself in two directions: against internal decay, and against external threat or domination. Some of those inspired by the new emphasis wrote and wrought against the abuses in Muslim society. Others preached and fought against its new infidel rulers. The rise of Sayyid Ahmad Barelawi (1782-1831) and the failure of his martial exploits against the Sikhs in the Punjab; the *Faraiziyah* movement of Bengal and the 1857 Mutiny of India can be seen as attempts to reinstate the old Muslim dominance. The dream of revival of Muslim political power remained into the twentieth century to haunt the community.

However local, these nineteenth-century Indian movements might be in the details of their particular development, in this they were typical of the whole Muslim world, recognizing and trying to reject corrosion within and aggression without. The latter has remained through a hundred and fifty years a dominating threat to Islamic society: pressing on different areas with differing force, in varying forms, but in essence it's constant. Almost every Islamic movement, in almost every part of the Muslim world, throughout that period has been in some way a variation on this double theme.

Al-Afghani. These two tendencies—internal reform and external defense—are typified and fused in a person whose outstanding figure is central to the nineteenth century Muslim world, Jamal ad-Din al-Afghani (1839-1897)[131]. Since he was reputed also for his classical Islamic learning, he may be said to represent the traditional Islam as well. In fact, he is supremely comprehensive, the complete Muslim of his time.

---

[131] For a partial bibliography, see Hisham A. Nashshabah thesis, "Islam and Nationalism in the Arab World: a selected and annotated bibliography", 1955; and Sharif al-Mujahid, "Sayyid Jamal al-Din al-Afghani: His Role in the Nineteenth century Muslim Awakenning", 1954, Karachi, Pakistan.

Geographically, his career encompassed Iran, India, Turkey, the Arab world as well as the European West. He was both Sufi and Sunni and preached reconciliation with Shi'a. He was himself active in both internal reform and external defense. He inspired political revolutionaries and venerable scholars. He advocated both local nationalism and pan-Islam. A very great deal of subsequent Islamic development is adumbrated in his personality and career. By Afghani's time the internal inadequacies were more pronounced, and the inner penetration and outer pressure of Europe had both proceeded much further. He realized that the entire Islamic world, not just this or that part of it, was threatened; and by the West as a powerful, dynamic entity. He saw that in comparison with the European entity, the entire Islamic world was weak. He realized that in a sense the Islamic world was threatened by its own weaknesses.

We cannot follow the detail, but must give due weight to the substance of his direct political agitation against European imperialism, particularly British, to which Afghani devoted himself in London, Paris, and at home. It was zealous and telling. He seems to have been the first Muslim revivalist to use the concepts, "Islam" and "the West" as antagonistic historical phenomena. This antinomy has since become quite standard in virtually all Islamic rhetoric. It would be fruitful and revealing to explore the growth in the Muslim consciousness of the specter of the West as an accusing, menacing power. It was in Afghani that this menace became explicit; and later Khomeini's revolution in Iran became active on this slogan.

In addition to internal reform and external defense, his re-calling of erstwhile Muslim grandeur has become a third dominant trait of modern Islam. The activism that characterized him has been a marked quality of the subsequent Islamic development since. It was given more or less explicit formulation by the poet Iqbal, and practical embodiment in numerous movements, such as the *Ikhwan* (Brotherhood) in the Arab world, the *Khaksar* in India, the *Kashani* in Iran, the *Darul Islam* in Indonesia, for instance. In fact, it has colored a very great deal of modern Islam, whose renascence has been more ebullient than thoughtful, and indeed has been aimed more at recapturing the vitality than at redefining the content or even the methods of faith.

Later Developments:

Later development of the trends—reactivation and reform within and defense without—was vigorous and widespread. Much of it was directly or indirectly related to the *Wahhabis*, *Waliyullah* and *Afghani*. Some was more or less parallel and independent. But all, of course, was complex. It would be false to oversimplify recent Islamic moves, constraining them into a neat common pattern. At the same time it is misleading to omit from the specifics of each the generalized Islamic form and impulse which relate them to the until living past and to each other.

Of the active group endeavor, one might mention the *Sanusi* movement in Libya in 1842, the *Mahdi* movement in the Sudan from 1881, the Irani movements of 1890's, the *Sarekat* Islam and the *Muhammadiyah* in Indonesia from 1911, the Indian *Khilafat* movement in 1918-1924, and so on. Each local manifestation has had its own immediate causes, in the economic, political, and other factors of the particular area. Yet each also fits into a total pattern such as aspiration towards a revival of Islamic glory and more particularly as aspects of the vast protest against internal decline and external encroachment. These are political, organizational, or mass movements which were all directed toward that historical nostalgia, the dream of ancient glory. This trait has been much developed throughout the Muslim world since.

THE RISE OF RADICALS

Introduction

During the 1950s and 1960s, radical Sunni Muslim thinkers, especially in Egypt (where the Muslim Brotherhood had been active since 1928), managed to fuse their sense of pessimism with political activism, turning their desperation into a plan of action. Spurred by the soul-searching that followed the Arab world defeats at the hands of Israel in 1948 and 1967, the radicals shaped a new, more radical Islamist ideology calling for revolutions and violence. They saw the ills of their society resulted from the fact that the Arab world had become a land of apostasy and profanation. During this period, Islamists developed the idea that the war against Israel was not the true, meaningful *Jihad*. In order to defeat Zionism, a holy war first had to be waged against the forces that had brought Islam to its current state of decline. This war had to be fought against the Arab world'σ secular, apostate, nationalistic regimes.

During the next twenty years, radical Muslims concentrated on fighting their regimes. They directed their violence not only against the leaders of those states (the assassination of Egyptian president Anwar Sadat in 1981, for example), but also against the state-appointed religious establishment and the nations; economic interests (including attacks on Western tourists, which were meant to destroy the local tourism industries). Arab regimes have been doing battle against radical Muslims since the 1950s. Arab governments threw many of them in jail, in some cases torturing and even executing their leaders.

A turning point in this struggle was the execution, of Sayyid Qutb in 1966 one of the key leaders of the Muslim Brotherhood. Qutb, a literary critic and educator, developed in the 1940s and 1950s many of the ideas of radical Islam that until guide the movement today. As a young man, Qutb was drawn to the ideas of pan-Arab nationalism, the notion that all Arabs should be united under one rule. In fact, prior to the 1956 revolution, he befriended Gamal Abdul Nasser, the eventual Egyptian president, who even attended some of Qutb's lectures. Coming later to the conclusion that nationalism alone could not provide sufficient answers to the ills of Arab society, Qutb turned to radical Islam. Qutb was sentenced to death after serving several prolonged jail sentences during which he suffered unthinkable abuses.

Qutb's teachings continued to inspire Sunni radicals years after his execution. Among other violent acts inspired by Qutb's words of hate, his pupils assassinated President Sadat in October 1981 and made several attempts on the life of President Hosni Mubarak. "I have killed the Pharaoh", declared the young Muslim radicals who killed Sadat, but even the assassin's bullets failed to destroy the repressive Arab states.

In 1990s, Sunni radicals turned their attention away from the destruction of Arab regimes, which had been their main concern since the 1940s and 1950s, and abandoned their hopes to transform their own societies. Their expectations of eventual victory for Islam and their personal sacrifices, jail terms, piety, and acts of violence toward that end had been of no avail. Even the Islamic revolution in Iran failed to reverse the tide. Obstinate Islamic movements were defeated in Algeria, Tunisia, and Egypt. Even Saudi Arabia, the most religiously orthodox Arab state, chose to suppress its radical Muslim opponents.

The turning point in this process of rethinking strategy was the Persian Gulf War. The rage and resentment toward the West—long present in the Middle East—became much more pronounced. For the Muslim world, not only was America now directly meddling in internal Arab affairs, but as the dominant power in the world, it was spreading sedition in the region, turning one Arab regime against another. Their new partnership with the West made them seem invincible. To overpower these states and cleanse them, radical Islam would first have to defeat the American and their allied patrons.

Therefore, to bring Islam back to the realm, the region would first have to be cleansed of the infidels. Thus the first step in sanitizing the Middle East from the apostasy that was polluting it would be to declare war on America. There was American presence in Saudi Arabia in the 1990s, including the bombing in Riyadh in November 1995 and the attack on the Khobar Towers in Dhahran in June 1996, the bombing of the American embassies in Tanzania and Kenya in 1998, and the attack on the USS Cole in Yemen in October 2000. There was even a failed dress rehearsal for the events of September 11, in the 1993 attack on the World Trade Center, led by Rahman. The sheik, who had been previously implicated in the murder of Sadat, had found asylum in New Jersey. Radical Islam was not only fighting the West, but it was also learning to use the freedoms of the West against its host.

But Middle Eastern violence is not turned only against Western targets. Much of it, in fact, is a broad resignation born of recognition of its own tyranny, poverty and shortcomings. In turn, most of that violence is a result of pervasive brutality employed by governments and turned inwards, against the impoverished and oppressed people of the Arab world. Its targets are mostly the Arab youth, and more recently even pre-adolescence children.

The Palestinian war has become a cult which normalizes death and terror. The homicide bombers do not die a patriotic death. Life is not sacrificed for the protection and defense of Arab or Palestinian interests. Indeed, no borders are protected, no enemy, real or imagined, will be defeated. Killing oneself in order to spread fear in the hearts of one's enemies and targeting civilian population will not win the war, or even a specific battle. At best, it will spread terror and create a new Arab national ethos of a questionable nature. This is an ethos whose only myth is that of young people and children who were talked into dying a dishonorable death for the sake of regimes that declared war against their own people; regimes that inflame the fire of hate and beat the drums of war so that their people will not declare their own war against them.

A peculiar partnership, a common interest, arose between the repressive regimes of the Middle East and the repressed, often radical Muslim opposition. For the regimes, directing Arab resentment outward and co-opting the message of the radicals would successfully channel local fervor and bitterness toward the West and Israel and stifle the potential re-emergence of domestic assassinations and terror that could be directed against the regimes. While many Arab regimes crushed their opposition ruthlessly, they did little to address the conditions that fueled its fervor, namely the failure of their corrupt and repressive form of governance. Fomenting anti-Western and anti-Israel sentiments was thus a matter of survival for these failed, incorrigible regimes, a way of riding the tiger and deflecting the growing resentment among their impoverished, oppressed populations. In essence, the very regimes that the West considered friends—such as Saudi Arabia, the Palestinian Authority, Egypt, and

Syria—decided to blow the fire of hate, to encourage anti-Semitic and anti-Western sentiments among their people.

Supporting and aiding terror was not only a matter of survival for many Arab regimes, it was also a tool used to tighten their grip on their populations and stave off revolution. These regimes had good reason for concern. The dictators of Syria, Iraq, and even Egypt, all of whom came to power as a result of military coups, decided in the mid-1990s to turn their revolutionary republics into dynastic monarchies. Anti-Americanism provided these regimes with a cloak behind which to hide their true designs for both their families and their societies. So anti-western violence and war became tools used frequently by Arab regimes in order to guarantee their staying in power.

This is part of a region-wide drift toward an explosion which has much more to do with the nature of the regimes and leaders of the region than it was about specific grievances over U.S. or Israeli policy.

Not only Arafat, but also the leadership of the PLO is entirely dependent on confrontation for survival and political identity. As Palestinian society descended into political enslavement, it remained entwined with a vibrant, free democracy—Israel. Part of the PLO's conflict with Israel is the unavoidable conflict between a nation symbolizing freedom and a regime extinguishing it. The regime rightly sees a danger, if not existential threat, in the example of a free nation. So it lashes out at the free nation to destroy it as a form of twisted self-defense.

The same is true of Syria, another terror master who engages in violence against the West in order to starve off revolution. Like many other regimes in the region, Syria is becoming more, not less, oppressive of its own population. After President Bashar Al-Assad came to power in July 2000, many in Syria believed that a new dawn, an age of greater openness might be awaiting Syrian society.

If we look at the politics of the region as a whole, in other words, what we see is an epidemic of tyranny. Arab autocracies encourage violence domestically by blocking peaceful change, and export violence by using state-controlled media to deflect demands for accountability with propaganda against the United states, Jews, or the West. Therefore, our war against terror must be a war against tyranny. Only when we bring freedom and orderly politics to the region it will cease being a threat to the well-being of the West.

Al-Qaida and the 9/11

On September 11, 2001, 19 Muslim hijackers took over four U.S. domestic flights, successfully crashing two of the planes into the World Trade Center two towers and one into the Pentagon building. The fourth flight, believed to be intended for Washington, D.C. target, crashed in rural Pennsylvania after passengers overpowered the hijackers. The September 11 hijackings are unquestionably the most devastating terrorist attacks on the United States to date. Terrorist organizations—chiefly al-Qaeda—carried out attacks on the U.S. and its allies throughout the last few years of the twentieth century. The 1993 World Trade Center bombing by Al—Qaeda was the first of many terrorist attacks upon Americans during this period. Subsequent attacks included the 1996 Khobar Towers bombing in Saudi Arabia, and the 1998 bombings of US embassies in Tanzania and Kenya. Also in 1998 came the World Islamic Front declaration of 23 February 1998, entitled "*Jihad* Against Jews and Crusaders", which stated the Front's "ruling to kill the Americans and their allies—civilians and military—is an individual duty for every Muslim who can do it in any country in which it is possible to do it." Led by Osama bin Laden, Al-Qaeda formed a large base of operations in Afghanistan, which had been ruled by the Islamic extremist regime of the Taliban since 1996. In October of 2000 the USS Cole bombing occurred, followed by the September 11 attacks. The attacks of 9/11 created an immediate demand throughout the United States for a decisive response, leading to an invasion of Afghanistan which removed the Taliban from power and ended al-Qaeda's use of the country as a terrorist base.

What made the Sept. 11 attack possible—and so unexpected and terrifying—was the willingness of suicide terrorists to die to accomplish their mission. September 11 was monstrous and shocking in scale, and unique in modality. For more than twenty years, terrorist groups have been increasingly relying on suicide attacks to achieve major political objectives. "From 1980 to 2003 terrorists across the globe waged seventeen separate campaigns of suicide attacks, including those by Hezbollah to drive the United States, French and Israeli forces out of Lebanon; by Palestinian terrorist groups to force Israel to abandon the West Bank and Gaza; by the Liberation Tigers of Tamil Eelam (the Tamil Tigers) to compel the Sri Lankan government to accept an independent Tamil homeland; and by al-Qaeda to pressure the United States to withdraw its combat troops from the land of the two holy mosques, Saudi Arabia."[132]

Foreign occupation and national resistance, more than the religious differences are the main factors leading to the rise of terrorist campaigns. In the case of al-Qaeda versus the United States, there is a religious difference between the rivals and no doubt that the United States is a democracy having an open society, more congenial for terrorist activities. American military presence, defined as heavy combat operations on the homeland of Muslim majority countries for a sustained period prior to the onset of al-Qaeda's suicide terrorist campaign against the United States in 1995 seems to be the standard cause for terrorist campaigns.

This standard comports with the meaning of "occupation". It defines American military presence from the perspective of the terrorists, who are likely to fear the possibility that foreign control may be imposed by force and to suspect that security guarantees to the autocratic rule actually may indicate American intention to defend the regime against revolution. This is Osama bin Ladin's view of the role of US troops on the Arabian Peninsula; although it is not the perspective of the United States, which, in most of the relevant cases, would see itself as supporting a friendly government. In his famous 1998 fatwa, *"Jihad Against Jews and Crusaders,"* Osama bin Laden asserted:

" . . . For over seven years the United States has been occupying the lands of Islam in the holiest of places, the Arabian Peninsula, plundering its riches, dictating to its rulers, humiliating its people, terrorizing its neighbors, and turning its bases in the Peninsula into a spearhead through which to fight the neighboring Muslim peoples. We issue the following *fatwa* to all Muslims: The ruling to kill the Americans and their allies—civilians and military—is an individual duty for every Muslim who can do it in any country in which it is possible to do, in order to liberate the al-Aqsa Mosque and the holy mosque (*Makkahh*) from their grip, and in order for their armies to move out of all the lands of Islam, defeated and unable to threaten any Muslim."[133]

---

[132] Pape, Robert A., *"Dying to Win: The Strategic Logic of Suicide Terrorism."* Random House, New York. P.5

[133] Osama's Fatwa in World Islamic Front Statement, *"Jihad Against Jews and Crusaders"*, Feb. 23, 1998.

By this standard, Saudi Arabia, Oman, the United Arab Emirates, Bahrain, Kuwait, Qatar, and Turkey all qualify, because the United States has stationed combat troops on the soil of each, or in adjacent countries, continuously since 1990. Afghanistan and Uzbekistan also qualify, since the US has stationed combat troops on their soil since 2001.

Further, al-Qaeda's suicide terrorists from Egypt, Pakistan, Morocco and Indonesia are associated either with efforts to topple the national government or with national liberation movements to establish greater political autonomy for local Muslim populations. In Egypt, Islamic militants have used violence in attempts to overthrow the local government, including the assassination of President Anwar al-Sadat in 1981 and the attempted assassination of President Hosni Mubarak in 1995.[134] In Pakistan, former President Pervez Musharraf has faced numerous assassination attempts since joining America's war on terrorism in 2001.[135] From 1999 to 2001, Indonesian Muslim militias waged an intense campaign of indiscriminate violence to stop East Timor, a predominately Catholic region, from gaining independence.[136]

Understanding that suicide terrorism is mainly a response to foreign occupation and/or causes of national liberation, rather than the product of Islamic fundamentalism, have important implications for how the United States and its allies should conduct the war on terrorism. Since the root cause of suicide terrorism does not lie in an ideology, even among Muslims, spreading democracy across the Persian Gulf is not likely to be a feasible solution so long as foreign combat troops remain on the Arabian Peninsula. Thus, the question is: can we find a lasting solution to suicide terrorism that does not compromise our core interest in maintaining access to one of the world's key oil-producing regions?

Suicide attacks of Sunni factions to Shi'a and vice versa in Iraq are not instigated by the Islamic fundamentalism. Similarly, the suicide attacks by Kurdish freedom fighters in the southeastern Turkey[137] are

---

[134] Nachman Tal, "Islamic Terrorism in Egypt," appeared in *Strategic Assessment* (Tel Aviv), vol.1, No.1 (March, 1998).

[135] *"Pakistan: Country Report"* (London: Home Offi ce, United Kingdom, Oct. 2004).

[136] *"The Roots of Jama'a Islamiyah";* (CNN: Feb. 26, 2004).

[137] Sunday, July 27, 2008. News from Istanbul, Turkey-Two bombs exploded minutes apart in an Istanbul square packed with people Sunday night, killing 13 and injuring

not caused by the Islamic fundamentalism. The Shi'a-Sunni conflict in Iraq is an ethnic struggle for supremacy of political power and resources while the later is the Kurdish fighting for freedom and self-rule.

Proponents claim that Islamic fundamentalism is the principal cause of suicide terrorism and that this radical ideology is spreading throughout Muslim societies, dramatically increasing the prospects for a new, larger generation of anti-American terrorists in the future. Hence, the US should install new governments in Muslim countries in order to transform and diminish the role of radical Islam in their societies. This logic led to widespread support for the conquest of Iraq and Afghanistan and is promoted as the principal reason for regime change in Iran, Saudi Arabia, and other Persian Gulf states in the future.

While the goal of this strategy is correct, its premise is faulty. American security depends critically on diminishing the next generation of anti-American Muslim terrorists. However, Islamic fundamentalism is not the main cause of suicide terrorism, and conquering Muslim countries to transform their societies is likely to increase the number coming at us. The stationing of tens of thousands of American combat troops on the Arabian Peninsula from 1990 onward make al-Qaeda suicide attacks against Americans, as declared in bin Laden's 1998 *fatwa*, including the horrible crimes committed on 9/11, from five to twenty times more likely. Hence, the longer American troops remain in Iraq and in the Persian Gulf in general, the greater the risk of the next Sep.11.

The idea that all Muslims around the world are anti-American because Islam encourages hatred for American values for democracy and free markets does not square with the facts. Indeed, robust evidence shows that American foreign policies, not revulsion against Western political and economic values, are driving anti-Americanism among Muslims. Significant numbers of Muslim migrants from fundamentalist Muslim countries to Europe and America negates this hate theory.

The underlying reason is not discontent with Western political or economic values. Rather, the taproot is American foreign policy toward Middle Eastern countries. "Overwhelming majorities across a range

---

about 70 in what the city governor said was a terror attack. Kurdish rebels belonging to the Kurdistan Workers' Party, or PKK, have been fi ghting for self-rule in southeastern Turkey since 1984. The violence has killed tens of thousands of people since then.

of Muslim countries believe that the United States conquered Iraq to control its oil or to help Israel rather than to end terrorism or promote democracy, and they fear that their country might be next."[138]

The idea that Islamic fundamentalism is on the verge of world domination and poses a realistic threat to impose Islamic laws in the United States and Europe is pure fantasy. Some radicals may harbor such delusions. But these are delusions nonetheless. The United States and Europe are overwhelmingly Christian countries and will remain so.

Osama bin Laden was fighting a war with the USA, in the same way as the USA was later fighting a War on Terror. War of any kind has its own moral rather no moral of common practices of our society. It has its own rules and practices which are in contrast with the norm of our society. The following incidence pushed Osama to wage war with the United States:

In 1970, the PLO was expelled from Jordan, in what was known as the Black September. Large numbers of Palestinians moved into Lebanon after the Black September, joining the thousands already there. Tensions between Israel and PLO led Israel to invade Lebanon in the 1982 forcing the PLO to withdraw again, this time to Tunisia. During the war, Israeli allies Phalangists committed the Sabra and Shatila massacre, and around 3500 unarmed Palestinians were killed by the Phalange while the Israeli troops surrounded the camps with tanks and checkpoints, monitoring entrances and exits.

"God knows it did not cross our minds to attack the towers, but after the situation we saw in Lebanon became unbearable—and we witnessed the injustice and tyranny of the American-Israeli alliance against our people in Palestine and Lebanon—I thought about it. And the events that affected me directly were that of 1982 and the events that followed—when America allowed the Israelis to invade Lebanon, helped by the U.S. Sixth Fleet. *As watched the destroyed towers in Lebanon, it occurred to me, punish the unjust the same way: to destroy towers in America so it could taste some of what we are tasting and to stop killing our children and women."*[139]

---

[138] Pape, Robert A., *"Dying to Win: The Strategic Logic of Suicide Terrorism."* Random House, New York; p.244.

[139] The Guardian (London), Oct. 30, 2004. The emphasis is author's.

But this act of terror by Osama reversed into more killings of men, women and children by the United States in the name of War on Terror in many states of Africa and Middle East, including Iraq and Afghanistan. War leaves no victors, only victims. By this equation none is innocent.

Osama is dead, but the cause he upheld is *not*. Others will take his place and may already have. If the world is to prevent the rise of more Osamas, it must change its strategy to the festering cancer of injustices and oppressions in the Middle East and elsewhere. Now that the so-called architect of 9/11 is gone, the US should have no business in Afghanistan-Pakistan, Iraq and elsewhere. Bin Laden has taken with him to his watery grave the West's raison d'être for its imperial project.

Radicalism in Egypt

Recently, on Sunday, Oct.9, 2011, 25 people were killed, mainly Coptic Christians and more than 300 injured when a protest demonstration by Copts was attacked by the army and thugs, sparking furious condemnation of the leadership's handling of the transition from Hosni Mubarak's rule. Copts were protesting on Sunday against a recent attack in which a renovated village church was attacked in the southern province of Aswan.

The local government in Egypt continued rounding up the Christians, including men, women and children in groups of 50 to 60 at a time. They were tied to doors and beaten, and women and children were tortured with electric shock devices to all parts of their bodies, according to the letter from Bishop Wissa. One 11-year-old boy, Roman Boctor, was hung upside down from an electric ceiling fan and tortured as the fan rotated. Police attempted to rape his 14-year-old sister, Hania, at the police station but her screams drew a crowd and the police stopped.[140]

Since two Christians were killed, on Aug. 14, 1998, around 1,200 Christians from the Al-Kosheh region near Luxor in Upper Egypt have been arrested and many of them tortured, according to the Egyptian Organization for Human Rights.

Bishop *Anba Wissa*, the Coptic spiritual leader of the El-Baliana region, and his priests made official complaints Aug. 19 and 20 to Lt. Said, a Secret Police inspector; to the governor of the Sohag District; and to the chief of the Department of Security. The police chief told them that

---

[140] "Egypt's Christians"; A Washington Times Editorial 11/4/98

the persecution would get worse as a result of the complaints, according to a letter from *Bishop Wissa* obtained by The Washington Times.

Eyewitnesses have reported that a green Skoda car pulled up outside the Coptic Church in Cairo shortly after midnight. Two men got out; one of them made a short phone conversation then left the scene. The explosion occurred almost immediately thereafter. The car carried a bumper sticker with the words "the rest is coming". At the time of the blast, several thousand Coptic Christians were attending midnight prayer service at the church at the occasion of the New Year for 2011. The explosion resulted in scattered body parts, destroyed cars and smashed windows.[141] 23 Coptic Christians were killed immediately following the explosion, and about 97 people—most of whom Christians—were injured.[142] This was the deadliest act of violence against Egypt's Christian minority in a decade, since the *Kosheh* massacre in 2000 that left 21 Copts dead. In the months prior to the massacre, the religious ambiance in Egypt had been clouded by anti-Christian propaganda, in particular regarding the public allegations that the Coptic Orthodox Church was storing weapons in churches and monasteries.[143] *Al-Awa* also accused the Coptic Church of holding 2 Christian women who supposedly converted to Islam as hostages. A wave of Muslim protests against Copts followed these allegations, including calls to boycott Coptic businesses and products. The Synod of Coptic priests in Alexandria described these allegations as "anti-Christian mobilization and lies." Hours before the explosion, Salafi Muslims held demonstrations in front of Alexandria's *Al Qa'ed Gohar* Mosque against the Coptic Orthodox Church and against Pope Shenouda III, repeating the Iraqi Al-Qaeda threats against Egypt's Coptic Orthodox Church.

Nigeria

During the last three weeks of June, several churches were burned, shops and homes looted and Christian property destroyed in *Yelwa Shendam*. Christians were chased out of the town and were forced to

---

[141] "Egypt bomb kills 21 at Alexandria Coptic church". *BBC News Online*. 1Jan. 2011. http://www.bbc.co.uk/news/world-middle-east-12101748.

[142] Ibid.

[143] Al Jazeera. September 15, 2010. http://www.aljazeera.net/NR/exeres/65471152-9030-4350-9448-79714469B785.htm. Retrieved September 22, 2010.

take refuge in *Jos*. Christians in the Plateau State of central Nigeria have been killed and forced from their land by extremist Islamic militants.

Attacks have been mounted against Christians in the area surrounding *Jos*, leaving several dead and many more wounded and displaced.[144]

Samuel Yunana's father, *Fayam*, was taken from his home, stabbed in the side of the stomach and told to convert to Islam. When he refused, his throat was slit. *Fayam* was among more than 700 people killed in the northern Nigerian city of *Maiduguri* during an uprising last week by a radical Islamic sect which wants *shari'a* (Islamic law) imposed across Africa's most populous nation.[145]

On December 25, 2009, *Umar Farouk Abdulmutallab*, a Muslim from northern Nigeria, attempted to blow up a crowded Northwest Airlines flight en route from Amsterdam to Detroit. This act of terrorism shines a spotlight on a growing culture of Muslim radicalization in Africa's most populous country.

Central and Northern Nigeria are feeling the brunt of this radicalization. Both Christians and Muslims in these areas have been victimized by warring militias, each claiming God's favor. More than 300 people were killed in a Christian-Muslim conflict that started on January 17, in *Jos*, Nigeria. *Jos* was also at the center of a similar crisis in 2008 that resulted in over 500 deaths.

In July 2009, *Boko Haram*, an Islamic extremist group, carried out attacks in Northern Nigerian states in which over 700 people were killed. One of *Boko Haram's* stated objectives is to impose strict Islamic law nationwide, including in the Christian-majority south. In the Northern Nigerian city of *Bauchi*, the Islamic sect *Izala* carried out targeted attacks against Christians, resulting in eleven deaths and over 3,000 persons displaced. The escalating violence has caused a state of humanitarian crisis in Nigeria.

For a first-hand account of the situation, the Hudson Institute and International Christian Concern co-sponsored **Reverend** *John Joseph Hayab's* appearance in Washington. Rev. *Hayab*, whose work is dedicated to peaceful reconciliation efforts, is founder of the Christian Awareness Initiative, a human rights organization focused on religious

---

144 Christian Solidarity World Wide, July 18 2002

145 MAIDUGURI, Nigeria | Mon Aug 3, 2009 11:24am EDT (Reuters).

reconciliation, and serves as head of the Kaduna State Christian Association of Nigeria. In his presentation, he addressed underlying factors contributing to Nigeria's Islam-Christian conflict and the situation of religious minorities.

Indonesia

No armed guards, no attempt to hide. Abu Bakr Baasyir, 71 years old, lives in a modest one-story home on the campus of the boarding school he helped found in the quiet village of *Ngruki*, amid the central highlands of the main Indonesian island of *Java*. He is the alleged spiritual leader of the militant Islamist group *Jemaah Islamiyah,* linked to at least a half dozen bombings in Indonesia over the last decade, including the devastating 2002 Bali nightclub blasts and, perhaps, the suicide bombings at Jakarta luxury hotels this past summer.[146]

Indonesia is the most populous Muslim country in the world, home to 207 million Muslims, and two-thirds larger than as many as all the countries of the Middle East combined. It is extremely devout; a recent Pew Global Attitudes survey found Indonesia as one of the world's most religious nations. It's also a thriving democracy, the third largest after India and United States. But it's a new democracy, until finding its legs—little more than a decade has passed since the country's virtual dictator, Suharto, was ousted. The end of his rule granted Indonesia new freedoms of expression, though it also unleashed radicals like *Baasyir*.

A year after the 2002 Bali bombings came the first Marriott hotel bombing in Jakarta, then in 2004 a strike on the Australian Embassy, also in Jakarta, and in 2005 a triple suicide attack, again in Bali. And just a few months ago from now, after a long gap, came the bombings at the Ritz-Carlton Hotel and once more the Marriott. These are scattered events in a vast nation. But in the words of one Indonesian proverb, "it takes just a little poison to spoil all the milk."[147]

Indeed, Indonesia's 17,500 islands can feel, at times, like so many marbles on a wobbly table. A subtle tilt and they'll all roll in one direction. For several decades, Indonesian society had been growing more overtly Islamic: Attendance at mosques swelled, and Muslim

---

[146] National Geographic Magazine INDONESIA: By Michael Finkel, Oct. 2009; p. 85.

[147] Ibid. p. 86.

dress became popular. In the late 1990s a growing number of district governments began enacting regulations inspired by *shari'a*, or Islamic law, and support for Islamic political parties was on the rise. Authorities have arrested at least 200 members of *Jemaah Islamiyah* in the past five years, although some dangerous fugitives remain at large.

The province of *Aceh*, on the western prow of Indonesian archipelago is best known for suffering the December 2004 tsunami. For centuries, the Aceh region has been recognized as one the most devout Muslim areas in all of Asia. Here, more than anywhere else in the islands, people observe a strict Islamic code of conduct. In 1999 the national government paved the way for Aceh to become the nation's first province to establish *shari'a* as criminal law.[148]

A widely distributed booklet, *A Brief Look at Shari'a Islam in Aceh,* outlines the rules. If you're caught gambling: 6-12 lashes, improperly mingling with the opposite sex: 3-9 lashes, drinking alcohol: 40 lashes, skipping three consecutive Friday prayers: 3 lashes.[149]

Fundamentalist Islam is fairly recent import to Indonesia. Islam originally came here the way most things come to islands—by sea. By the 12th century most of the traders taking Indonesian pepper and nutmeg and cloves to the West were Muslims from the Middle East. For Indonesians spices producers, converting to Islam had advantages—trading partners preferred fellow believers. The spread of Islam in Indonesia was gradual and peaceful. Scattered across some 3000 miles of ocean, the islands had hundreds of ethnic groups and religious practices. Islam helped integrate varied peoples and their customs into a single regional culture. By the time the United East India Company, run by the Dutch won control of the spice trade in the 17th century, Islam had spread to nearly all of Indonesia's coastal societies. "Islam was so successful coming to Indonesia because it was able to accommodate the existing culture and religions," says Syafii Anwar, executive director of the International Center for Islam and Pluralism in Jakarta. "Even in the architecture of the mosques, local style was incorporated."[150]

---

[148] Ibid. p. 88

[149] Ibid. 9. 89

[150] Ibid. p. 93

The end of Suharto's regime also intensified a schism with the Muslim community between those who supported the nation's traditional blending of Islam with local beliefs and those who sought to "purify" Islam, stripping away its regional flavor. That clash continues today, fueled in part by ideas and practices originating the strict *Wahhabism* of Saudi Arabia, which has funded Islamic universities and boarding schools throughout Indonesia.[151]

"Islam in Indonesia is a huge tent under which all voices can talk to each other," says Robin Bush of the Asia Foundation. Fringe groups, she points out, can receive an inordinate share of media attention and frighten people away from publicly denouncing them. They can even send suicide bombers into hotels. But their reach has not extended into the ballot box. Of course, that could change. Continued government corruption, another Suharto-like leader, a charismatic Imam who can rally the disaffected—any of these might shift Indonesia's balance. "If our secular government fails to deliver, *Jemaah Islamiyah* will have fodder to recruit," says Ismail.[152]

Jakarta (AsiaNews/Agencies)—A mob went on the rampage on the western outskirts of *Bogor* (West Java) early Sunday, attacking coffee shops, night clubs, small hotels and other businesses they accuse of "violating the sanctity of Ramadan," as part of a wider campaign by Islamic extremists to impose *Shari'a* on the largest Muslim country in the world. The province where the violence occurred is also the one where anti-Christian prejudice is strongest. Members of the infamous Islam Defenders Front (FPI) and Islam Defenders Force (LPI) took part in the attacks.[153]

Muslim mob closes Christian church in Indonesia. Jakarta, November 8, 2002 (Deutsche Presse-Agentur)—Church leaders in Bandung, West Java, have called on Indonesian authorities to intervene in the violent closure of a Christian church this week by a Moslem mob, a news report said on Friday.[154]

Seventeen Churches Closed Down in *Aceh*, 4 October 2002. The authorities gave no reason for these closures. Christians in Aceh have

---

151 Ibid. p. 93

152 Ibid. p.98

153 AsiaNews.it; 10/1/2007; retrieved 27 Sept. 2011

154 www.domini.org/openbook/ind/htm; retrieved 27 sept. 2011

been under increasing pressure since the implementation of *Shari'a* (Islamic law) in the province in March 2002. Although *Shari'a* regulations were only supposed to apply to Muslims, Christian women are being forced to conform to Islamic dress codes. As a result Christians are facing increasing difficulties and opposition.[155]

Forced Conversions, Circumcision in *Moluccas*, January 19, 2001. Conflict in the *Moluccas* is set to enter a third year with no end to the violence in sight. Disturbing new reports suggest Christian communities are facing forcible conversion and circumcision, adding a new dimension to a conflict that has already caused untold suffering. By conservative estimates at least 5000 have been killed and a further 500,000 displaced. Whilst the majority of *Moluccans* wish to see the conflict resolved, Islamist extremists and elements in the government and armed forces are widely believed to be behind the continuing violence.[156]

In a disturbing new development, hundreds of Christian families are being forced to convert to Islam or face death. Entire Christians villages are currently held captive by militants in East *Seram*, *Keswui* and *Teor* Islands facing the daily threat of violence.[157]

Jihad Warriors in the *Moluccas* Burn Christian Village: November 8, 2001. Four Christians and an army officer are feared dead following a brutal attack on a Christian village in the *Moluccas* islands of Indonesia. More than a thousand villagers were forced to run for their lives to the surrounding jungle as militant *Jihad* warriors burned their homes to the ground. The attack happened at *Waemulang*, the second largest Christian village on Buru island, on November 1, 2001. he villagers were attacked by a large militant force shortly after a visit to the region by Jafar Umar Thalib, a leader of a militant *Jihad* organization *(Laskar Jihad)*, which is largely held responsible for the continuation of the conflict in *Moluccas*.[158]

---

[155] /www.domini.org/openbook/ind20021004.htm; retrieved 27 Sept. 2011

[156] Ibid.

[157] Ibid.

[158] Ibid.

Taliban of Afghanistan

On September 30, 1996, the Taliban government decreed that all women should be banned from employment.[159] This had a devastating impact on household incomes, especially on vulnerable or widow-headed households, which were common in Afghanistan.

The Islamic Emirate of Afghanistan was founded in 1996 when the Taliban began their rule of Afghanistan and ended with their fall from power in 2001. The Taliban and its rule arose from the chaos of post-Soviet Afghanistan. It began as an Islamic fundamentalist politico-religious movement composed of students in the *Helmand* and *Kandahar* region of Afghanistan. Spreading from *Kandahar*, the Taliban eventually seized Kabul in 1996. By the end of 2000, the Taliban were able to capture 90% of the country, aside from the opposition (Afghan Northern Alliance) strongholds primarily found in the northeast corner of *Badakhshan* Province. The Taliban sought to impose a strict interpretation of Islamic *Shari'a law*.

One of the first acts of the Islamic Emirate was the murder of the former President of Afghanistan, *Muhammad Najibullah*. Before the Taliban had even taken control of Afghanistan's capital they sent out a squad to arrest, torture, mutilate and murder *Najibullah*, leaving his body hanging from a street lamp outside the presidential palace for two days.

Women were forced to wear the *burqa* in public, because, according to a Taliban spokesman, "the face of a woman is a source of corruption" for men not related to them. In a systematic segregation, women were not allowed to work, they were not allowed to be educated after the age of eight, and until then were permitted only to study the Qur'an. Women seeking an education were forced to attend underground schools, where they and their teachers risked execution if caught.[160]

Women were not allowed to be treated by male doctors unless accompanied by a male chaperone, which led to illnesses remaining untreated. They faced public flogging and execution for violations of the Taliban's laws.[161] The Taliban allowed and in some cases encouraged

---

[159] UNHCR-Chronology of Events; January 1995-February 1997

[160] Lamb, Christina. "Women Poet; 'Slain for her verses', *The Sunday Times*, November 13, 2005

[161] "100 Girls' Schools in Afghan Capital Are Ordered Shut", *The New York Times*, June 17, 1998

marriage for girls under the age of 16. Amnesty International reported that 80 percent of Afghan marriages were considered to be by force.[162]

From the age of eight, women were not allowed to be in direct contact with men, other than a close blood relative, husband, or in-laws (*mahram*).[163] A woman who was badly beaten by the Taliban for walking the streets alone stated "my father was killed in battle . . . I have no husband, no brother, no son. How am I to live if I can't go out alone?"[164]

Elementary education of children, not just girls, was shut down in Kabul, where virtually all of the elementary school teachers were women. Thousands of educated families fled Kabul for Pakistan after the Taliban took the city in 1996.[165]

The female employment ban was felt greatly in the education system. Within Kabul alone the ruling affected 106,256 girls, 148,223 boys and 8,000 female university undergraduates. 7,793 female teachers were dismissed, a move that crippled the provision of education and caused 63 schools to close due to a sudden lack of educators.[166]

The decree that no male doctor should be allowed to touch the body of a woman under the pretext of consultation was soon introduced.[167] With fewer female health professionals in employment, the distances many women had to travel for attention increased while provision of ante-natal clinics declined.

In October 1996, women were barred from accessing the traditional *hammam*, public baths, as the opportunities for socialising were ruled un-Islamic. Nasrine Gross, an Afghan-American author, stated in 2001 that it has been four years since many Afghan women had been able to pray to their God as "Islam prohibits women from praying without a bath after their periods".[168] In June 1998, the Taliban banned women from attending general hospitals in the capital.

---

[162] A Woman among Warlords; Wide Angle, accessed 12/11/07

[163] Michael Griffin (2001). *Reaping the Whirlwind: The Taliban movement in Afghanistan.* London: Pluto Press, pp6-11/159-165.

[164] *My forbidden face: Growing up under the Taliban.* UK: Virago Press pp29-107.

[165] Ahmed Rashid; *Taliban* (2000), p.106

[166] *¹*Michael Griffin (2001). *Reaping the Whirlwind: The Taliban movement in Afghanistan.* London: Pluto Press, pp6-11/159-165.

[167] Latifa *My forbidden face: Growing up under the Taliban.* UK: Virago Press pp29-107.

[168] Afghan Women's Request for Recognition at the U.N

Family harmony was badly affected by mental stress, isolation and depression that often accompanied the forced confinement of women.

The Taliban closed the country's beauty salons. Cosmetics such as nail varnish and make-up were prohibited.[169] In October 1996, a woman had the tip of her thumb cut off for wearing nail varnish.[170]

In 1999, a mother of seven was executed in front of 30,000 spectators in Kabul's Ghazi Sport stadium for allegedly murdering her husband. She was detained for three years pending investigation prior to the execution.[171]

Maulvi Qalamuddin, a huge Pashtun tribesman with enormous feet and hands, a long thick nose, black eyes and bushy black beard that touches his desk while he talks, heads his Department of the Promotion of Virtue and Prevention of Vice in the center of Kabul. In the streets, people just call the department's thousands of young zealots, who walk around with whips, long sticks and Kalashnikovs, the religious police. "The day I (the author) visited him for a rare interview in the summer of 1997, he had just issued an edict reading, 'Stylish dress and decoration of women in hospitals is forbidden. Women are duty-bound to behave with dignity, to walk calmly and refrain from hitting their shoes on the ground.'"[172] 'Women are not allowed to work in any field except the medical sector. No Afghan women have the right to be transported in the same car as foreigners', the edict continued. Education for boys is also at a standuntil in Kabul because most of the teachers are women, who now cannot work. An entire generation of Afghan children is growing up without any education.

When the Taliban first entered Kabul, the religious police beat men and women in public for not having long enough beards or not wearing *burqa* properly.

The Department is modeled on a similar government organization in Saudi Arabia and it has recruited thousands of young men, many of them with only a minimum *madrassa* education from Pakistan. The Department is also the Taliban's most effective intelligence agency.

---

[169] PBS, Taliban Women, March 6, 1998

[170] *I* Michael Griffin (2001). *Reaping the Whirlwind: The Taliban movement in Afghanistan.* London: Pluto Press, pp6-11/159-165.

[171] The Taliban Human Rights Watch in the Wall Street Journal 14/7/2010

[172] Ahmed Rashid's TALIBAN; Yale University Press; 2001; p.105

Qalamuddin admitted that he has thousands of informers in the army, government ministries, hospitals and Western aid agencies. 'Our stall all has experience in religious issues. And we are an independent organization and we don't take advice from the Justice Ministry or the Supreme Court as to what we should implement. We obey the orders of the Amir Mullah Mohammed Omar.'[173]

Qalamuddin's edicts are broadcast regularly on Radio Shariat (formerly Radio Kabul) and cover every aspect of social behavior for the population. One addresses public attendance at sports events. 'All onlookers, while encouraging the sportsmen, are asked to chant Allah-o-Akbar [God is Great] and refrain from clapping. Game should be interrupted at prayer time. Both the players and spectators should offer prayers in congregation', said the edict. Kite flying, once a favorite pastime in the spring for Kabuli, is until banned as are all sports for women. For the Taliban anyone questioning these edicts is tantamount to questioning Islam itself. For any question coming from foreign aid workers, they simply said, 'You are not Muslim, so you have no right to discuss Islam.' 'The constitution is the *Sharia* so we don't need a constitution. People love Islam and that is why they all support the Taliban and appreciate what we are doing,' said Attorney General Maulvi Jalilullah Maulvizada.[174]

The plight of Afghan women and Afghan society as a whole began well before the Taliban arrived. Twenty years of continuous warfare with Soviets had destroyed Afghan civil society. Illiteracy was a major problem before the Taliban appeared, affecting 90 per cent of girls and 60 per cent of boys. There were huge swathes of rural Afghanistan where schools had been destroyed in the war and not a single one remained. Within three months of the capture of Kabul, the Taliban closed 63 schools in the city affecting 10300 girls, 148000 boys and 11200 teachers, of whom 7800 were women. They shut down Kabul University sending home some 10,000 students of which 4000 were women. By December 1998, UNICEF reported that the country's educational system was in a state of total collapse with nine in ten girls and two in three boys not enrolled in school.[175]

---

[173] Ibid. p.106.

[174] Ahmed Rashid's Interview with Maulvizada, Kabul, June 1997; Ibid. Taliban, p. 107.

[175] Ibid. p. 108.

The Taliban leaders were all from the poorest, most conservative and least literate southern Pashtun provinces of Afghanistan. In Mullah Omar's village women had always gone around fully veiled and no girl had ever gone to school because there were none. Omar and his colleagues transposed their own milieu, their own experience, of lack of it, with women to the entire country and justified their policies through the Qur'an.

The Taliban's new model for a purist Islamic revolution has created immense repercussions, in Pakistan and to a more limited extent in the Central Asian Republics. Pakistan, an already fragile state beset by an identity crisis, an economic meltdown, ethnic and sectarian divisions and a rapacious ruling elite that has been unable to provide good governance, now faces the specter of a new Islamic wave, led not by the older, more mature and accommodating Islamic parties but by neo-Taliban groups.

By 1998, Pakistani Taliban groups were banning TV and videos in towns along the *Pashtun* belt, imposing *Sharia* punishments such as stoning and amputation in defiance of the legal system, killing Pakistani Shi'a and forcing people, particularly women to adapt to the Taliban dress code and way of life. Pakistani leaders, then, appeared to be oblivious of the challenges and continued to support the Taliban. In Central Asia, like *Tajikistan* and *Uzbekistan*, new-Taliban militants were being hunted by the police in the *Ferghana* valley, which borders both countries.

The Taliban and their supporters present the Muslim world and the West with a new style of Islamic extremism, which rejects all accommodation with Muslim moderation and the West.

As a global terror network, Al Qaeda is attracting an alarmingly high number of militants to operate its 'franchises' in Punjab under the Taliban brand name. Some of these franchises are already out on a rampage. Through a series of recent attacks on civilian and security targets, they have shown that they are as ruthless as their *Pakhtun/ Pashtun* **counterparts in** Afghanistan and as resourceful as their Al Qaeda mentors. Almost all the terror attacks in Pakistan-Punjab over the last two weeks, including the one on GHQ in Rawalpindi, carry their mark. Even in incidents where they are not the main attackers, they are believed to have put together all the logistics by supplying weapons, procuring transport and arranging board and lodging for the assailants.

Reports that two of their top commanders have been arrested should, therefore, mean that they have suffered a setback. The arrests come in the wake of the nabbing of another Punjabi Taliban commander, Aqeel alias Dr Usman, who is said to have masterminded the GHQ attack.

Nevertheless, this does not mean that they have been dealt a fatal blow. The tentacles of the Punjabi Taliban have spread across the province through the activists of banned sectarian organizations and the veterans of *Jihad* in Kashmir and Afghanistan. The arrest of a few leaders cannot render their network ineffective. From *Kahuta* in north Punjab to Rahimyar Khan in the south, the entire province is strewn with radicalised individuals whose ranks appear to swell, even as they lose some of their leaders. One wonders what strategy the state has in mind to curtail the terror tactics of these militants and to neutralize their organizations. If the government and its law-enforcement agencies fail to act promptly, they may soon find that it is too late to root out the menace.

Saudi Arabia

Saudi Wahhabism, as it spreads throughout the Islamic diaspora, has been likened by one terrorism expert to "kindling for Usama Bin Laden's match."[176] The terrorist attack of 9/11 awakened Americans to a growing movement by extremists within the Islamic world—a movement motivated by a radical political doctrine that can be best thought of as Islamist totalitarianism. Of the 19 terrorists of 9/11 attacks on the US soil were all Muslim and mostly Saudis. It has become quite clear that extreme Islamist ideologies have been gaining adherents throughout the world. It is equally clear that much of this extremist religious thought is originating from and being spread by the Saudi Arabia's Islamist sect known as *Wahhabism*.

The United States and the Saudis had forged a mutually beneficial alliance, even before President Franklin Roosevelt's historic meeting with King Abdulaziz al-Saud aboard the USS Quincy north of the Suez Canal on February 14, 1945, The House of Saud had been helpful to

---

[176] Former Treasury official David D. Aufhauser, "An Assessment of Current Efforts to Combat Terrorism Financing," Statement before the Senate Committee on Governmental Affairs, June 15, 2004, available at http://hsgac.senate.gov/public/index. cfm?Fuseaction=Hearings.Testimony&HearingID=3a5f7334.

the American war effort during World War II, and both nations were later on the same side during the Cold War. As recently as the 70's, the world of US-Saudi relations was a reasonably close and relaxed one. The serious bumps along the road began with the Saudis' 1973 oil embargo against us—essentially punishment for our efforts in that year to provide Israel with emergency help when she was attacked by her Arab neighbors. But the United States and Saudi Arabia continued to be strategically interdependent—our protection, our dollars, and our technology for their oil. Today, however, the relationship has become strained to the breaking point by the Faustian bargain the House of Saud has made with its *Wahhabi* establishment. The watershed year was 1979, when Ayatollah Khomeini seized power in Shiite Iran and Sunni extremists took over the holiest of Islam's shrines, the Great Mosque in Makkahhh, which was under the protection of the Saudi King. The threatened Saudi monarchy lost no time—and has spared no expense—in shoring up its legitimacy as the rightful and only defender of the faith. This is a claim it had made for well over half a century, since seizing the holy cities of Makkahhh and Madina from the Hashemites. From the 1980s onward, in return for the protection of their own powers and privileges, the Saudi royal family chose not only to accommodate *Wahhabi* views about propriety, pious behavior, and Islamic law, but effectively to turn over education in the Kingdom to the *Wahhabi* establishment.

We need to end our dependency on oil, the international market for which is Saudi-dominated. An increasing share of our payments for oil, along with others', finds its way to Saudi Arabia. The billions that Saudis provide annually to their *Wahhabi* sect for global expansion comes from these petrodollars. Thus, when we pay for Middle Eastern oil today, this Long War in which we are engaged becomes the only war the U.S. has ever fought in which we pay for both sides.

This report compares textbooks from the Saudi Ministry of Education, which are posted on its website as this is issued, with those analyzed in our 2006 study, *Saudi Arabia's Curriculum of Intolerance*, and shows that the same violent and intolerant teachings against other religious believers noted in 2006 remain in the current texts. This analysis is issued as the deadline that nears for the removal of intolerant teachings from all Saudi textbooks. This commitment stems from the Saudi government's "confirmation" of policies that were publicly announced and lauded as "significant developments" by the U.S. State Department in July 2006, and are to be implemented in full by the start of the 2008-2009 school year.

In May 2006, the Center for Religious Freedom, with the Institute for Gulf Affairs, released a ground-breaking report (as shown below) that analyzed excerpts from a dozen textbooks published by the Saudi Ministry of Education and used at that time in the Saudi public school curriculum. Saudi Arabia also disseminated these texts internationally, including to some 19 academies founded by Saudi Arabia and chaired by the local Saudi ambassadors in or near major foreign cities, one of which is the Islamic Saudi Academy (ISA) outside Washington, D.C.

The 2006 report concluded:

"The Saudi public school religious curriculum continues to propagate an ideology of hate toward the 'unbeliever,' that is, Christians, Jews, Shiites, Sufis, and Sunni Muslims who do not follow Wahhabi doctrine, Hindus, atheists, and others. This ideology is introduced in a religion textbook in the first grade and reinforced and developed in following years of the public education system, culminating in the twelfth grade, where a text instructs students that it is a religious obligation to do 'battle' against infidels in order to spread the faith."[177]

The twelve point list below is taken directly from the 2006 report and applies equally to the Saudi textbooks for the 2007-2008 year that are currently posted on the website of the Saudi Education Ministry—www2.moe.gov.sa/ebooks/index.htm.

Regarding Sunni, Shiite, Sufi and other non-Wahhabi or non-Salafi Muslims, the textbooks:

1. Condemn the majority of Sunni Muslims around the world as "bad successors" of "bad predecessors."[178]
2. Condemn and denigrate Shiite and Sufi Muslims' beliefs and practices as heretical and call them "polytheists".178
3. Denounce Muslims who do not interpret the Qur'an "literally."[179]

---

[177] 2008 Update: Saudi Arabia's Curriculum of Intolerance; www.hudson.org.

[178] *Monotheism, Tenth Grade*. Kingdom of Saudi Arabia. Ministry of Education. Education Development, 1426-1427; 2005-2006, p. 67;.

4. Command Muslims to "hate" Christians, Jews, polytheists, and other "unbelievers," including non-Wahhabi Muslims, though, incongruously, not to treat them "unjustly."[180]

   Now teaches that a true believer "worships God alone, loves the believers, and hates the infidels."

6. Teaches that "the Jews and the Christians are enemies of the [Muslim] believers"179 and that "the clash"180 between the two realms "continues until the Day of Resurrection."181

7. Instructs students not to "greet,"182 "imitate,"183 "show loyalty to,"184 "be courteous to"185 or "respect"186 non-believers.

9. Instruct that "the struggle between Muslims and Jews"187 will continue "until the hour [of judgment],"188 that "Muslims will triumph because they are right," and that "he who is right is always victorious."189

11. Teach the Protocols of the Elders of Zion as historical fact and relate modern events to it.190

---

179 Ibid, p. 66 and p. 149.

180 Ibid, p. 49 and p. 148

181 *Hadith and Islamic Culture: Management, Social Studies, Natural History, and Technical Studies (Boys), Twelfth Grade.* Kingdom of Saudi Arabia. Ministry of Education. Education Development, 1426-1427; 2005-2006, p. 59 and p. 63.

182 Ibid. Eleventh Grade; 1426-1427; 2005-2006, p. 66. And p. 94.

183 *Monotheism, Eighth Grade.* Kingdom of Saudi Arabia. Ministry of Education. Education Development, 1426-1427; 2005-2006; p. 45.

184 Ibid. p. 14 and 15.

185 *Hadith and Islamic Culture: Management, Social Studies, Physical Sciences, and Technical Fields (Boys), Eleventh Grade.* Kingdom of Saudi Arabia. Ministry of Education. Education Development, 1426-1427; 2005-2006, p. 66 and 1428-1429; 2007-2008, p.94.

186 Ibid. p. 66.and p.94.

187 *Hadith, Ninth Grade.* Kingdom of Saudi Arabia. Ministry of Education. Education Development, 1426-1427; 2005-2006, p. 148.

188 Ibid. 1426-1427; 2005-2006, p. 148; 1428-1429; 2007-2008, p. 148.

189 Ibid.1426-1427; 2005-2006, p. 49; 1428-1429; 2007-2008, p.149.

190 *Hadith and Islamic Culture, Tenth Grade (Boys).* Kingdom of Saudi Arabia. Ministry of Education. Education Development, 1426-1427; pp. 103-104 and 1428-1429; 2007-2008, pp. 104-105.

12. Discuss Jews in violent terms, blaming them for virtually all the "sedition" and wars of the modern world.[191]

There is also a lesson from a tenth grade text on *Jurisprudence* now posted on the Saudi Ministry of Education website that sanctions the killing of homosexuals and discusses methods for doing so.

These texts teach students that there exist two incompatible realms—one consisting of true believers in Islam, the monotheists, and the other of infidels or unbelievers—and that these realms never coexist in peace. They assert that unbelievers, such as Christians, Jews, and Muslims who do not share Wahhabi beliefs and practices, are hated "enemies," and that true believers should aid and show loyalty only to other true believers. These texts teach that Christians, Jews, and others have united in a war against Islam that will ultimately end in the complete destruction of these infidels. The books promote global *Jihad* as an "effort to wage war against the unbelievers." Some Saudis themselves have linked the Kingdom's educational curriculum to patterns of violence in young Saudi men.

Saudi Arabia's religious legitimacy, through the custodianship of the two Islamic holy shrines, and its vast oil wealth enable it to exert unprecedented influence in the Muslim world. Saudi religious texts are being disseminated worldwide through the internet and other means. This means that millions of Muslim students are being indoctrinated from textbooks that some Saudis themselves have linked to religious violence. Largely due to such educational materials, Saudi Wahhabi extremism threatens to become a mainstream or even the dominant expression of Islam among the world's 1.3 billion Muslims. While the Saudi state has recently initiated a program to re-educate some Islamic terrorists, it appears to be educating even greater numbers with a religious curriculum that legitimizes the "violent repression" and "physical elimination" of the other.

Saudi government sponsorship of textbooks that promote violent and intolerant teachings constitutes a threat to American interests, and violates both international and bilateral human rights obligations that Saudi Arabia has freely assumed. The Saudi state's international agreements—in particular its confirmation to the United

---

[191] Ibid. 1426-1427; 2005-2006, p. 104-105 and 1428-1429; 2007-2008; pp. 105-106.

States government that it would remove all intolerance from its textbooks—give jurisdiction over this matter to the U.S. Department of State. All the books used in this study are in Arabic and were translated by two independent translators. Photocopies of all the excerpts in their original Arabic, side by side with the English translations, are available on our website at http://www.hudson.org/religion.

These textbooks are used in Saudi public school classrooms in elementary, middle, and high school levels. They are part of the government's religious curriculum, which can encompass up to five courses in the upper grades, thus comprising a significant part of the Saudi school day. In addition, the texts are disseminated through the internet and other means by Saudi Arabia for use around the world. For example, the Saudi religious curriculum is followed by the network of some 19 international academies founded by the Saudi government, each chaired by the local Saudi ambassador.[192] At the beginning of the 2007-2008 school year, the Saudi academy outside Washington, D.C., stated in its web brochure that it used the Saudi Ministry of Education "curriculum, syllabus and materials" for its Islamic and Arabic studies classes.[193] In June 2008, USCIRF released its analysis of seventeen of the Washington-area Saudi academy textbooks on religion, finding that they appeared to be Saudi Ministry of Education textbooks, containing some alterations but until with identical wording in many sections of the texts. The Federal Commission observed the use of correction tape or fluid and cutting and pasting in the textbooks, "but not sufficient revision to remove all objectionable material." The Washington-area Islamic Saudi Academy, with a student body approaching 1,000, states on its website that its mission is to be "the premier educational institution" for the American Muslim community. Its goal appears to be establishing in the United States, as well as other countries, a homegrown leadership for the next generation of adherents of the Saudi Wahhabi sect of Islam.

Saudi state curriculum for many years has taught children to hate "the other" and support *Jihad*. For example, a book for third-year high school students published by the Saudi Ministry of Education that was collected from the Islamic Center of Oakland in California, teaches

---

[192] www.hudson.org/religion.

[193] Ibid.

students, to prepare for *Jihad* in the sense of war against Islam's enemies, and to strive to attain military self-sufficiency: '*To be true Muslims, we must prepare and be ready for Jihad in Allah's way. It is the duty of the citizen and the government. The military education is glued to faith and its meaning, and the duty to follow it.*' [194]

The same hostility toward "infidels" as propagated in official Saudi Islamic publications and *fatwas,* surfaces repeatedly in statements by Muslim terrorists. A prime example occurred on May 29 and 30, 2004, when a terrorist squad went through the compound of foreigners in Khobar, Saudi Arabia, segregating the Muslims from the non-Muslims (mainly Christians and Hindus) before slitting the throats of the latter, and in some cases, beheading them. To the remaining terrified Muslims the slaughterers calmly explained how certain verses in the Koran should be read and understood to preach hatred of "unbelievers." Their explicit aim was to cleanse the land of Prophet Muhammad of Christians and polytheists.[195] While Saudi officials were quick to denounce this ruthless act of terror, it followed logically from the state's relentless indoctrination in hate ideology.

The Saudis' totalitarian doctrine of religious hatred—now planted in many America mosques—is inimical to our tolerant culture, and undermines the war on terrorism by providing the intellectual foundation for a new generation of Islamic extremists.

Pakistan

Recently, *Salmaan Taseer* (1944-2011) the Governor of Punjab in Pakistan, was gunned down by his own bodyguard on Jan. 4, 2011 in Islamabad, only because of his opposition of Pakistan Blasphemy Law.[196] Also the recent bomb blast in a local mausoleum in Pakistan and bomb explosion in the Coptic Church in Egypt to express a section of Muslim's hate against Muslims and Christians shows the utter battle going within *Ummah.*

---

[194] Ibid.

[195] Ibid.

[196] The Islamic Republic of Pakistan uses its Penal Code to prohibit and punish blasphemy against Islam. The Criminal Code forbids defiling the Quran, defaming Prophet Muhammad, and forbids damaging or defiling a place of worship or a sacred object and provides penalties for blasphemy ranging from a fine to death.

Sectarian violence in Pakistan sparks up occasionally between the predominant *Sunnis* and *Shi'as* minority. *Shi'a* in Pakistan make up 5% of the total Muslim population, while the remaining 95% is Sunnis. In the last two decades, as many as 4,000 people are estimated to have died in *sectarian* fighting in Pakistan, with 300 in 2006 alone.[197] Among those blamed for the sectarian violence in the country are mainly Sunni militants such as *Sipah Sahaba, Jaish-e-Muhammad, Jama'at-e-Isami* and members of *al Qaeda* who are supported by the Arab World[198] and Iranian-backed Shi'a militant groups such as *Tehrik-e-Jafria* and others.[199] However, predominant Sunni terrorist groups are often blamed for frequent attacks on minority *Shi'as, Ahmadis,* Christians and their religious gatherings resulting in reprisal attacks by them.

In the 1990s and 2000s, sporadic violence resulted from disputes over control of Pakistani mosques between Barelwi and Deobandi.[200] In May 2001, sectarian riots broke out after Sunni Tehreek leader Saleem Qadri was assassinated by the Sipah-e-Sahaba Pakistan, a Deoband-affiliated terrorist group.[201] In April 2006 in Karachi, a bomb attack on a Barelvi gathering to celebrate the *Mawlud* (Prophet's birthday) killed at least 57 people.[202] On February 27, 2010, *Barelvis* celebrating *Mawlud* in Faisalabad and Dera Ismail Khan were attacked by militants believed to be affiliated with the Taliban and Sipah-e-Sahaba, again sparking tensions among the rival sects.[203]

The blasphemy laws are used fairly routinely to harass those considered "improper Muslims" such as the *Ahmadis* who are subject to onerous restrictions under law. Although *Ahmadis* regard themselves as Muslims and observe Islamic practices, a 1974 Constitutional amendment during the time of Zulfiqar Ali Bhutto declared *Ahmadis*

---

[197] "Shiite-Sunni conflict rises in Pakistan". *David Montero. February 2, 2007. http://www. csmonitor.com/2007/0202/p01s02-wosc.html. Retrieved* 2011-01-15

[198] Hussain, Zahid (2008). *Frontline Pakistan: The Struggle With Militant Islam*. Columbia University Press. p. 93

[199] "Pakistan's Militant Islamic Group" *BBC News.* January 13, 2002. http://news.bbc. co.uk/2/hi/south_asia/1758534.stm. Retrieved 01-15-2011.

[200] ^ Bomb carnage at Karachi prayers, BBC Online, 11 April 2006

[201] Ibid.

[202] Special Coverage of Nishtar Park bombing, Jang Group Online

[203] The widening split, Express Tribune, April 26, 2010

to be a non-Muslim minority because, according to the Government, they do not accept Prophet Mohammed as the last prophet of Islam. In 1984 the Government passed an amendment prohibiting *Ahmadis* from calling themselves Muslim and banning them from using Islamic words, phrases, and greetings. The punishment for violation of this section is imprisonment for up to 3 years and a fine.[204]

In addition to it, an exhaustive list of violations in Pakistan, apart from Blasphemy, relates to Universal Human Rights, child abuses, intolerance and persecution of minorities, woman's persecution under *Hudood* Ordinance, and ethnic, sectarian, civil and religious blood-lettings and killings throughout Pakistan.

---

[204] Ibid.

MUSLIMS IN CONFLICT
WITH ISLAM

Introduction

Despite the tragedy of September 11, and the subsequent terrorist acts against Western targets throughout the world, despite the clash-of-civilizations mentality that has seized the globe, despite the blatant religious rhetoric resonating throughout the halls of governments, there is one thing that cannot be overemphasized. What is taking place now in the Muslim world is an internal conflict among Muslims, not an external battle between Islam and the West. The West is merely a bystander—an unwary yet complicit casualty of a rivalry that is raging in Islam over who will write the next chapter in its story. This internal struggle is taking place not in the deserts of the Arabian Peninsula, but in the developing capitals of the Muslim world—Tehran, Cairo, Damascus, Baghdad, Islamabad and Jakarta—and in the cosmopolitan capitals of Europe and the united States—New York, London, Paris, and Berlin—where that message is being redefined by scores of first-and-second generation Muslim immigrants. By merging the Islamic values of their ancestors with the democratic ideals of their new homes, these Muslims have formed what *Tariq Ramadan* (the Swiss-born intellectual and grandson of *Hasan al-Banna*) has termed the "mobilizing force" for the Islamic Reformation.

All great religions have grappled with these issues. One need only recall the Europe's massively destructive Thirty Years' War (1618-48) between the forces of the Protestant Union and those of the Catholic League to recognize the ferocity with which interreligious conflicts have been fought in Christian history. The awful war during which nearly a third of the population of Germany perished was a gradual progression in Christian theology from the doctrinal absolutism to the doctrinal pluralism of the early modern period, and ultimately, to the doctrinal relativism of the Enlightenment. This remarkable

179

evolution in Christianity from its inception to its Reformation took fifteen bloody centuries.

Some fourteen hundred years of rabid debate over what it means to be a Muslim; of passionate arguments over the interpretation of the Qur'an and the application of Islamic law; of trying to reconcile a fractured community through appeals to Divine Unity; of tribal feuds, crusades, and world wars—Islam has finally begun its fifteenth century.

The Un-Islamic Violence and Extremism

The violent activities of the extremist groups today show to the non-Muslim world an un-Islamic face of Islam. There are two dimensions of the issue. The nature and the scale of violence recorded to by these outfits are un-Islamic *per-se*, because the Qur'anic messages throughout advocate compassion for all humanity (57:27) and restraint in the use of force (2:194). These activities have become doubly offensive against the scriptural commands, when these are shown as 'holy war' *Jihad*, and are packaged in religious vocabulary. Divine commands, *"Fight in the cause of Allah those who fight you, but do not transgress limits; for Allah does not love transgressors"*[205] lays down three requirements for '*Jihad*', a fight only in the cause of the faith, fight as defensive, and fight without excessive violence. Each of these is violated in the terrorist acts perpetrated by these outfits.

These are, therefore, heretical. Even the Prophet's name is used (such as, *Jaish-e-Muhammad* and *Sipah-i-Sahaba*) which is downright blasphemy. However, the voice of sanity, and the opinions of jurists and *ulama* are not raised against the sacrilegious use of religious principles and precepts. These activities may have legitimate personal goals and objectives, if at all, but they have no relationship with the name and faith of Islam. These are resorted to for self and only self purposes.

Unfortunately, the trend of using religion for non-religious goals is not new, and can be traced since medieval times. Muslim invaders entered non-Muslim domains; they described the war as 'holy' even though the goal was acquisition of land, kingdom, and wealth. This trend needs to be reversed. It is easy to understand its effect on the non-Muslim mind. If Muslims themselves consider such violence as sanctioned by their

---

[205] Q. 2:190.

faith, it is difficult to blame the non-Muslim world for viewing Islam as a religion which stands for violence rather than for peace.

Islamic terrorist organizations exist across the world, and have carried out attacks from South Asia across the Middle East, in Europe, Southeast Asia, and the United States, since at least 1983. These organizations use several tactics, including suicide attack, hijacking, kidnapping and execution, and recruit new members through the internet. The best-known organization is Al-Qaeda, which envisions a complete break from the foreign influences in the Muslim world and the creation of a new Islamic caliphate, and which carried out the September 11 attacks.

The laws of *Jihad* categorically preclude wanton and indiscriminate slaughter. The warriors in the holy war are urged not to harm non-combatants, women and children, "unless they attack you first." A point on which they insist is the need for a clear declaration of war before beginning hostilities, and for proper warning before resuming hostilities after a truce. What the classical jurists of Islam never remotely considered is the kind of unprovoked, unannounced mass slaughter of noncombatant civil populations that we saw in the recent past in the Muslim and non-Muslim countries of Europe and America. For this there is no precedent and no authority in Islam. Indeed it is difficult to find precedents even in the rich annals of human wickedness." [206]

The question is: why should Muslims be surprised, incensed or feel the world does not understand Islam, if the practices of stoning women to death or beheading Muslims who open up to other beliefs, persists? A resounding majority of the British population (75%) believes that "Islam is negative for Britain." This sentiment is not confined to the British. We are witnessing unprecedented movements across Europe, against the infringement of Muslim culture, religion and dress code on European societies. Europeans and outspoken Americans are taking actions to ban Muslim cultural encroachment on their lives and on their democratic values. Blinded by their small victories and perceived religious supremacy, Muslims in their homelands and in other parts of the world, do not seem to take notice of other peoples' impatience with their unsolicited way of life.

Muslims in the West are seen as a threat to Western culture, way of life and economic stability. In a scientifically based survey taken

---

[206] *Jihad* in Hadith; www.PeacewithRealism.org., retrieved 3/13/11.

by the Islamic Education and Research Academy (IERA), a Muslim polling entity, found that their religion and its adherents are immensely resented in the United Kingdom. The poll revealed that a staggering 94% of British citizens see Islam as a repressive religion, especially for women. The surveyors, like most Muslims, attributed this negative view of Islam and Muslims, to non-Muslims' misunderstanding of their religion. IERA's senior researcher *Hamza Tzortzis* said, "We wanted to do something positive with the survey results rather than just say, 'It's so sad'. So, the organization's strategy is to give a new realm of possibility for people to comprehend Islam, have a proper respect for Islam and see the human relevance of the faith."

The question is: what do Muslims want non-Muslims in Britain, America and the rest of the world, to know about Islam that could change their negative views of Islam? Based on what non-Muslims see on the news, experience and hear in the streets, in mosques, in Muslim schools in Britain, let alone in Iraq, Pakistan, Yemen, Somalia, Afghanistan, Iran, and Saudi Arabia, the overwhelming majority of the British (77%) do not want to be associated with Islam. Unlike most Muslims, the majority of Westerners relate to each other through social interaction, merits, common values, tangible contributions and tolerance of differences. Most Muslims, relate to others through religious orientation.

Is it any wonder, the West wants to prevent Islam from taking root in their democracies?

There is an escalating conflict within and between Muslims societies over different interpretations of Islam and religious rituals. Muslim on Muslim killings, the destruction of minorities' holy shrines and other cultural heritages, as well as the ongoing carnage in Pakistan, Afghanistan, Yemen, Iran and other Muslim countries, are but some examples of bloody conflict among Muslims. The rampant oppression of Muslim and non-Muslim minorities in all Arab and non-Arab Muslim countries bears witness to a religion mired in contradictions and at odds with itself and, by extension, with the rest of the world, especially the West.

In reaction to the recent destruction of one of Sufi Islam's oldest and most revered shrines in Pakistan, a Saudi Muslim wrote, "For whatever reason, the cancer of extremism is fast eating into the vitals of the entire Muslim world. A lunatic fringe has hijacked their faith and claims to speak on their behalf and all Muslims can do is wring their hands in helplessness. In their long and eventful history, Muslims have never faced a greater challenge to their identity and existence. This sickness within is far more dangerous than what they confront from without. Where are Muslim voices of reason and sanity? Where are our leaders, our *Ulama,* our intellectuals and our Islamic centers, when we need them so badly? Why don't they come out in the open to speak out against this distortion of our faith and morbid celebration of death? If their voices aren't heard, they must shout from the rooftops but speak they must. There's no other way to stop this madness. This is no time to hide."[207]

Perhaps no other faith abhors and warns against violence and injustices of all kinds and strife as Islam does. In fact, if Islam means acceptance or submission to the will of God, it also means peace literally. More important, it preaches moderation[208], restraint[209] and reason in everything we do, even in our devotion and prayers. It warns us that killing one innocent human being is akin to killing all humanity and saving one innocent life is like saving mankind. The Qur'an constantly cautions us that Allah does not like those who spread strife and chaos on earth. We're told killing a fellow human being is waging war against God and Allah promises them harshest punishment.

But we have been here before and heard and said it all, haven't we? In fact, we keep repeating this stuff *ad nauseam* like parrots without anyone taking us seriously. While Muslims earnestly hold forth on the real teachings and message of Islam, a weary world looks away in disgust as the jackals in straitjackets continue to kill in our name and in the name of God. They could go on waxing lyrical on the peaceful nature of the great faith and its liberating teachings but the world looks not at their scriptures but at their actions, or rather of those who claim to be Muslims and shed innocent blood with impunity.

How long will this go on? And who's going to stop this endless dance of devil? Pakistan was created in the name of Islam and won after millions of human sacrifices and at a monumental price. This endless spilling of innocent blood is therefore not only tragic but an assault on Quaid-e-Azam's vision for Pakistan. From mosques to *madrasas* and from mourning Shi'a to Ahmadi shrines, no one is safe.

---

[207] www.ArabNews.com

[208] Q. 16:125

[209] Q. 16:127-128

Are Muslims a Threat in the West?

Introduction

The inroads made by Islamism in the non-Muslim West, are no less impressive, if not as well known. It would not be an exaggeration to argue that in both Europe and North America the leadership of traditional Islamic institutions such as mosques, Islamic centers, schools, and charities is for the most part in the hands of Islamists who espouse a radical ideology not only virulently opposed to basic Western norms, but also at odds with Islam as truly practiced for most of its history.

The growth of Islamism in the United States started in 1963 with the founding of the first Islamist organization in North America, the Muslim Student Association (MSA) at the University of Illinois at Urbana-Champaign by a group of Muslim Brotherhood immigrants with the help of the Muslim World League and Saudi money. Following this initial beachhead, some two dozen spinoff organizations from the MSA were established in the United States in the two decades that followed. As a result, virtually all currently existing Muslim political organizations in the country are the ideological progeny of the original Islamist set-up, despite claiming that they are independent. What's more, these organizations not only share an identical ideology, but also continue to maintain close operational ties and interlocking directorships. The specific areas of activity analyzed include, first, proselytizing and indoctrination (*dawah* and *tarbiyya*) to convert non-Muslims to Islam, with special emphasis on populations and groups (prisoners, minorities) believed to be alienated from mainstream society; second, the attempt to radicalize moderate Muslims; and third, infiltrating infidel society and its political and social institutions through political and electoral activism, outreach activities directed toward police and law-enforcement institutions, alliances with radical left and anti-establishment groups, and efforts to undermine state and federal legislation designed to defeat Islamic extremism and terrorism. The role of the *Tablighi Jama'at* and its *Deobandi* creed in proselytizing among prison inmate populations receives special attention.

Washington has failed to see radical Islamist ideology, rather than terrorism, as the key enemy and has been singularly unsuccessful in its efforts to conduct "public diplomacy" during the two terms of the Bush administration and continuing under the present administration. The main enemy is radical Islamist ideology or 'Islamism'. A change of emphasis would allow us to see clearly that defeating this enemy cannot be accomplished by counter-terror strategies alone, but requires a sophisticated strategy to defeat the ideology of Islamism by delegitimizing it in the eyes of its current and potential supporters in the Muslim community. The essential prerequisite to achieving this objective is to understand the nature of the threat presented by radical Islam, its ideological underpinnings, and its strengths and weaknesses. The possibility of mounting a political warfare campaign against radical Islam based on the premise that Islamism is an enemy of traditional Islam is most needed. A well-crafted political warfare strategy directed at Islamism's detrimental effects on Muslims themselves promises significant payoffs.

Muslims in Europe
The rise of radical Islam in Europe, and especially Western Europe, is closely tied to the explosive growth of the Muslim immigrant populations in the continent. While the efforts to establish Islamist organizations and networks, such as those of the Muslim Brotherhood, under Said Ramadan predated the waves of Muslim immigration in the 1960s and 1970s, it was the massive numbers of new immigrants, more often than not concentrated in compact Muslim ghettoes, that created the ideal conditions for spreading Islamist ideology. An understanding of the radicalization problem is intimately connected with the Muslim immigration and consequent population explosion phenomenon in Europe.

What is beyond dispute is that in the past half a century or so the Muslim population in Western Europe has exploded from less than a quarter million in the early 1950s, to between 15 and 20 million today (2011). While that until represents only three to four percent of the EU-27 (497 million), it is a rapidly growing population that has also become progressively radicalized. This has led to various speculations about the implications of this trend by governments and various experts.

185

As already mentioned, most European governments, except Great Britain, provide statistics on neither Muslim fertility rates nor total populations. Nonetheless, available data, however incomplete, shows beyond much doubt that the Muslims are dramatically younger as a group, with fertility rates that are two and even three times higher than those of native Europeans, and are also growing fast on account of legal and illegal immigration. In the town of Bradford, for instance, the Pakistani and Bangladeshi Muslim population increased from 47,430 and 13,300 in 1991, to 69,121 and 21,000 in 2001, or 46 percent and 59 percent respectively in just ten years.[210] The Pakistani and Bangladeshi share of the total population grew to more than 20 percent.

Very similar fertility rates are reported in France, where according to figures for 1999 provided by the French statistical agency INSEE, the main Muslim national groups had birth rates as follows: Algerians—2.57, Moroccans—2.97, Tunisians—2.90, Turks—3.21. Concrete evidence of the greater fertility of German Muslims, the majority of whom are Turks, is provided by the fact that in 2005 approximately 10 percent of the 685,795 babies born in Germany had Muslim parents, even though Muslims make up only 4 percent of the overall population.[211] By the same token, the fertility rates of the Maghreb nationals in France should not be dramatically different from those of the sizable Moroccan, Tunisian, and Algerian diasporas in Spain, Italy, and the Netherlands. Overall, the probable European Muslim TFR of between 2.50 and 3.00 will result in natural increase of the Muslim population of approximately 1.5 to 2 percent per annum. This compares to the EU average Fertility Rate of 1.5 which, as mentioned, leads to a loss of two and a quarter million people per year in the EU.

The second factor contributing to non-native population increase in Europe has traditionally been legal immigration. There have been two waves of post-WWII large-scale Muslim influx into Europe: "post-colonial" and "guest worker" immigration. The first involved the former citizens of the colonial possessions of Great Britain, France, the Netherlands, and other European nations who qualified for immigration. This is how large numbers of people from Pakistan,

---

[210] "The Impact of Chain Migration on English Cities," available online at www. migrationwatchuk.com/pdfs/migrationtrends/9_13_impact_of_chain_migration.pdf.

[211] www.focus.de/politik/deutschland_aid_52269.html.

Bangladesh, India, Algeria, Indonesia, and elsewhere settled in Europe in the aftermath of de-colonization. Then, as European economies recovered from wartime devastation and went into "economic miracle" overdrive, millions of "guest workers" were recruited as cheap labor for the booming economies of Western Europe in the 1950s and beyond. These two waves of immigration set the stage for today's large Muslim diasporas communities.

A clear majority of new immigrants from outside of Europe now arrive through family reunification. In the United Kingdom, which accounts for some ten percent of the total EU Muslim population, for example, there were close to fifty thousand new arrivals via spousal migration in 2001, most of whom were Muslims.[212] Muslim chain migration in all of the EU thus could be as high as half a million per annum, a figure that exceeds the natural population increase.

The final quasi-legal immigration category that contributes significantly to the growth of EU's Muslim populations is political asylum. The total number of asylum applicants in the EU is estimated at 6.6 million since 1980, which is about the same as the number of legal labor migrants in this period.[213] Current asylum seekers are mostly Muslims from North Africa and the Middle East. Asylum thus continues to be a "process of mass population movement as never intended."[214]

Illegal Immigration

Finally, the Muslim populations in Europe are augmented by large-scale illegal immigration. The estimates most often mentioned by European Union authorities are three million for the total number of illegal residents in the EU and five hundred thousand per annum in new arrivals. All in all, natural increase, chain migration, asylum seekers, and illegal immigration easily contribute over a million to the growth of the EU Muslim population every year, and the actual figure is probably considerably higher. The Muslim population is thus set to increase by at least 50 percent every decade. It will likely double from its 2001 level

---

[212] Data from the UK Home Office cited in D.A.Coleman, "Facing the 21st Century: New Developments, Continuing Problems," Paper presented at the European Population Forum, Geneva, Switzerland, January 12-14,2004, p.43.

[213] D.A. Coleman, op. cit., p. 43.

[214] D.A. Coleman, op.cit. p. 46

by 2015 and double again by 2030. By that year, the majority of young people in most large European urban centers will be Muslims.

The Urban Dimension

Perhaps the most significant and politically salient characteristic of the Muslim Diaspora populations in Western Europe is the fact that they are overwhelmingly urban and tend to be concentrated in the largest cities of the region.[215] This heavy concentration of the young Muslim populations in the key political, economic and cultural centers of Europe has the potential of endowing them with political and economic clout that may exceed their numbers when compared with those of the ageing and shrinking native cohorts.

The Radicalization of European Islam

How did the radicalization of socio-political phenomenon come about in a society that prides itself on being the embodiment of tolerance, compassion and social cohesion? The radicalization of European Muslims was the result of a combination of political, economic, and social factors and policies and their intended and unintended consequences, both within and without the European context. The stage was probably first set by the unrealistic belief of European governments that the millions of Muslim "guest workers" were sooner or later going to go home voluntarily. Thus, for many years, no European government entertained the possibility of long term settlement for the immigrants nor took even elementary acculturation and assimilation measures. Turkish state officials, for example, were given monopoly over the religious institutions and education of Turkish *gastarbeiter* in Germany on the assumption that Islam was a foreign religion and thus of no concern to the German government, and a similar arrangement was made by France with the Algerian government. Things went as far as a 1982 treaty between France and Morocco obligating French judges to use Moroccan Islamic statutes in adjudicating family law cases for Moroccan immigrants. The "temporary" guest workers were thus encouraged to maintain their separate ethnic, linguistic, and cultural identities and organize separate sports and cultural institutions and even labor union and political organizations.

---

[215] In stark contrast, the native Muslim populations in Eastern Europe are primarily rural.

Nonetheless, it was in this general period that a number of important developments took place that decisively influenced the course of Islam in Europe and the West. The first and most important one, as already discussed, was the strategic alliance between Muslim Brotherhood organizational and conspiratorial skills and Saudi money, which resulted in the founding of a number of key Saudi front groups promoting radical Islam in the West and the establishment of the first Islamist networks in both Europe and North America under *Ikhwan* ideological tutelage. As in the case of the *Ikhwan*, Saudi Arabia was and is the key financial benefactor of all of them, subsidizing thousands of *Deobandi* madrassas in Pakistan and many Islamist institutions in Britain, from the Leicester Islamic Foundation to the Dewsbury mosque and European headquarters for the proselytizing Islamists of *Tablighi Jama'at*.

The Saudi government and its domestic, regional and international Islamic charities and agents have been working on all fronts to unite and mobilize the faithful against non-Muslims, especially in the West. It has been widely documented that the Saudi government has been paying for most Muslim institutions and groups throughout the world for decades and this financing has intensified since the 9/11 attack on the U.S. by mostly Saudi princess and/nationals.

The Saudi government is using its petrodollar revenues not to modernize its society, but instead to promote its austere brand of Islam, *Wahhabism*. The Saudi ruling family uses a variety of channels and methods, especially the Muslim World League among others, to spread *Wahhabism* throughout the world, including in the U.S. The Saudi government's objective is to establish extremist and loyal Muslim communities throughout the world on which it could rely to promote the Saudi ruling elites' interests. They have succeeded in achieving this goal in many Muslim and non-Muslim countries. The only beneficiaries of united Muslims would be the Saudi autocrats and theocrats.[216]

Below are just a few direct quotations from *Wahhabi* literature published in Saudi Arabia that is freely available in many European mosques and Islamic centers.

---

[216] www.freedomhouse.org/religion: retrieved 01-15-2011.

- On democracy: "democracy is the very embodiment of unbelief," and "an evil system, and we have been ordered to reject evil."
- On interfaith dialogue: It is a "sinful call" because it "breaks the wall of resentment between Muslims and unbelievers."
- On freedom of religion: It is forbidden, because "it allows the denial of Islam." Accepting any religion other than Islam makes you an apostate and "you should be killed, because you have denied the Qur'an."
- On infidels: "Believers must hate them because of their religion . . . and always oppose them in every way according to Islamic law."
- On moderate Muslims: "whoever believes that Christians and Jews worship God is an infidel" and "he who casts doubt about their infidelity, leaves no doubt about his own infidelity."
- On Europe: "Muslims must be protected from the barbarian culture of Europe."[217]

Hidden behind such rhetoric is a well-thought-out strategy that the *Wahhabis* and their Muslim Brotherhood and *Deobandi* allies have pursued with considerable success. It aims first to control and dominate the Muslim establishment in the various countries through a network of interlocking organizations and umbrella groups. As a result, the Muslim communities in many European countries today are completely dominated by Islamist elements despite frequent protestations to the contrary. The Muslim Council of Britain, for example, pretends to be a moderate umbrella group of Muslim organizations and is often called upon as an interlocutor for the government on behalf of the Muslim community. In fact, even a perfunctory look at its affiliates reveals that virtually its entire membership is made up of Wahhabi, Deobandi, Ahle Hadith, Jamiat-e-Islami, and Muslim Brotherhood groups and their spinoffs. The same is true of Germany, where the IGD, various Saudi-sponsored groups, and the Turkish radical organization *Milli Goeruesh* completely dominate the organizational terrain in close cooperation.

---

[217] All of these quotations are taken from "Publications on Hate Ideology Invade American Mosques," Center for Religious Freedom, Freedom House, Washington D.C., 2005.

A 2005 French education ministry study, known as the *Rapport Obin*, describes existing conditions in public schools near the ghettoes that are hard to reconcile with their physical location in the middle of Europe. According to the study, Islamists known as "grand frères" (big brothers) enforce a strict Islamic dress code that prohibits make-up, dresses, and skirts. They also forbid any co-educational activities and make going to the cinema, the swimming pool, or the gym all but impossible for Muslim girls. The punishment for refusal to conform is often physical violence and beatings. And this, says the report, is a relatively protected environment compared to what girls experience outside of school. No less disturbing is the picture the report paints of the spread of the kind of religious obscurantism that one normally associates with Wahhabi zealots. Thus, Muslim students are said to often refuse to study Voltaire or read Madame Bovary, acknowledge even the existence of other religions, or sing, dance, draw faces or even right angles because they resemble the cross. English is hated as the "language of imperialism."[218] Almost identical conditions in German schools, particularly in the treatment of girls, are reported by the German-Turkish sociologist *Necla Kelek*.

How far this separatism has proceeded could be judged by the existence of what the French call *zones sensibles*. These "sensitive zones," which officially number 750 with some 4 to 5 million inhabitants, are mostly Muslim ghettoes that are increasingly beyond the writ of French law.[219]

The immediate repercussions of this troubling phenomenon are already visible in the fact that the continent is no longer just a transit point for terrorists, but has itself become a breeding ground for all manner of Islamic extremists and *Jihad*ists. With hundreds of European-born and raised extremists documented to have already taken part in terrorist activities in all the hotbeds of *Jihad*ism worldwide, this is and should be a matter of serious concern. Frightening as terrorist activities are, though, they are unlikely by themselves to present a systemic challenge

---

[218] Jean-Pierre Obin, "Les signes et manifestations d'appartenance religieuse dans les établissements scolaires," Ministère de l'Education Nationale, Paris, June 2004.

[219] During the 2005 riots in the Paris suburb of Clichy-sous-Bois, the first building to be burnt was the police station. It was later revealed that the station was not attended at night, since it was deemed too dangerous to do so.

to the European order. For they are, after all, but the symptoms of the much deeper malignancy of a quasi-totalitarian Islamist ideology on the march that presents a real and vastly greater threat. To put it simply, if the kind of radical, uncompromising and violence-prone worldview currently on display in Muslim ghettoes remains dominant among European Muslims as they become a majority of the young urban cohorts by 2025 or earlier, it is very difficult to see how Europe could continue to be governed effectively as a modern, democratic and secular polity.

A resounding majority of the British population (75%) believes that "Islam is negative for Britain."[220] This sentiment is not confined to the British alone. We are witnessing unprecedented movements across Europe, against the infringement of Muslim culture, religion and dress code on European societies. Europeans and outspoken Americans are taking actions to ban Muslim cultural encroachment on their lives and on their democratic values.

A fanatical terrorist has escaped being thrown out of the UK because it would breach his human rights. Hate-filled Siraj Yassin Abdullah Ali, graded the highest possible risk to the public, was released after serving just half of his nine-year sentence for helping the July 21 bombers. He now mingles freely among the Londoners his co-plotters tried to kill six years ago. Government officials are desperate to deport the Islamic fundamentalist back to his native Eritrea but have been told they cannot because he could face 'inhumane treatment or punishment'. Ali was convicted of helping a gang of five Al Qaeda suicide bombers in their bid to repeat the carnage of the attacks of July 7, 2005, two weeks later. The case is the latest to highlight how human rights laws have left the authorities powerless to remove some terrorists and convicted criminals.

Ismail Abdurahman, 28, who hid the bomber Hussain Osman for three days, escaped being deported to his native Somalia after judges feared for his safety. Abdurahman is also living at a bail hostel in London despite the protests of police and Home Office officials. The release of Ali and Abdurahman underlines the challenges faced by police, probation, and MI5. Under Article 3 of both the European Convention

---

[220] www.cdhr.info;(website of Center for Democracy and Human Rights in Saudi Arabia; Dated Dec. 11, 2010; retrieved on 01-15-2011.

on Human Rights, and Labour's Human Rights Act, individuals are protected against torture, inhuman or degrading treatment. The clause allows foreign terror suspects to fight deportation on the grounds that they would be tortured in their home countries if returned. In February, Lord Carlile warned that European judges have turned Britain into a 'safe haven' for foreign terrorists. 'They should be deported instantly back to where they came from.'[221]

---

[221] 'Terrorist we can't kick out': Chris Greenwood, Mail Online, Sept. 25, 2011

EPILOGUE

The problem of political Islam is a huge human tragedy currently in the making. The final solution may be larger in scale than any global social/political upheaval experienced to date. Islam, as it is known today, will not disband nor experience some sort of spontaneous intellectual, spiritual, or democratic renaissance. The seeds of conflict and war were planted a long time ago, have been maturing for centuries, and are now fully ripe. To date effective corrective activity has been postponed as the weed deliberately deceives.[222]

This is the image of Islam today seen from the unsympathetic eye. This is neither wholly untrue, nor wholly true. What image can one make in a world of war and destruction, fire and flames, wanton killings of men and women, old and young, innocents and culprits by suicide bombers. And what an irony that this drama is staged both by the 'terrorists' and those fighting 'war on terror' alike. Killing of innocents multiply in either side, either way.

Fighting enemy is a necessary evil in Islam. But it is only permissible in self-defense: *"Fight in the cause of Allah those who fight you, but do not transgress limits; for Allah does not love transgressors."*[223] Peace is preferable in spite of humiliation and loss of life: *"But if the enemy inclines toward peace you (also) incline toward peace, and trust in Allah."*[224] For Muslims, Treaty of *Hudaybiyah* was highly humiliating,[225] but the Qur'an calls it *'a manifest victory'* over the mighty tribe of

---

[222] www.wikiislam.net; *Islam Undressed: The Gathering Storm*; retrieved 10/12/2011.

[223] Q. 2:19

[224] Q. 8:61

[225] One of the terms of the Treaty read, "whoso cometh unto Muhammad of Quraysh without the leave of his guardian, Muhammad shall return him unto them; but whoso cometh unto Quraysh of those who are with Muhammad, they shall not be return." (Muhammad, Martin Lings; 1983; p. 253)

Quraysh and their affiliates.[226] The conversion of pagan tribes of Arabia from idolatry to Islam was so unprecedented in number and places in this period of peace that the enemy had to void the treaty before its expiry. Peace was the utmost priority for Islam, although the ethical justification for going to war is abundantly emphasized in the scripture. The Qur'an would appear to be one of the earliest documents which addressed the question of essentiality of war.

It is not our intention or our competence to predict the future development of Islam. Since the religion is alive and dynamic for more than the last fourteen hundred years. One can safely say that Islam will have future development—development of militancy or peace and prosperity—depending on the future course of socio-political trends of history.

Just what line of development the Muslims will next hew for Islam. Its adherents torn between a loyalty within and world without—a loyalty that they cherish but do not know quite how to apply, and a world by which they find themselves surrounded but with which they do not know quite how to cope? Or will they perhaps emotionalize it into a closed system, by which they retreat from modernity into a fanaticism of crippling isolationist violence? Or will they construe it into an open, rich, onward vision, an effective inspiration for truly modern living; bringing themselves spiritual integrity and fulfillment, and their societies progress with justice and honor in the world?

On questions such as these will turn not only the religious but also the worldly welfare of the Muslim people. Worldly problems cannot be solved by men whose ideological and moral outlook is inappropriate to their solution. The direction in which Islam moves is highly relevant to all other developments. The economic, political, military, demographic, and other kinds of question that press on each of the various Muslim nations cannot be underestimated by anyone familiar with the area or concerned with the welfare of its people. It would be absurd to belittle these issues. Yet, none of them is more consequential than the religious question. Indeed, all go hand in hand. The various factors intertwine not only in jointly determining the progress of the Islamic world, but in determining each other.

---

[226] Q. 48:1

Roughly since the Second World War, every major Muslim community in the world has been in charge of its own affairs—as effectively as is feasible in the kind of world in which we live. Muslims, like others, are not free from outside pressures, but they are as free as can be devised or imagined. What they now do and become is as close as possible to their own doing and being. The economic, political, social, cultural, and spiritual development on which they are now embarked constitutes a history that is Islamic in a renewed, full sense.

Freedom and responsibility are within a context of determined circumstance. An Islamic economic system were one that a Muslim community should or would adopt if it were isolated. This approach is unfruitful; it is irrelevant on a large scale. To take the isolationist approach would signify that Islam is irrelevant to the kind of world in which we all live. A truer recognition is surely that Muslims' "independence" will mean not isolation but renewed internal strength and a growing Islamic influence on the rest of mankind, as well as vice versa. Freedom is participation. A faith that is alive is a faith for men and societies that are involved.

The evolution of Islam is to be seen in this total context. Their whole contemporary enterprise is mighty: constructing a new life at the outset of twenty-first century. One has yet to work out what is the meaning of religion in a new world that comprises with network of roads and dams, industrial complexes and technical institutions, and responsibility for them. It is not slight for a religion whose genius it is to apply its moral imperatives to day-to-day living, to wed the ultimate meaning of life to the society in which one participates, to seek justice in the midst of machines and modernity.

Division between civilizations are no longer valid, and that modern civilization, though it got under way first in the West, is spreading throughout the world and is transforming or superseding older cultural patterns for both West and East. Secularism, as indeed modernity in general, would be not a Western device but a new and universal one, which all civilizations are in process of assimilating. To illustrate this for Islam the secular Turkish could be cited. Similarly in Indonesia and Malaysia, secularism and Islamic-oriented policies could be seen as alternatives, in favor of the former. In this view the mundane welfare of the Muslim peoples would seem to depend not on their interpretation of Islam but rather on social processes independent of religious consideration.

The question as to what kind of Islam Muslims will next construct is real and meaningful. To this the answer is not easy and simple. Whatever one may believe about Islam's transcendental essence, yet the earthly manifestation of Islam, both temporal and spiritual, is the creation of Muslims. The tendency in recent Islam has been to stress man's freedom.

The faith of Islam has responded positively to the vicissitudes of history. This is confirmed both by doctrine and by observation. When beset by the threat of complete annihilation from the pagan Arab tribes, the Qur'an asks the believers, *"Fight in the cause of Allah those who fight you"*(2:190). The ever-changing situations of hostility with the tribal Arabs, and with the Jewish and the Christian tribes made the revelations of the Medinan period more strident than those of the earlier period. These revelations command the believers to fight for survival and to defend themselves and their faith. With the fight for survival gradually advancing toward the age of conquest during the period of Pious caliphs and Umayyads, Muslim warriors fought with the Persians and Romans in the battlefields of Qadisiyyah (637), Ajnadayn (634) and Yarmuk (636) taking from their hands Syria, Iraq and Egypt. With the end of hostility with the Romans and Persians began the age of consolidation and prosperity during the period of Abbasid of Baghdad, Fatimid of Egypt, Umayyad of Spain and Mongols of India, when the world saw such a magnificent civilization flourishing in Damascus, Baghdad, Cairo, Cordova and Delhi which surpassed the cultural heights reached earlier by Sassanian and Byzantine kingdoms. "But what has rendered the Abbasid age especially illustrious in the world annals" says Prof. Hitti, "is the fact that it witnessed the momentous intellectual awakening in the history of Islam and one of the most significant in the whole history of thought and culture."

The future of Islam in the events of the forthcoming world can be estimated on the basis of its past resilience towards historic changes. Islam is not the only civilization that has potential to cope with the changing circumstances of the world events. What distinguishes Islam is its attitude of ethical trends in social and political justice. The need of the hour is to protect the values embedded in pristine Islam and not let them be corrupted by misuse for political ends. This, to be sure, is the real challenge which Islam faces today.

Bibliography

"Kuran, Timur, *Why the Middle East Is Economically Underdeveloped—Historical Mechanisms of Institutional Stagnation*"

Abdulhak Adnan, *La Science chez les Turcs Ottomans* (Paris: 1939).

Abu Zahra, *Al-madahi al-islamiyya* (Cairo: Maktabat al-Adab).

Ahmed Rashid's TALIBAN; Yale University Press; 2001.

Al-Banna, Hasan. *Five Tracts of Hasan Al-Banna (1906-1949)*. Translated by Charles Wendell. Berkeley: University of California Press, 1978.

Al-Bukhari, *al-Jami' al-Sahih*, English translation.

Alhaji A.D. Ajijola, *Introduction to Islamic law*. Karachi, Pakistan : International Islamic Publishers, 1989.

Ali Umlil; *Islam et etat national* (Casablanca: 1991).

Al-Mas'udi, *Muruj-az-Zahb* vol. 4.

Al-Masudi (896-956), *Muruj adh-dhahab wa ma'adin al-jawahar (Eng. The Meadows of Gold and Mines of Gems), a world history. vol. 3.*

Al-Shafi'i, *Kitab al-Umm,* Cairo ed. Vii, Eng. Translation.

Al-Tarmidi, Sunan al-Tarmidi, B: 27; H: 1130.

Ameer Ali, *A Short History of the Saracens,* McMillan, London, 1949;

Anwar al-Jundi, *Muhakamat fikr Taha Husayn* (Cairo: Dar al-Islam, 1984).

Berg, Herbert. *"Islamic Law."* Berkshire Encyclopedia of World History (2005)

Bernard Lewis, *"Ottoman Observers of Ottoman decline,"* in Islamic Studies (Karachi), 1962;

Bernard Lewis; *What Went Wrong?* Oxford University Press,

Bernard Lews, *Islam in History: Ideas, People and Events in the Middle East,* Chicago, 1993.

Browers, Michaelli and Kurzman, Charles, eds. *"An Islamic Reformation?"* Lanham, MD, Lexington Books, 2004.

Brynjar Lia, *Architect of Global Jihad: The Life of al-Qaida Strategist Abu Musab al-Suri* (New York; Columbia Univ. Press, 2008)

Caetani, Leon; *Principe di Teano: Annali dell' Islam* (Milano 1905) vol. iii.

Chris Horrie and Peter Chippindale. *What is Islam? A Comprehensive Introduction*, Virgin Books, 1991.

Dayal, Lakshmeshwar, *The Truth About Islam: A Historical Study,* Anamika Publishers, New Delhi, 2010.

Dollinger, *The Gentile and the Jew,* vol. 1

Fawaz Gerges, *The Far Ememy* (Camnridge, England, 2005)

Fazlur Rahman, *ISLAM,* 2nd Ed. 1979; Uni. Of Chicago Press, Chicago.

Fazlur Rahman's *ISLAM & MODERNITY: Transformation of an Intellectual Tradition;* Univ.of Chicago Press, Chicago and London, 1984

Francis Robinson, *Atlas of the Islamic World since 1500*; Oxford, 1982,

Hamzeh, A. Nizar. *"Qatar: The Duality of the Legal System,"* *Middle Eastern Studies*, Vol. 30, No.1, January 1994

Hisham A. Nashshabah thesis, *"Islam and Nationalism in the Arab World: a selected and annotated bibliography",* 195.

I. Goldziher, *Muhammedanische Studien,* 1961, vol.2

Imam al-Qurtubi; *Al-intiqa' fi fada'il* . . . . (Beirut: Dar al-Ilmiyya).

Imam Feisal Abdul Rauf, *What's Right with Islam*; New York, Harper, 2004.

J.Schacht and C.E. Bosworth, *The Legacy of Islam,* 2nd Ed., Oxford Univ. Press, Oxford, 1974

Kenneth Cragg; *The Event of the Qur'an;* OneWorld, Oxford, 2006

Khushwant Singh, *A History of the Sikhs*, Princeton, 1963

Khutabat-I Sir Sayyid, Bada'un, 1931;

Kidwai, Shaikh M.N., *"Woman under Different Social and Religious Laws"* Seema Publications, Delhi, 1976.

Kitab al-Tamhid, Cairo 1947 English translation.

Kuran, Timur; *The Absence of the Corporation in Islamic Law—Origins and Persistence*

Kuran,Timur; *"The Logic of Financial Westernization in the Middle East,"* Journal of Economic Behavior and Organization,Vol. 56 (2005).

Kurzman, Charles, ed. *Liberal* **Islam***: A Sourcebook.* Oxford and New York: Oxford University Press, 1998.

Leila Ahmad, *Women and Gender in Islam,* Yale Univ. Press, 1992.

Lenormant, *Ancient History of the East,* vol. ii.

Lloyd, Trevor Owen (1996). *The British Empire 1558-1995.* Oxford University Press.

Lutfi Pasha, *Asafname,* edited with a German translation by Rudolf Tschudi, Berlin, 1910.

M. Rafiq Khan, *Islam in China,* Delhi, 1963.

Mark Juergensmeyer, *Terror in the Mind of God* (Berkeley: Univ. of California Press, 2003).

Michael C. Hudson, *Arab Politics,* Yale, 1977,

Muhammad 'Abduh, quoted in H.A.R.Gibb's *Modern Trends in Islam,* Chicago 1946,

Muhammad 'Abduh, *Risala al-Tawhid*; Eng. Translation.

Muhammad Arkoun, *"Rethinking Islam",* translated and edited from French to English, Robert D. Lee.

Muhammad Asad, *Islam at the Crossroads,* Delhi 1934.

Muhammad Hashim Kamali, *"Punishment in Islamic Law: A Critique of the Hudud Bill of Kelantan, Malaysia."*

Otto, Jan Michiel; *Shari'a and National Law in Muslim Countries: Tensions and Opportunities for Dutch and EU Foreign Policy.* Amsterdam University Press, 2008.

P.M. Holt, *The Mahdist State in the Sudan,* 1881-1898, Oxford, 1958.

Rafiq Zakaria. *"The Struggle Within Islam: The Conflict between Religion and Politics,"* Penguin Books, New Delhi, India, 1988.

Reza Aslan, *"How to Win a COSMIC WAR: God, Globalization, and the End of the War on Terror."*

Risalat al-Islam, Cairo, 1368/1949;

Risale-i Kocu Bey (Istanbul: 1860), translated in German in 1861.

Sayyed Qutb, *Milestones* (Birmingham, England: Maktabah, 2006)

Shahrastani, *Al-milal wa al-nihal*; (Beirut: Dar Sa'b, 1986);

Shahrastani, *Al-milat wa al-nihal* (Beirut: Dar Sa'ab, 1986) vol.1.

Sharif al-Mujahid, *"Sayyid Jamal al-Din al-Afghani: His Role in the Nineteenth century Muslim Awakenning",* 1954, Karachi, Pakistan.

Sir Muhammad Iqbal, *The Reconstruction of Religious Thought in Islam,* 1944, Lahore.

Smith, Simon (1998). *British Imperialism 1750-1970*. Cambridge University Press.

Syed Ameer Ali, *A Short History of the Saracens*; Macmillan, London, 1949.

T.W. Arnold, *The Preaching of Islam*, Kitab Bhavan, New Delhi, India, 1999;

Tafsir Ibn Kathir. Tafsir for Ayah 33:53 in web tafsir.com

The Council of the Academy of Islamic Studies, Hyderabad, Deccan, India, *Toward Reorientation of Islamic Thought: A Call for Introspection, 1954.*

Thomas W. Arnold, The Preaching of Islam; Kitab Bhavan, New Delhi, 1999.

Virginia H. Aksan, *"Ottoman Political Writing, 1768-1808,"*

W. Montgomery Watt's *Muhammad at Madina*, Oxford Univ. Press, London, 1956.

Wright,Tom (JANUARY 5, 2011). *"Leading Pakistani Politician Killed"*. The Wall Street Journal.

Ziauddin Sardar, *The Future of Muslim Civilization,* London, 1979,

Index

The author, currently retired for health reason, has a Master's degree in History and Civilization from Karachi University, Pakistan. Subsequently, he entered as Research Fellow in the Islamic Research Institute of Pakistan and also taught undergraduate classes in the History of the subcontinent of India-Pakistan. He is currently living in the United States for the last two decades and has previously published two other books, (i) Muslims in America: What Everyone Needs to Know, and (ii) Believers and Brothers: A History of Uneasy Relationship. He and his wife are living in Fort Lauderdale, Florida, have four children and seven grandchildren, all in the United States.